Real Sister

• •

Stereotypes, Respectability, and Black Women in Reality TV

EDITED BY JERVETTE R. WARD

Rutgers University Press

New Brunswick, New Jersey, and London

Library of Congress Cataloging-in-Publication Data
Real sister : stereotypes, respectability, and Black women in reality tv / edited by Jervette R. Ward.
     pages cm
   Includes bibliographical references and index.
   ISBN 978–0–8135–7507–0 (hardcover : alk. paper) — ISBN 978–0–8135–7506–3 (pbk.
: alk. paper) — ISBN 978–0–8135–7508–7 (e-book (epub)) — ISBN 978–0–8135–7509–4
(e-book (web pdf))
   1. Reality television programs—United States—History and criticism. 2. African American
women on television. I. Ward, Jervette R., 1983– editor. II. Title.
   PN1992.8.A34R43 2015
   791.45'60973—dc23
   2015002731

A British Cataloging-in-Publication record for this book is available from the British Library.

Visit our website: http://rutgerspress.rutgers.edu

Manufactured in the United States of America

For My Grandmothers, My Mother, and My Sisters—
Truly Phenomenal Women

Alice C. Ward
Earnestine Cullens Jones
Brendalyn D. Ward
Brena C. Ward
Jenell M. Ward
Jenae D. Ward

Contents

Acknowledgments

I am incredibly thankful for my husband, Kenneth Ellis, and our daughter, McKinley. Their support of my work never ceases to amaze me, and their love gives my life meaning. My parents, Jarvis and Brendalyn Ward, and my siblings, Brandan, Brena, Jenell, and Jenae, always keep me grounded, and for that I am truly thankful. My grandparents, Alice C. Ward, Earnestine Cullens Jones, and Walter Jones make me feel special and loved each and every day, and I am exceedingly grateful for them. To all my numerous extended family and friends far and near, I send much gratitude for your encouragement—I will not get into trouble by making a list.

My University of Memphis family, especially Verner D. Mitchell and Ladrica Menson-Furr, have been tremendously influential—thank you. My colleagues at the University of Alaska Anchorage (UAA) have made my work life a wonderfully satisfying experience. I especially thank my dean, John Stalvey; my associate dean, Jeane Breinig; and my initiators into UAA life, Toby Widdicombe and Marva Watson. My former colleagues at Pine Manor College, Bill Stargard and Melinda Ponder, introduced me to Boston and provided a place for this book idea to bloom—many thanks. My undergraduate research assistants, Emily McNulty, Emi Hall, and D'ana Castro, have been incredibly helpful over the years—thank you. My former student and artist Danielle "DEL!" Steffensen created the art for the cover, and I greatly admire her work.

Thank you to all of the wonderful scholars who have contributed to this book and made it possible. In addition, I am exceedingly grateful to the Rutgers University Press team and my sponsoring editor, Lisa Boyajian, for her commitment to this book project and for her guidance. Blessed Beyond Measure!

Real Sister

Introduction

The Real Scandal

• •

Portrayals of Black Women
in Reality TV

JERVETTE R. WARD

American television viewers have recently become enamored with the ABC primetime hit *Scandal*, which features Kerry Washington portraying Washington, D.C., fixer Olivia Pope. Pope is based on the real-life fixer Judy Smith, but *Scandal* is unique in that it is the first show in forty years to cast a Black female lead in a network drama. The success of *Scandal* paved the way for Viola Davis to portray Annalise Keating in *How to Get Away with Murder*, another new and successful ABC drama with a Black female lead. Other networks now have picked up on the trend, and even Fox has joined in the action with Taraji P. Henson portraying Cookie Lyon on the new hit *Empire*. Yet, even as the scandalous actions of Pope, Keating, and Lyon have engrossed the nation because of the novelty of the leads, the jaw-dropping action, and the sharp dialogue, Black women have become prevalent in another genre—reality TV—and their portrayals in this genre are even more scandalous than Pope's, Keating's, and Lyon's. Yet, in the midst of the scandalous action on reality TV there are also positive representations of Black womanhood, if one is willing to look for them. Pope occasionally is presented as the image emancipator of Black women, yet she also embodies many negative stereotypes about Black women. Tom Burrell argues:

> *Scandal* is basically a continuing perpetuation of the stereotype of a black woman whose libido and sexual urges are so pronounced that even with an education and a great job, and all these other things, she can't control herself. So, she's basically a reincarnation of Bess from *Porgy and Bess*; she's the female in *Monster's Ball*; she's the sexual predator and aggressor. It basically plays into the whole sexual stereotype of black women that's been around from the very beginning, and that basically gives permission for them to be sexually exploited. (qtd. in Desmond-Harris)

Critics and viewers debate whether the image of Pope is beneficial, yet the arguments usually converge on the idea that there must be balance in the representations of Black women. Just as viewers and critics demand balance in scripted television, reality TV must also present more nuanced representations of Black womanhood.

Reality TV is a broad genre that encompasses a wide variety of shows. For the sake of this book, a working definition is needed, and the article, "Reality-Based Television Programming and the Psychology of Its Appeal," provides it:

> We offer the following definition of *reality-based television programming*: programs that film real people as they live out events (contrived or otherwise) in their lives, as these events occur. Such programming is characterized by several elements: (a) people portraying themselves (i.e., not actors or public figures performing roles), (b) filmed at least in part in their living or working environment rather than on a set, (c) without a script, (d) with events placed in a narrative context, (e) for the primary purpose of viewer entertainment. (Nabi et al. 304)

This definition provides a solid framework for the study of this genre.

I must admit—I did not start watching reality television, in particular *The Real Housewives of Atlanta* (*RHOA*), of my own free will. One of my former colleagues talked about the show for months, and I saw the commercial promos on television; however, I stood strong and refused to watch. She kept saying, "Just try it." But, as Nancy Reagan advised in the 1980s, I just said "NO!" Yet, one weekend, one of my sisters came to town for a visit, and before I could stop her, she turned my television to *The Real Housewives of Atlanta* and told me that she could not miss that week's episode. We only had one television and our living/dining/kitchen area was an open floor plan, so I was "forced" to watch the show. Every few minutes I would utter some words of shock and disdain. My sister looked at me with pity and simply informed me that she knew that I would watch the show next week. With the utmost dignity, I informed her that she was incredibly mistaken and that I would never allow such a thing to occur. However, at the same time a week later, my television miraculously found itself on the same station as *The Real Housewives of Atlanta*. I called my former colleague and my sister to inform them that I held them both fully responsible for my downfall into reality TV. I then proceeded to watch the next several seasons. I now regularly tune in to see what NeNe, Cynthia, Kandi, and Phaedra are up to each week. Even as I watched each week's episode, I refused to admit publicly that I watched the shows. As I told a friend one day, "I will *deny* ever watching the show if it comes up with someone—especially if it is an academic arena." Yet, I began to notice a trend when I gathered with other Black women in the academy—many were watching at least one of the shows, but they would carefully admit to viewing. One of the contributors to this book calls this the reality TV intellectual speakeasy. In these conversations, we voiced significant issues with reality television, yet we all tuned in weekly for our "guilty pleasure."

My level of discomfort about watching reality television reached a new height one day while I was sitting on a plane. As I looked around my cabin, I noticed a white woman who looked to be in her late thirties settling in for the long flight by watching *The Real Housewives of Atlanta*. As much as I enjoy watching the show, I became immediately embarrassed and horrified at the idea of this white woman laughing at the antics of the Black women that I laugh at and with on a regular basis. I felt ashamed, yet I immediately began to wonder *why* I felt ashamed. Was I falling prey to respectability politics? Would this white woman have felt ashamed if I had logged onto my computer and began watching *The Real Housewives of New Jersey* or *The Real Housewives of New York City*—two shows that feature white housewives who also act in outlandish ways? My shame and discomfort stemmed from my recognition of the influential nature of TV. In her article "African American Stereotypes in Reality Television," Tia Tyree writes, "In essence, television and reality television programming, in particular, can be an informational tool for audiences to gauge who they are, who others are in their society as well as what is or is not socially acceptable behavior" (397). Tyree's discussion of how audiences can use reality TV as a shibboleth for society underscores the need to further analyze the portrayal of Black women in the genre. I recognized that I was concerned with how the portrayal of Black women on *RHOA* might affect the perception of all Black women. As a scholar, this concern led to a desire to further explore the genre, specifically due to its prevalence in society. Tyree continues, "In the early 1990s, reality television was a fledgling television genre beginning to catch the attention of American viewers. Twenty years later, reality television is a mainstay on television airwaves and seemingly the format of choice for many networks" (394). Leigh H. Edwards seconds Tyree's assertion by writing, "Once considered a fad or copycat genre, reality TV now dominates American television programming and has become a lasting staple" (Edwards 1). This firmly entrenched television arena now significantly presents images of Black women, yet stereotypes and respectability politics abound.

Reality television is in essence a form of touristic reading. Touristic reading is usually applied to works of fiction, yet as many of the contributors to this book argue, reality television only skirts reality. Rosemary V. Hathaway discusses the theory of touristic reading and describes it as:

> The fallacious practice whereby a reader assumes, when presented with a text where the writer and the group represented in the text are ethnically different from herself, that the text is necessarily an accurate, authentic, and authorized representation of that "Other" cultural group. But the touristic reading is a snapshot, a still photo (with the emphasis on "still"), a cultural portrait that selectively edits out signs of dynamism or contention, both within the text and within the culture "represented" by the text and features only what the reader wants to see. (172)

Reality TV then becomes an opportunity for people to observe others not like themselves, which often leads to the reinforcement of stereotypes—this observation could also be one of class or sex and not just race. Touristic reading must then directly correlate to respectability politics. Tourists look for the best and brightest of a location, and locations acquiesce by seeking only to showcase the best they have to offer. Hathaway partially frames her discussion using the widely analyzed review of Zora Neale Hurston's *Their Eyes Were Watching God* by Richard Wright. Hurston's most famous work offers up Black characters who speak in dialect and who might not be "the best" the race has to offer. Wright accuses Hurston of creating minstrel characters who exist only for the pleasure of the white reader. Hathaway writes, "Hurston's case is especially poignant because her literary career was largely underwritten by white patrons and because the issue of how best to 'represent the race' was an ongoing debate among Harlem Renaissance writers" (172). Hathaway, like many other scholars, points out that Richard Wright and Alain Locke both expected Hurston to adhere to some form of respectability politics: "As with Wright's review, Locke's seems to demand of Hurston a certain kind of conformity or allegiance to a cause. Clearly this is unreasonable weight to put on a novelist, largely because it is typically not a demand made of white writers" (175). Just as Hathaway argues that it is unreasonable to place the burden of the race on one novelist, it is also unreasonable to place the burden of the race on reality TV stars. Therí A. Pickens continues Hathaway's argument in "Shoving Aside the Politics of Respectability: Black Women, Reality TV, and the Ratchet Performance." Pickens writes, "To be respectable is to be policed by oneself and a larger black community so that one is deemed worthy of equal treatment. Implicit in the ideology of respectability lingers the idea that it is not possible to remain individualized as a black person: one's individual will and desires must be subordinated to the political and social uplift of the collective. In many ways, the parameters defining black respectable behavior have not changed much since the nineteenth century" (2). Pickens goes on to succinctly explain both the role of the viewer and of the performer when one is adhering to rules of respectability. She argues, "The relationship between the ratchet performer and the audience rests on an implied contract in which both parties are aware that the ratchet violates the norms of respectable behavior" (4). Pickens contends that reality TV stars, in particular Tamar Braxton from *Braxton Family Values*, use their ratchet or unrespectable behavior as a type of capital to advance their careers.

Reality TV has become a battleground of stereotypes, respectability politics, and ratchet capitalization, and in this ever-expanding genre, Black women are playing increasingly prevalent roles; however, the portrayal of Black women on many shows consistently presents negative and stereotypical images. From *The Real Housewives of Atlanta* to *Basketball Wives* to *Love and Hip Hop Atlanta*, Black women are shown as angry, violent, ghetto, and loud. In the chapter "Divas, Evil Black Bitches, and Bitter Black Women: African-American Women in Postfeminist and Post–Civil Rights Popular Culture," Kimberly Springer discusses one of the earliest famous Black women reality TV stars, Omarosa Manigault. Manigault's diva antics have in some ways become the ratchet meter by which to judge all Black women reality TV stars, and the stereotype persists (81). Tyree addresses these stereotypes:

> When African Americans are framed in stereotypical ways within reality television, those actions and behaviors can be translated as "real" elements of the programming by those who engage in the people-watching process. Further, if these distorted negative images of African Americans go unchecked in the lives of some audience members, it can cause issues when they interact with members of the stereotyped group. (408–409)

Because of the influencing nature of reality TV, it is imperative that scholars specifically focus on the portrayal of Black women in this genre.

Around the same time as the aforementioned flight, my former colleague Ladrica Menson-Furr called me because her local Fox News station wanted to interview her on camera about the new show *Married to Medicine*. Fox was interested in the Black female academic response to the show. My colleague was not only concerned about admitting on national television that she watched reality television, but she was also concerned with how the English academic world would respond to scholarly discussions on a much maligned genre—even if the genre had been deemed respectable by media studies. After many phone conversations and debates, she warily decided to do the interview, and she succinctly discussed how stereotypes of Black women have existed for centuries. In the interview with Brooke Thomas, Menson-Furr states, "If we allow these forms of entertainment to say this is who we are, then we're helping to perpetuate the image. I think when you take power and you say well that's just one particular characterization that an individual has been cast and is being paid to perform then we're able to say, 'well this is not a true stereotype'" (qtd. in Thomas). Shortly after the interview, the two of us presented at a conference together at which we continued the conversation about the portrayal of Black women in reality TV with several other Black female academics. Many admitted to watching and enjoying the shows, yet all felt slightly uncomfortable watching and, more important, admitting to watching. Even as we laughed and gasped at the shows, our critical academic minds often thought about all of the academic and theoretical issues that are problematic about the episodes—Sapphire stereotypes, the angry Black woman, and many other tropes appear on the screen. Our discomfort with the shows was mirrored in a study done by Lisa K. Lundy, Amanda M. Ruth, and Travis D. Park. Participants were concerned with the lack of morals and deception that are a part of reality television (Lundy, Ruth, and Park 216). They write, "As a result of the 'moral corruption' demonstrated through RT [reality TV] programming, many participants expressed concerned about the impact the popularity of this television genre will eventually have on society" (217). And, like us, participants in the study even admitted to feeling silly for discussing reality television (219). Yet, each week the number of viewers of these shows continues to rise. In his article "So You Think You Can Think," Dominic Pettman writes, "Even if we loathe reality TV, and claim to never watch it, that doesn't mean we haven't all been engulfed in its logic, mannerisms, motifs, conventions, and conceits." People of all walks of life are tuning in every week to see what happens on reality TV, and often their gaze is focused on Black women. Even though it is fairly common to hear people publicly and disdainfully avow that they do not watch reality television, people are watching. The enticing nature of reality TV is discussed in the article "Simply Irresistible: Reality TV Consumption Patterns." The authors write:

> The first theme that emerged from the data was the underestimation of RT viewing. Initially, participants denied watching much RT; in fact, RT was rarely mentioned when participants were asked to describe the type of television shows that they typically watched. Instead, shows that were typically mentioned included adult and teenage drama, sports broadcasting, comedy sitcoms, and news shows. However, over the course of the focus group discussions, it was evident that participants watched (or were at least familiar with) more RT shows than first indicated. Despite the fact that participants from each focus group listed only half a dozen reality shows at the beginning of the focus groups, at least 25 different RT shows were discussed throughout the focus groups as shows that were watched on a regular basis. One participant realized this phenomenon in saying, "I didn't think I watched this much or knew this much about reality television, but apparently I was wrong." (Lundy, Ruth, and Park 213)

The research by Lundy, Ruth, and Park clearly shows that reality TV has gripped the American public, and that grip does not appear to be loosening any time soon. However, Black middle- and upper-class women often try to distance themselves from these shows, and there are endless blogs, websites, and news articles that bemoan the antics of many of the reality television women—for example, the online articles "VH1 Hates Black Women," "VH1 Hates Black Women Part 2," and "From 'Julia' to 'NeNe': The Impact of Reality TV on Black Women" all rail against the problematic portrayals of Black women in reality TV. These attempts at respectability politics reached full force once VH1 aired the now canceled show, *Sorority Sisters*. Black sororities collectively voiced their outrage at the antics of the cast members who represented some of the oldest and most historic Black Greek organizations. The outrage led to the quick cancellation of the show and several of the stars of the show were dismissed from their sororities.

In the midst of all the reality television bemoaning and watching, there has not been a book written by female academics that analyzes the various issues that exist in the portrayal of Black women in reality television. Once I returned home from the aforementioned conference, I began to explore the possibility of collecting a series of chapters that explore all of the issues discussed in the conference conversations. I also wanted to delve deeper into some of the issues we had yet to discuss in an interdisciplinary fashion. The interdisciplinary aspect of this volume is one of its strengths as scholars from different disciplines provide a richer and deeper analysis of the topic. There are other books that deal with the broad subject of women in reality television and with reality TV in general. Rachel E. Dubrofsky's *The Surveillance of Women on Reality Television: Watching The Bachelor and The Bachelorette* discusses two shows that primarily feature a white cast, while Jennifer L. Pozner's *Reality Bites Back: The Troubling Truth about Guilty Pleasure TV* examines the broad societal effects of reality television. *Reality Gendervision: Sexuality and Gender on Transatlantic Reality Television*, edited by Brenda R. Weber, explores gender stereotypes in both the United States and Great Britain. Books that address reality television in general are also increasingly popular. *Reacting to Reality Television: Performance, Audience and Value* by Beverly Skeggs and Helen Wood looks at both the audience and the performers of reality TV, while Annette Hill's *Reality TV: Audiences and Popular Factual Television* explores audience response to and discussion of the genre. *Better Living through Reality TV: Television and*

Post-Welfare Citizenship by Laurie Ouellette and James Hay is a textbook on the genre; Mark Andrekevic's *Reality TV: The Work of Being Watched* explores the voyeuristic aspects of reality TV; *Understanding Reality Television,* edited by Su Holmes and Deborah Jermyn, details the history of reality TV, but its publication in 2004 limits its scope, but *The Tube Has Spoken: Reality TV and History,* edited by Julie Anne Taddeo and Ken Dvorak and published in 2010 expands that historical arc. *Reality Squared: Televisual Discourse on the Real,* edited by James Friedman, looks at the impact of reality TV. *Makeover Television: Realities Remodelled,* edited by Dana Heller analyzes shows that seek to transform, which is loosely similar to *Exposing Lifestyle Television: The Big Reveal,* edited by Gareth Palmer. June Deery's *Consuming Reality: The Commercialization of Factual Entertainment* explores the economic structure of the genre, and Misha Kavka's *Reality TV* addresses the historical aspects of the genre and her *Reality Television: Affect and Intimacy* looks at the *effect* of reality TV and how it creates intimacy. All of these books have contributed greatly to the study of reality television; nevertheless, a book that focuses solely on the representation of Black women in reality television is sorely needed. Black women are a large part of the viewing public, and there are a growing number of reality television shows that primarily feature them. The lack of a book on this topic begs the question of whether academics are cutting themselves off from a portion of American culture that has no indication of going away. Edwards argues, "Critical attention to reality TV is important given not only the high number of viewers but also the passion of fan devotion" (12). Critical attention to Black women in reality TV is also important.

Reality TV has a special power in its ability to address current societal issues. Edwards writes, "Because reality TV can be produced and edited in weeks while scripted programs can take months, it can respond more quickly to sociocultural changes" (12). Yet, this special power also makes it difficult to write a book on a subject that is changing every day. Even though this book addresses particular shows, it exists to bring attention to the larger issues in the genre. *Real Sisters: Stereotypes, Respectability, and Black Women in Reality TV* is a series of chapters by women academics that critically analyzes the portrayal of Black women in reality television. The style of this book is academic in approach and meticulously researched, yet it is written in accessible, jargon-free language in order to attract the serious general reader, members of literary discussion groups and book clubs, viewers of reality television, and graduate and undergraduate students in courses or programs that explore women's issues and women's creativity, African American studies, gender and women's studies, popular culture, and media studies. This volume walks a fine line between highly academic commentaries and easily approachable language for students.

The central argument is that reality television has taken hold of the viewing public and that the portrayal of Black women in reality television is often a stereotypical, negative image that needs to be discussed, analyzed, and at times negated. This book also addresses the often-discussed question of whether Black women of reality television are victims or entrepreneurs. In the age of Michelle Obama, the image of Black women in the media has never been more popular or problematic. Discussing Black womanhood in the reality world domain is a new and exciting opportunity. In the White House, four polished Black women have become a firm fixture in American culture and offer a counterview to the image of Black women that is often portrayed in the media; yet, even as Michelle Obama presents a well-educated and sophisticated image to the public, she regularly praises Beyoncé, a woman who sings "Bow Down, Bitches" while prancing around in a nipple-styled body suit. Given this sphere of contrasting images and ideas, this book exists to develop and to expand upon the image of Black womanhood in reality television.

Black womanhood has been "problematic" for generations, and its very existence is often debated. In "Looking Back from Zora, or Talking Out Both Sides My Mouth for Those Who Have Two Ears," P. Gabrielle Foreman writes, *"Black womanhood* is an oxymoronic term. Black *womanhood*, indeed Blacks' very humanity in this era, is anything but presumed. Black femininity, then, has to be forcefully asserted" (651). Even though Foreman is writing about American slavery in the nineteenth century, the argument could still apply to present culture. In the article "Hearing Anita Hill (and Viewing Bill Cosby)," John Fiske discusses the famous televised hearings that occurred before Clarence Thomas took his seat on the Supreme Court. Fiske writes:

> The meanings of femininity, for instance, depend upon their racial articulations and on their class ones: femininity may be an axis of unity among all women, but its intersections with the axes of race and class produce differences that may disrupt that unity. Being a Black woman in the United States is necessarily different from being a white woman because of the different histories that lie behind each social identity or point of intersection. (104)

Fiske concisely presents a media adaptation of the Matrix of Domination—oppression based on race, class, and gender. Because of these different histories and experiences, it is necessary for the experiences and representations of Black women in reality TV to be discussed and analyzed. Some might suggest that there should be a discussion of white women in reality television as a framework for this text; however, there is no need to do so in this volume because there are many other works in which they are discussed in detail. This book exists solely to discuss the portrayal of Black women—the first book-length volume to do so. To use white reality television women as a framework becomes an "othering" of Black women. Black women do not need to be placed in opposition to white women or women of other races to be worthy of analysis.

Reality television's mixed message of Black womanhood presents a unique opportunity for scholars. The principal aim of this book is not to argue for or against Black reality television; rather, the goal is to inspire a more nuanced and scholarly discussion of the effects of reality television on the image of Black women in society. Edwards writes, "Reality TV reverses classic narrative. Instead of trying to make characters seem real, it turns real people into characters, using predictable and repetitive narrative frames" (17). This creation of character is one of the primary reasons reality TV must be careful about racial stereotypes. Edwards further explains, "Reality shows bank on larger-than-life cast members who draw in viewers with their emotional outburst, conflicts, and melodramatic resolutions. Indeed, character is one of the main driving engines for the success of a reality show" (17). These character representation and character stereotypes of Black women are why this book exists and why analysis must take place.

However clichéd, this book looks at the good, the bad, and the ugly of reality TV. In chapter 1, "Black Women: From Public Arena to Reality TV," Sheena Harris opens the book by discussing the history of the representation of Black women in the public arena. She uses Saartjie Baartman, also known as the Hottentot Venus, as the foundation of discussion of the infamous booty-gate between Phaedra Parks and Kenya Moore on the *Real Housewives of Atlanta*, yet she also addresses *Flavor of Love, I Love New York*, and *Love & Hip Hop Atlanta*.

In chapter 2, "Selective Reuptake: Perpetuating Misleading Cultural Identities in the Reality Television World," LaToya Jefferson-James builds upon Harris's argument by addressing some of the prevalent character creations that affect Black women in reality TV. She begins by explaining how the genre became so prevalent in society, yet she primarily focuses on the characterization of the Pimp, the Sapphire, and the Preacher while analyzing the gender ideals that divide Black men and women. She also discusses the patriarchal, misogynistic, and capitalistic culture of reality TV. She frames her argument inside a discussion of the creation of the genre. Jefferson-James continues Harris's analysis of *Flavor of Love* and also discusses *Preachers of L.A.*

Alison D. Ligon expands the conversation to fashion and takes the discussion to the bridal salon in chapter 3, "Striving to Dress the Part: Examining the Absence of Black Women in Different Iterations of *Say Yes to the Dress.*" Through an analysis of the various *Say Yes to the Dress* shows, she argues that the shows present a modern version of the Cinderella story that often excludes Black women. Yet, even as these shows present a retake of an old idea, they allude to the persistent question of the marriageability of Black women.

Chapter 4, "The Semiotics of Fashion and Urban Success in *The Real Housewives of Atlanta,*" by Cynthia Davis, connects the *Real Housewives of Atlanta* phenomenon to the nineteenth- and twentieth-century fashion magazines that were marketed to Black women. Her chapter continues to build upon the historical foundation laid by Jefferson-James and Harris. Davis draws parallels between the fashion and lifestyle magazine articles that gave hair and clothing tips to the current Louboutin culture that is displayed on *RHOA.*

In chapter 5, "Homes without Walls, Families without Boundaries: How Family Participation in Reality Television Affects Children's Development," Detris Honora Adelabu creates the transition from weddings and fashion to a discussion on reality TV family life. In particular, she examines the impact of reality TV on the development of Black children who are cast members of the shows and loyal viewers. Adelabu argues that through the viewing of and participation in reality TV, children develop a skewered understanding of African Americans and what it means to be Black in America. She focuses mainly on the image of Black family life in *Basketball Wives, Hollywood Exes,* and *RHOA.*

Monica Flippin Wynn searches for positive representations of Black women in chapter 6, "Where Is Clair Huxtable When You Need Her? The Desperate Search for Positive Media Images of African American Women in the Age of Reality TV." As she gazes longingly back at Clair Huxtable from *The Cosby Show,* Flippin Wynn looks for and finds a reality television

Clair in Tiny from *T.I. & Tiny: The Family Hustle*. Flippin Wynn returns the discussion to *Flavor of Love*, yet she quickly moves to an analysis of *Tiny & Toya, T.I. & Tiny: The Family Hustle, Tia and Tamera, Welcome to Sweetie Pie's*, and *Raising Whitley*. She argues that there are positive representations of Black women on reality TV, yet the shows that present them are often not as popular as the shows that present negative portrayals. Flippin Wynn suggests that if one is willing to move beyond what is popular, it is possible to find positive representations.

Preselfannie E. Whitfield McDaniels discusses the hierarchy that viewers have created in reality TV. In chapter 7, "Questions of Quality and Class: Perceptions of Hierarchy in African American Family-Focused Reality TV Shows," she begins by discussing *Being Bobby Brown*, but she primarily focuses on *Tia & Tamera, The Sheards, Braxton Family Values*, and *T.I. & Tiny: The Family Hustle*. McDaniels situates these shows in opposition to *Keeping Up with the Kardashians*, the *Tequila Sisters, Here Comes Honey Boo Boo*, and *Duck Dynasty*.

Chapter 8, "Contemplating *Basketball Wives*: A Critique of Racism, Sexism, and Income-Level Disparity," by Sharon Lynette Jones discusses arguably one of the more popular reality television shows. *Basketball Wives* exists in direct opposition to the positive media images that Flippin Wynn discusses in chapter 6. Jones argues that instead of participating in and creating meaningful dialogue on major societal issues, the show trivializes racism, sexism, and income-level disparities. Jones, a self-proclaimed fan of the show, presents a detailed critique of the women while challenging the show to better address these issues in the future.

Chapter 9, "Exploiting and Capitalizing on Unique Black Femininity: An Entrepreneurial Perspective," focuses on the financial aspects of reality television shows. Terry A. Nelson examines why African American women choose to participate in the shows, and she places her argument firmly in an entrepreneurial business framework. Using social identity theory, resource-based view theory, and optimal distinctiveness theory, she argues that Black women reality TV stars are strategically using the resources at their disposal to become financially successful. Her arguments primarily address the shows *RHOA, Hollywood Exes*, and *Married to Medicine*.

Chapter 10, the final chapter of the book, pays homage to the ubiquitous reunion episodes that conclude many of the seasons of popular reality TV shows. Even Kevin Hart spoofs the idea of a reunion show in his reality TV parody, *The Real Husbands of Hollywood*. Yet, "Reunion Chapter:

A Conversation among Contributors" is no spoof; the final chapter is a casual academic conversation among all ten of the book contributors. This chapter provides readers with further discussions of earlier chapters and briefly presents new areas of analysis. The "Reunion Chapter" offers a touch of verisimilitude to the book and is presented in a way that is familiar to viewers of reality television. Collectively, this book presents readers with new and exciting ways to discuss reality TV—readers will not view reality television the same ever again.

Works Cited

Abrams, Sil Lai. "From 'Julia' to 'NeNe': The Impact of Reality TV on Black Women." *Grio*. NBC Universal 5 June 2013. http://thegrio.com/2013/06/05/from-julia-to-nene -thoughts-on-the-impact-of-reality-tv-on-black-women/.

Desmond-Harris, Jenée. "*Scandal* Exploits Black Women's Images?" *The Root* 13 Oct. 2012. http://www.theroot.com/articles/culture/2012/10/black_television_stereotypes_tom _burrell_interview.html.

Edwards, Leigh H. *The Triumph of Reality TV: The Revolution in American Television*. Santa Barbara: Praeger, 2013.

Fiske, John. "Hearing Anita Hill (And Viewing Bill Cosby)." *Channeling Blackness: Studies on Television and Race in America*. Ed. Darnell M. Hunt. New York: Oxford UP, 2005. 89–136.

Foreman, P. Gabrielle. "Looking Back from Zora, or Talking Out Both Sides My Mouth for Those Who Have Two Ears." *Black American Literature Forum* 24. Women Writers Issue (1990): 649–666.

Hathaway, Rosemary V. "The Unbearable Weight of Authenticity: Zora Neale Hurston's *Their Eyes Were Watching God* and a Theory of 'Touristic Reading.'" *Journal of American Folklore* 117.464 (2004): 168–190.

Lundy, Lisa K., Amanda M. Ruth, and Travis D. Park. "Simply Irresistible: Reality TV Consumption Patterns." *Communication Quarterly* 56.2 (2008): 208–225.

Nabi, Robin L., et al. "Reality-Based Television Programming and the Psychology of Its Appeal." *Media Psychology* 5.4 (2003): 303–30.

Pettman, Dominic. "So You Think You Can Think." *Inside Higher Ed* 26 Aug. 2013. https:// www.insidehighered.com/views/2013/08/26/essay-teaching-about-reality-tv-turning -course-reality-tv.

Pickens, Therí A. "Shoving Aside the Politics of Respectability: Black Women, Reality TV, and the Ratchet Performance." *Women & Performance: A Journal of Feminist Theory* (2014): 1–18.

Robertson, Iyana. "Beyonce's Gold 'Nipple' Bodysuit Made of 30,000 Swarovski Crystals." *Vibe* 18 Apr. 2013. http://www.vibe.com/2013/04/beyonces-gold-nipple-bodysuit-made -30000-swarovski-crystals/.

Springer, Kimberly. "Divas, Evil Black Bitches, and Bitter Black Women: African-American Women in Postfeminist and Post–Civil Rights Popular Culture." *Feminist Television Criticism: A Reader*. Ed. Charlotte Brunsdon and Lynn Spigel. 2nd ed. Berkshire: Open UP, 2008. 72–92.

Thomas, Brooke. "Reality vs. *The Real World*." *Myfoxmemphis*. Fox Television Stations 1 May 2013. http://www.myfoxmemphis.com/story/22133072/reality-vs-the-real-world.

Tyree, Tia. "African American Stereotypes in Reality Television." *Howard Journal of Communications* 22.4 (2011): 394–413.

Warren, Franchesca. "VH1 Hates Black Women." *Black and Married with Kids*. Black and Married with Kids 19 June 2012.

———. "VH1 Hates Black Women Pt. II: Self Hate Is One Powerful Drug." *Black and Married with Kids*. Black and Married with Kids 22 June 2012.

1

Black Women

• •

From Public Arena
to Reality TV

SHEENA HARRIS

In 1810, the young Khoikhoi, Saartjie Baartman, was enslaved after a European-led commando killed her father and husband in Cape Colony, South Africa, which immediately left Baartman an orphan and a widow. Less than six months later she arrived as a slave in England where she was forced to shock and entertain London audiences with nude performances. She performed in London's Fashion District at the top of the Hay-Market to a high society audience who paid two shillings to see her body. She possessed a large buttocks and elongated labia, and she was soon given the stage name Hottentot Venus. Baartman's oversized posterior was featured on the stage in Piccadilly, where she was forced to flaunt her nude body in colored garments exposing most of her posterior. Her naked body was treated like an exotic creature that overemphasized sexuality. Britain's upper crust gazed at, sought after, lusted for, and was fascinated with what many had considered to be a part of a human menagerie. According to her biographer Rachel Holmes, "To behold the figure of Venus, or to hear her name, was to be prompted to think about lust, or love. At the same time, the word Hottentot signified all that was strange, disturbing, alien, and possibly, sexually deviant" (ch. 1).

In North America as in England, the Black female body was degraded to the status of less than cattle—from the slave block where they were publicly degraded, inspected, sexually desired, and sold to the highest bidder, to the plantation where they became the objects of their new masters' desires. According to Melissa Harris-Perry, "The myth of black women's unrestrained sexuality operated in both slavery and freedom as a means of justifying racial and gender exploitation" (ch. 1). Nearly fifty years after Baartman, Sojourner Truth, a former slave, abolitionist, and author, stood before a public crowd while baring her nude breast and asked "Ain't I a woman?" (hooks 58). In comparison, Baartman was forced onto the public stage because of limited choices: a return to South Africa, where surely she would have resumed a life of servitude, or continued exploitation in England, where she at least received a small wage and an inkling of freedom. Baartman chose the latter, but it was a decision that drove her to alcoholism in order to cope with the debilitating and often unbearable "reality" of her exploited life. Many people of the period talked about the lasciviousness of Black women, yet in all of Baartman's pictures she maintains the utmost dignity and pride despite her servitude.

Baartman's life is a deep contrast to the many "booty shots" of today that have been glorified on reality TV where many of the women are brazenly sexual in their stance and facial expression. White people profited from the body of Baartman, yet in contrast Black women now are profiting from their own bodies while standing in similar stances to her forced stance. In this way, reality television stars perpetuate both consciously and unconsciously the same forces that were used for generations to oppress Black women in American society. The lens of "reality" television that attempts to show real experiences does much to depict a community of Blacks who have advanced and a sector of Blacks masquerading as authentic. These representations are helping to reinforce negative stereotypes surrounding Black women in American popular culture. Is the fact that Black women can call the shots on their bodies and make a profit from them the equality that was fought for, or is it still enslavement in a more complex cultural and financial system that still profits while giving reality characters the crumbs from their proceeds?

During the 2012 season 5 premiere of the *Real Housewives of Atlanta* (*RHOA*), reality television star Phaedra Parks declared, "In our culture behinds have always been desired" when referring to Black women throughout American history. Since the start of her reality career, Parks has strongly emphasized her fondness for "donkey booties." A Georgia native, she insists that "there are a lot of different types of booties. . . . You got your SpongeBob SquarePants. . . . You got big round donkey booties that just come off the back. . . . Black men like a donkey booty, so if you want a black man, you gotta put some meat and potatoes on them bones" (qtd. in Faller). Parks, a lawyer to the stars, used her love for the buttocks to launch a workout video that emphasized the maintenance of the butt; however, before production, she solicited the help of her fellow *RHOA* cast member Kenya Moore, a former Miss USA. Before the two could settle on a workout regimen, they were embroiled in a too-hot-for-TV controversy. Moore eventually left the Parks production and launched her own workout video, featuring the maintenance of a "stallion booty." The debate over the physical maintenance of a donkey booty versus that of a stallion booty, sparked ratings and found its way center stage in the reality television craze.

There are others who have profited from their association with the Black community. In November 2014, Kim Kardashian, who is known for her "black-like features," attempted to "break the Internet" with her naked cover in *Paper* magazine. The public display of the Black female body as exotic and sexually desirable is not a new phenomenon. Historically, many of the stereotypes surrounding the body and the image of Black women generally have been persistent in American popular history. Jewell writes, "Racist legacies that fixate on the sexuality of Black women have meant that black women's responses have often involved suppressing or dissembling discussion about bodies and sexuality" (intro). The *RHOA* stars Parks and Moore perpetuate the public culture surrounding the Black female's body as exotic and oversexualized. They, along with other Black reality stars, provide a trajectory for deconstructing and reinforcing visual misrepresentations of black women. According to scholar bell hooks: "American women have been socialized, even brainwashed, to accept a version of American history that was created to uphold and maintain racial imperialism in the form of white supremacy and sexual imperialism in the form of patriarchy. One measure of the success of such indoctrination is that we perpetuate both consciously and unconsciously the very evils that oppresses us" (120). hooks's analysis serves as an interesting reference point in discussing the evolution of Black women on the public stage and the rise of reality television. Historically Black women, after the American Civil War, took to the public arena in an attempt to defuse many of the negative stereotypes that made it virtually impossible to claim full citizenship rights. In a white male–dominated society, Black women did not have a full range of public representation (Harris-Perry ch. 1).

The image of Black women within reality television is a continuation of exploitation in historical identification, and it complicates the narrative of Black womanhood especially in a self-professed "postracial" society. Black women's reality and the media's portrayal of them are sometimes at odds with one another. It begs one to question whether or not reality television stars speak for the entire Black community or simply for themselves. Is reality the mask used by a capitalistic society that garners lavish and fictitious dreams of wealth, fame, and self-respect, which makes it okay to publicly feed into the most debilitating stereotypes of the century? In many ways, reality television gestures toward the fictional portrayal of middle-class and elite Black women in an attempt to represent a shared experience among Blacks. It is a display that forces viewers to integrate the suppression of Black women's independence and the extent to which Black women still subscribe to notions of the popular culture's definitions of true womanhood.

Given the plethora of reality television shows since the early 2000s, it seems an opportune time to examine how these shows, particularly those with a majority Black female cast, construct themselves as a genre, and are, in turn, being constructed by critics, viewers, and the continued maintenance of white supremacy. Several of the most viewed successful reality shows of this recent period—VH1's *I Love New York, Love and Hip Hop: Atlanta* (*LAHHA*), and Bravo's *The Real Housewives of Atlanta*—contain elements of truth that signify a "real" depiction of Black women as elite, wives, and refined. However, after viewing Black women within this particular genre, the question becomes how much exploitation Black women are projecting and how much is being forced upon them. Such depictions tend to be problematic to the real experience of Black women as a body of people. The reality television genre is so far from real that it is more of a symbolic gesture of an imagined elite status that many of the women grapple with but never truly understand.

Historically, a refined culture played a big part in whether or not the new social class would be accepted into the main body of elites. Today, however, through reality television, a new class of seemingly elite Black women has surfaced. They are vastly different from the Black women who took to the public arena at the turn of the century and whose status, in turn, carried with it a public and cultural responsibility (Giddings vi; Jackson 14–18; Neverdon-Morton 2; White 161). It was the responsibility of the Black elite to go into the community and help in the uplifting of the race (Harlan 161). Unfortunately, these ideas are now being overshadowed by the glitz and glam of a rising popular culture. Reality star Black women of today, especially those from the South, are more concerned with self-gratification than the perceived continued maintenance of harmful stereotypes. Linnethia Monique Johnson, better known as NeNe Leakes on *RHOA*, is an excellent example of this class structure. While it is unclear just how rich Leakes is, she never passes up an opportunity to remind the viewing public, "I'm rich, bitch." Leakes has continued to build upon her *RHOA* fame. She starred in season 18 of *Dancing with the Stars* and has had recurring roles on *Glee* and *The New Normal*.

Reality television has provided an avenue for this new class of elites to showcase the grandeur, possessions, and an affluent quality of life, while the viewing public makes a mockery of them and their lack of a more refined behavior generally associated with the upper class. Whether intentionally or simply by default, reality television allows those who participate to influence the decisions, rationale, and race consciousness of the masses. It offers a plausible alternative—or break from reality—for many poor Blacks in a society structured around their failure. Who would have thought that people would be more immersed in the imagined drama of others than in their own lives? Reality TV has captured the sensationalism surrounding the derogatory image of Black women and has helped to reinforce age-old stereotypes about their place—or lack thereof—in the public arena.

Throughout the years, scholarship has sought to correct many of the myths and stereotypes to which women in the public arena were subjected. Notions that African American women, both rich and impoverished, were unfit to shape public culture has persisted for generations. Do Black women have the ability to redefine respectable behavior and gender roles as they relate to Black culture? Do Black women generally attempt to fit into a predesigned media box that rarely takes their history, body image, and culture into perspective? Finally, how have Black women used the reality television craze to bring authentic Black female culture to the forefront of American society? Justin M. Jhally argues:

The whole process of watching television [has] social influence. Television provides us with pictures of the world, of our world, and the knowledge that most of these pictures are fictional does not immunize us from believing in them. The beliefs we form become part of the context within which we understand who we are. To understand prime-time television, then is to understand an important part of the way we view the world and ourselves. (ch. 1)

The arrival of reality television has been both influential and detrimental to the image of Black women. According to the scholar K. Sue Jewell, "Mainstream media have historically served the interest of the privileged, who have defined African American women and other disenfranchised segments of the population as possessing certain values, belief systems and lifestyles that do not entitle them to receive societal resources, but account for their marginal status in salient societal institutions" (intro). Within the evolution of Black popular culture, the continued impact of segregation, disfranchisement, and the changing composition and influence of intragroup class relationships on Black women are rarely considered. Certainly reality television has done much to stimulate our imaginations with animated characters, drama, suspense, and in those rare occasions, love. Since the onset of Black women as a main subject within this genre, Blacks have found their way to this guilty yet pleasurable prime-time entertainment.

From the reemergence of Public Enemy's hype man Flavor Flav's *Flavor of Love*, which aired on VH1, American audiences of all races, ages, and economic backgrounds regretfully, and often in secret, tuned in faithfully as they watched, talked about, and became completely engrossed in the seemingly "real" love life of Flavor Flav. Loosely based on the dating show *The Bachelor*, twenty women lived in a California mansion and simultaneously group-dated the outdated and semi-famous rap star until the winner was chosen. Within three seasons the hype man, who wore an oversized clock around his neck, admonished African Americans to never forget "what time it was." *Flavor of Love*, publicized as a dating game show, brought on female contestants who were expected, publicly and without filter, to prove their love for Flavor Flav. In return, the aging star would have group and one-on-one dates with all of the young contestants in a process that took speed dating to new heights. Despite the criticism that the show received, its second season finale ratings listed it as the second-highest nonsports basic cable television show of 2006. VH1 had an instant hit through the oftentimes "Stepin Fetchit"–like character of an American celebrity. *Flavor of Love* helped with spin-off shows like *I Love New York, Charm School*, and *I Love Money* (Stanley).[1]

Although *Flavor of Love* is often rejected by the masses of the Black middle class, it is an interesting way to discuss the rise of Black women in popular culture as it relates to the reality television world. Flavor Flav's misuse of the Black body is not uncommon. Black women have been exploited and recurrently placed at the bottom of the social totem pole in American society. From earlier forms of popular media, males within society often defined the roles of Black women. White and Black newspapers alike considered the female platform not only to reside within the domestic sphere but also to be docile and subservient. According to excerpts from articles in the *Freedom's Journal*, the first African American–owned and –operated newspaper, Black women were admonished to "employ yourself in household affairs. Wait till your husband confides in you, and do not give your advice till he asks it. Always appear flattered by the little he does for you.... A wife may have more sense than her husband but she should never seem to know it" (Sterling 220; see also King 39). Historically, women have been taught to know their place.

Despite the fact that these sentiments were being spread throughout the nineteenth century, many of them found their way center stage in reality television. It could also be argued that these nineteenth-century newspaper reports on how and what Black women should be certainly could not foresee the rise of reality television. Although *Flavor of Love* helps to chronicle one of the first negative depictions of Black women in the new reality culture, the show also does much to signify class debates as well. The women on *Flavor of Love* were willing to do anything for the attention of Flavor Flav. One woman allegedly defecates on the floor as a cry for attention from both Flavor Flav and the reality television audience. How much of these actions can actually be seen as "real" and authentic experiences? An emphasis on the factual has always been a contested issue within the Black community. From slave narratives, to newspapers, and finally to reality television, the reality genre exists at the generic crossroads between what is real and what is fiction. When Flavor Flav entered into living rooms around the world, many conscious Blacks immediately began to engage in public discourses about the "perceived" reality of one man's love life and how that projection of "truth" would affect the larger community. More important, how would his negative depiction of women, primarily Black women, be socially crippling and take Blacks back two hundred years to when Baartman stood center stage in Piccadilly, England, as men and women stood mystified and aroused by her half-naked physique and confident posture?[2] The marketing of reality television shows as the general experiences of Black women is also problematic. They further suggest that Black women are uncultured, primitive, and lack sophistication. They emphasize the extent women of color would go in their pursuit of fame, love, and stardom.

VH1's *I Love New York* was a direct spin-off of *Flavor of Love.* Tiffany Pollard, better known by the stage name New York, went to extreme measures to gain the attention and affection of Flavor Flav. There was no limit to her "reality" character. Pollard was willing to fight, curse, and engage in sexual intercourse in order to prove her devotion to Flav. After two whirlwind seasons of self-degradation, the generous producers of VH1 offered Pollard her own official show—*I Love New York.* Similar to *Flavor of Love,* Pollard participated in the public display of dating nearly twenty men at the same time until she selected her "true love." Pollard's character in many ways performed as a modern-day minstrel show. Similar to how Thomas "Daddy" Rice blackened his face with charcoal and ridiculed Black folk, Pollard's "reality" buffoonery projected an image of a subordinate Black humanity and created a psychological sense of Black inferiority.[3] Yet, her ratings, just as Flavor Flav's ratings, imply that Black people in blackface represented a desired genre of television, which was authenticated through the fact that the characters were Black and accepted as true representations of the larger "body" of Blacks—the Black community.

Pollard does not represent an anomaly. Nearly sixty years after the demise of slavery, Black men and women were continually in a battle to redefine negative stereotypes about the ability, equality, and ambitions of Blacks. Black women, unlike white women, had to be careful not to be seen as too promiscuous and worldly because then all women would be judged by the few—respectability politics. According to clubwoman Margaret Murray Washington, third wife of race leader Booker T. Washington:

> Moreover, you can no more find the "average" Negro woman than you can multiply eggs by treaties. Just as eggs are different from treaties, so good Negro women are different from bad Negro women, and no average can be struck. The best we can do is to estimate the size of the various groups of Negro women, but even this is not enough; the influence, efficiency, significance of one superior woman's life may be indefinitely more than that of ten dull

drudges. And so the statistical method could not do justice to this essentially human problem; statistics negate individuality. (*Outlook* magazine)

However, with the growing genre of Black inclusion in American popular culture, it became that much more difficult to conceal the "bad eggs" within the race from the public: "Earlier forms of popular culture, especially minstrelsy, had also shaped perceptions of African Americans and circumscribed the careers of Black artists . . . but . . . in an age of commercialized leisure and proliferating technologies of mass" media, the intensity of negative stereotypes of blacks only grew (Brundage 2). Still, at the onset of *I Love New York*'s first season in January 2007, and despite the one-sided historical depiction of Black women as oversexualized, Pollard entertained the public's continued fascination with the negative sensibilities of Black womanhood. She did this similar to the way that the Hottentot Venus's exotic persona entertained European men in the nineteenth century and the way that American Black women were characterized as desexualized or oversexualized. These myths, through the popular mass media, have lived into the twentieth century through minstrel characters like Pollard. However, the burden of the race cannot be placed on the shoulders of one female who in many ways is a minnow in a larger sea of exploiters. However, her voice is powerful in telling her own story, despite the exaggerated scenes.

VH1's *Love and Hip Hop: Atlanta* (*LAHHA*) presents another fascinating discourse on the public sphere, race, body image issues, and class. It plays into the popular fixation of Blacks as primitive and in desperate need of love. *LAHHA* is a spin-off from the original *Love and Hip Hop: New York*, which focused on men in the hip hop industry and the women who love them. *LAHHA* offers many of the same problematic representations of Black female imagery as other reality television shows. *LAHHA* focuses on the love affairs of a few artists who live in the Atlanta area. The most notable male on the show is Steven Jordan, who goes by the stage name Stevie J. He is a figure who plays into all of the negative stereotypes that are associated with Black males and their treatment of Black women. While *LAHHA* does little to show the historical consciousness of the characters being presented, they do present the effects of years of oppression on the Black family. According to Jordan, he mistreats women because his mother neglected him as a child. Joseline Hernandez, a former stripper and prostitute, accepts and understands Jordan's situation because her parents abandoned her and forced her to endure a life on the streets. Finally, Oluremi "Mimi" Faust, the owner of a cleaning service, "Keep It Clean," and the mother of Jordan's fifth child, consistently subjects herself to his abuse because he insists that he cannot control his womanizing ways. Jordan is an oversexed Black male who represents many of the ills within the Black community. On numerous occasions Jordan tells the women in his life that he is the driver of his bus and they can choose to stay on or get off. With more than five children from several different women, his most recent "baby momma," Faust, has appeared in all three seasons. The viewing audience is forced to sit back and watch as Jordan, a Grammy Award–winning manager and producer, lies to and manipulates Faust. If she did not know about the deceit in season 1, after season 2 it is clear that she is a willing participant in Stevie J.'s reality show of exploitation.

The plot only thickens with each episode of *LAHHA*. During season one, the American public learns that Jordan and Hernandez were expecting a child. This whirlwind takes viewers into the season two finale when Hernandez publically admits that the two have issues because of their mothers and they plan to help each other out of their downward spiral. Hernandez's loyalty and understanding of Jordan's inability to be faithful, honest, and racially conscious causes him to find comfort in her character and to marry her. Shortly thereafter he has a public affair with B. Mae, an aspiring rapper on the show. This foursome represents only one of the dysfunctional love stories found within this reality television show.

The question arises once more: Why cannot reality television simply be looked at as pure entertainment? Perhaps in a society that does not benefit from the continued maintenance of Black exploitation, reality television could just be seen as pure entertainment. However, within American society it continues to serves as a problematic representation that exploits Blacks in exchange for entertainment. Within the various depictions of women and their relationships with men, the Black female body is continually put on public display. Her class and occupation are called into question, and without a doubt the Black women within these reality shows do much more than depict singular lives within American culture. The singular view becomes a collective view. They inadvertently lead the outside world to believe without question the historically popular images of Black women as second-class citizens. What *LAHHA* offers the general public is anything but an authentic representation of Black culture. Perhaps if reality TV offered a full range of Black female representation, the debates would be more balanced. However, it is deeply rooted in the real monstrosity of the nineteenth-century minstrel show and it makes a mockery of wives, the elite, motherhood, and the state of the Black family structure. Love? It is clear within these shows that no one loves their Black bodies and is therefore incapable of loving others. Sociologist E. Franklin Frazier calls it the inferiority complex and the quest for status within a race-based society. He writes, "Living constantly under the domination and contempt of the white man, the [Black woman] came to believe in [her] own inferiority, whether [she] ignored or accepted the values of the white man's world" or not (Frazier 130). Frazier's argument supports the fact that reality television cannot be simply looked at as pure entertainment.

Even in the age of President Barack and First Lady Michelle Obama and the full range of positive Black imagery available in American society, there is still an unexplainable fascination with reality television that plays up the negative stereotypes of African Americans. From the "Stepin Fetchit" characters of Flavor Flav and Stevie J. to the outspoken, oversexed, and often violent New York and the women of *LAHHA*, the imaginations and deepest fears of viewers were ignited. From the obvious minstrel stage of reality television, the viewing audience is taken to the arena of the southern "new Black elite." It is here that the plot would appear to have changed, but in most ways it remains the same. Black women and men dress up in clothes they cannot afford, eat at restaurants they cannot pronounce, purchase expensive homes that they cannot furnish and are later evicted from, question their identity, and exploit their own bodies. The women "take care" of the men, and they all engage in an uncontested level of violence that is unmated. The new Black elite, through these reality shows, represents the grave ill in American society in which Blacks continuously support notions of white supremacy and engage in an inferiority complex (Frazier 131). The real representations of Black life stand in sharp contrast to the "real" representations of reality television.

Beyond the construction and maintenance of "housewifery," Bravo's *The Real Housewives: Atlanta* (*RHOA*) mocks the term in its entirety. For many Blacks, however, Black women were never the "traditional" definition of housewives. They have worked outside of the home for generations. To the general public, however, they have been associated with such terms as *lazy, welfare queens, masculine*, and *ghetto*. These depictions grew from a long history of slavery, segregation, discriminatory public laws, racism, Jim Crow laws, and disfranchisement. According to W. E. B. Du Bois,

"The result of this history of insult and degradation has been both fearful and glorious. It has birthed the haunting prostitute, the brawler, and the beast of burden; but it has also given the world an efficient womanhood, whose strength lies in its freedom and whose chastity was won in the teeth of temptation and not in prison and swaddling clothes" (Du Bois ch. 7). White privilege, in contrast, allowed white middle- and upper-class women and men to continually shift and redefine their infrastructure. More important, an acknowledgment that not all Black women fall under this negative stereotype does not mean that "all" Black women are wholesome and without fault. However, it becomes extremely problematic when a few Blacks are used to define the larger Black community and the representation is negative.

RHOA offer the most complex trajectory to analyze the overarching problematic depiction of Black women in reality television. Through the "real" lives of five to six women (depending on the season), Bravo captures the seemingly real struggles, joys, failures, and everyday lives of Atlanta's finest. There are several different installments of *Real Housewives*, but the Atlanta series is surprisingly the highest-rated and the most-watched series on the network. What about the *RHOA* causes men and women of all economic statuses and ethnic backgrounds to faithfully tune in to watch the daily drama of NeNe Leakes, Phaedra Parks, Kandi Burruss, Kenya Moore, Cynthia Bailey Rhoa, Porsha Stewart (Williams), and a revolving door of others? All of these women represent some element of the wife, the single woman, lust, love, and sexuality. In many ways they also depict the negative impact of slavery on Black women and families. But do these women also represent progress?

Many ideas surrounding what constitutes a housewife are challenged within *RHOA*. All of the women have jobs and careers, except for Stewart, who appeared in seasons 4 and 5. She was married to ex-football quarterback Kordell Stewart and spends most of her time planning charity events. The other men on the show are depicted as the real "housewives." In an interview with television host Wendy Williams, Porsha Stewart confessed, "If anybody decided to be a 1950s wife, it was me. I was an independent woman. I had my own business. I was a boss. I had a lot of responsibility. When I met a man who I just cater to and just make him my world, I decided to be that way with him. I decided to make him and his son my everything. . . . So, that was all on me" (qtd. in *Sister 2 Sister*). In contrast, the other wives were more descriptive of the reversed roles of man and wife within the Black community. However, this stereotype suggests that the roles of Black women and men are different than those of white men and women and that education and discrimination play little within these gravely exaggerated representations.

Parks is married to conman Apollo Nida. They have two young boys and deal with the daily stresses of marriage, kids, infidelity, Parks's career, and Nida's criminal activity.[4] As previously mentioned, Parks with the help of her husband contracted to do a workout video, and their main coordinator was going to be Moore, a former Miss USA. Moore, unlike Parks, is not married and is seemingly jobless, which further muddles her qualifications to be on the show. Yet, controversy ensues over future proceeds of the video and the team splits. Strife between the two women begins immediately. Ultimately, Parks and Nida continue with their video. They decide on the name *Phine Body*. The video emphasizes the maintenance of the "donkey booty." Moore then commits to creating her own version of "phine" with the *Stallion Booty Bootcamp Workout Video*. The controversy became so heated that it went beyond reality television. While promoting her video on *Anderson Live*, Moore bashes the "donkey booty" video while also refuting claims that she supposedly bought her butt. During her appearance on *Anderson Live*, Anderson jokingly asks, "What's the difference between a Stallion Booty and a Donkey Booty?" Moore goes on to explain the difference between the two animals. Not once does she acknowledge the historical implications of seeing women in terms of as animal posteriors. Despite these truths, according to Amazon's purchasing site, Moore's video sales are topping the charts, and it would appear that the American people want a "stallion booty" too. Parks and Moore both seemed to be re-creating the Baartman experience, even though it may be argued that unlike Baartman they both controlled their own images and bodies.

The question surrounding reality television beckons the public to ask at what cost do Black women who are not housewives, who are not rich, who are violent, and who are not the "shared Black experience" speak for the majority of Blacks in the public arena? Many would argue that the depiction of Black women in reality television is part truth and part scripted, yet the continued willingness to be exploited is tied into basic needs of survival—an argument that is often used as an easy way not to be held accountable for one's actions. When compared to Black women within a historical context, it was survival when a mother slept with her owner so that he would not rape her daughter. It was survival when within the caste of slavery, women had no voice, no autonomy, and no space to cultivate who they were and who their daughters would be. Yet, during those times they understood the system. They knew that any wrong move would be the total destruction of their offspring, the destruction of their race, and their sex. So women created a public arena in order to make right what had been wrong for so many years. Today, however, there are no auction blocks, in the traditional sense; instead, now, there are television boxes that serve as incubators to the historically negative images of Black womanhood. The Black woman can still redefine the way she is viewed by the masses. Perhaps reality television will be the medium in which she can change the alarming negative perception of the Black community and the Black woman.

Notes

1 Public Enemy, which was formed in 1982, is well known for its tough criticism of popular media and the continued destruction of the Black community. However, once Flavor Flav made it to the stage of reality television, his "fight the power" and political overtones of injustice days were over. He had officially succumbed to the powers that be. He now helped in the public maintenance of white supremacy and in the continued destruction and treatment of Black women as second-class citizens.

2 Seemingly harmless, could reality television succeed in the total denigration of Black women in ways that the slave block, public newspapers, and Blaxploitation films could not?

3 Minstrel shows served as a form of white entertainment prior to the Civil War when dialect speech and caricatured images were becoming a popular "art form." During the 1830s and 1840s, Thomas "Daddy" Rice performed "Jump Jim Crow," from which the term *Jim Crow* originated.

4 Nida's career is unknown. After Nida was imprisoned for nearly five years, Parks and Nida married. However, his bad streak did not end with his nonviolent criminal offense. In 2014, he was arrested for and pled guilty to charges of fraud and identity theft.

Works Cited

Brundage, Fetzhugh, ed. *Beyond Blackface: African Americans and the Creation of American Popular Culture, 1890–1930*. Columbia: U of South Carolina P.

Du Bois, Darkwater: *Voices from Within the Veil*. New York: Washington Square Press, 2004.

Faller, Bonnie. "Hollywood Life by Bonnie Faller." Your Celebrity News, Fashion, and Beauty BFF. http://hollywoodlife.com/celeb/phaedra-parks/.

Fortini, Amanda and Jean-Paul Goude. "No Filter: An Afternoon with Kim Kardashian." *Paper*, 2014. Papermag.com. http://www.papermag.com/2014/11/kim_kardashian.php.

Frazier, E. Franklin. *Black Bourgeoisie: The Rise of a New Middle Class in the United States.* New York: Free Press, 1957.

Giddings, Paula. *When and Where I Enter: The Impact of Black Women on Race and Sex in America.* New York: HarperCollins, 1984.

Harlan, Louis. *The Making of a Back Leader. Vol. 1: The Making of a Black Leader, 1856–1901.* New York: Oxford U P, 1972.

Harris-Perry, Melissa V. *Sister Citizen: Shame, Stereotypes, and Black Women in America.* New Haven and London: Yale UP, 2011.

Holmes, Rachel. *African Queen: The Real Life of the Hottentot Venus.* New York: Random House, 2003.

hooks, bell. *Ain't I a Woman: Black Women and Feminism.* Boston: South End, 1981.

Jackson, David H. Jr. *Booker T. Washington and the Struggle against White Supremacy: The Southern Educational Tours, 1908–1912.* New York: Palgrave Macmillan, 2008.

Jewell, K. Sue. *From Mammy to Miss America and Beyond: Cultural Images and the Shaping of US Social Policy.* London and New York: Routledge, 1993.

Jhally, Sut, and Justin M. Lewis. *Enlightened Racism: The Cosby Show, Audiences, and the Myth of the American Dream.* Boulder, CO: Westview, 1992.

King, Wilma. *The Essence of Liberty: Free Black Women during the Slave Era.* Columbia: U of Missouri P, 1996.

Neverdon-Morton, Cynthia. *Afro-American Women of the South and the Advancement of the Race, 1895–1925.* Knoxville: U of Tennessee P, 1989.

Outlook, May 1904.

Sister 2 Sister, November 11, 2013.

Stanley, Alessandra. "On 'Flavor of Love' and 'Secret Lives of Women,' Jail Brides and Would-Be Rap Molls." *New York Times* 8 Aug. 2006. http://www.nytimes.com/2006/08/08/arts/television/08love.html?fta=y&_r=0.

Sterling, Dorothy, ed. *We Are Your Sisters: Black Women in the Nineteenth Century.* New York: Norton, 1984.

White, Deborah Gray. *Ar'n't I a Woman: Female Slaves in the Plantation South.* New York: Norton, 1985.

2

Selective Reuptake

· ·

Perpetuating Misleading
Cultural Identities in the
Reality Television World

LATOYA JEFFERSON-JAMES

"Selective reuptake" is frequently used in psychopharmacology and other areas of chemical dependency; however, I use it with the understanding that viewing reality television is itself an addiction in American culture. Therefore, it is dangerous to ignore reality television or dismiss it as harmless, fluff entertainment not worthy of academic interrogation. As a topic ripe for academic exploration, I cannot write about reality television shows as if they appeared simply because the zeitgeist was right. Like many phenomena of American culture, reality television became ubiquitous because it is cheap to make and profitable for the producers and companies. African Americans' rather late entry into the reality television game is a reflection of the need for greater profit. Culturally, reality television, including those shows that feature predominantly African American casts, does not deviate from the ideology of the hegemony. Further, it would be academically disingenuous to write of African American reality television shows—or any manifestation of current-day African American culture—as somehow divorced from American culture. For this reason, I chose to write about two particular shows, one secular and definitely profane, and the other a secularization of the sacred for less than pious purposes. Though they may appear radically different on the surface, they are both linked by misogynistic gender notions that have been scripted onto African American bodies and culture and continue to cause tension in the African American community.

Reality television shows with majority Black casts like *Flavor of Love* (*FOL*) and *Preachers of L.A.* are very much a part of the white supremacist, patriarchal, capitalistic ideology, though the faces are brown and many of them female; the subject matter is selective reuptakes of long-standing stereotypes that have followed African Americans since their first inclusions in film technology. The behavior of the casts and African Americans' record-breaking consumption of their antics are manifestations of African Americans' internalization of the dominant culture's view of them. African Americans condone and perpetuate their own subjugation with support of these shows while someone else profits. Many times, these shows make mockeries of Black manhood at the expense of Black womanhood. Sometimes, in the reality television world, Black males are selected who display and embody exploitative, predatory behavior. Other times, they are edited to create that familiar stereotype, which is then consumed by the audience. The roles of Black women support the dehumanization of Black males and are equally disturbing. They are cast between the unwitting supporters of their own oppression or the deserving Sapphires. Either way, Black women continue to be crystallized somewhere between Jezebel and Sapphire, and for twenty-first-century audiences who are unfamiliar with both these stereotypes, record-breaking consumption of these images seemingly support them.

First, reality television is a cheap and useful discursive tool for the hegemony. Many shows feature celebrities who have fallen from either grace or prominence, quasi-celebrities who are looking to increase their fame or paydays, overnight YouTube sensations, or ordinary people who are simply looking to break into show business or break out of debt. Reality television is also Hollywood's way of outsourcing jobs. By the 1980s, scripted television shows—which require writers, actors, editors, makeup artists, and other personnel—skyrocketed in production costs. With cable television offering audiences more choices and advertisers more competition, producers felt pressed: "Program producers (network production arms, major Hollywood studios, and the few small independent production companies) all faced rapidly rising costs in the 1980s" (Raphael 126). Producers were losing money and began deficit financing shows: hoping that the success of the first season would help them recoup their initial investment expenses. Economically, reality television shows made sense for several reasons during these times: first, "at a time when dramas routinely costs over $1 million per episode, and half-hour sitcoms cost $500,000 to $600,000 apiece, Reali-TV programs offered considerable savings in production costs, sometimes over 50 percent compared with fictional programming" (Raphael 131). Second, reality television shows did not need scripts, and therefore producers could totally eliminate that expense, and without the requirements for elaborate scripts and careful character development, reality television shows could be produced quickly. Third, producers recouped their investments expediently, sometimes with the airing of only a few episodes.

A fourth benefit of creating reality television shows was that producers did not have to hire and pay to retain top talent in order to make shows successful. Retaining talent for scripted shows represents a huge investment for producers. Ted Madger's description of a popular comedy's contracts demonstrates the magnitude of such investments:

> Take *Friends*, for example. In 1994, the six principal actors agreed to five-year contracts at $22,500 each per episode. At each renewal of the contract for *Friends*, the cast negotiated as a group, with threats to move on and pursue other projects. In 1999, each of the six actors was paid $125,000 per episode; the following two seasons, each received $750,000 per episode. For the 2002 season—the final year for the show—each cast member earned $1 million an episode, with each episode budgeted at $7.5 million. (144)

Though *Friends* is an extreme example, it represents the significant investment in labor producers make when they want to retain the top talent of Hollywood. Producers not only have to pay the talent, but also must abide by contractual stipulations set by the Screen Actors' Guild, and they may be held accountable for the way in which particular characters are written and portrayed on film through selective editing.

By dispelling with top-notch actors, producers avoided contractual obligations and unionized pay. Reality television stars receive modest pay; reports range from as low as $25,000 to as high as $80,000 per episode. Though this is nowhere near the amount of money former *Friends* star Jennifer Aniston and others make for television shows, it is much higher than the average American wage earner. For the disgraced or seemingly irrelevant celebrity or the average citizen, a few recorded sessions of personal humiliation may be well worth the cost. Furthermore, contracts for reality television stars are not laden with the unionized demands and image restrictions of Hollywood talent. Producers have free range to edit and portray reality stars in ways that maximize viewership with little regard for the harm their editing may bring to the stars' images.

Economically, this proliferation of reality television in an ailing economy seems sensible. However, it is also important to understand the concept of cultural domination and hegemony and the role that the media plays in advancing ideology. Hegemony, according to Antonio Gramsci, is simply the dominant culture and its ideals about how the world is ordered. The dominant culture uses various superstructures, including the environment and the economy, narratives and media outlets, schools and textbooks, law enforcement and legislation, and church and family in order to maintain its cultural preeminence in a society. Though force has been used historically to bring about domination for the hegemony, in this era media is an invaluable discursive tool for maintenance of dominance. On the one hand, the media help people conform to and accept their own subjugation as logical and natural through the repetition of certain narratives, ideas, and stereotypes. On the other hand, the dominant culture enjoys a sense of prestige in its own narratives about itself. It is presented in all facets, including the media, as *the* highest form of humanity, its history as *the* narrative of struggle and hope within the human family, its artistic/social/historical/cultural outputs as *the* definitive human activities, its phenotypical traits as *the* standards of beauty, and its gender roles as *the* proper sexual hierarchy. Other cultures are shown in proscribed, often two-dimensional roles that are in direct opposition to those images presented of the dominant culture. Taken together, these two opposing cultural representations, which may be ubiquitous via various media outlets in certain historical epochs, are accepted and internalized as "truth" by both the oppressor and the other. As Gramsci writes, this "'spontaneous' consent given by the great masses of the population to the general direction imposed on social life by the dominant fundamental group; this consent is 'historically' caused by the prestige (and consequent confidence) which the dominant group enjoys because of its position in the world of productions" (12). Accepting and supporting the dominant groups' perception of the other as truth is the "spontaneous consent" of which Gramsci speaks. Reality television, normally controlled by the dominant group, is economically and culturally consistent with the views of the dominant group. For instance, it is no coincidence that Americans are consistently shown the same repeating images of African Americans. Repetition through media over time helps to bring about unforced, spontaneous consent, and reality television shows, with their carefully placed stereotypes, is as much a part of this process as old-fashioned minstrel shows.

Economically, although reality television shows are cheaply produced, they play upon the class anxieties experienced by most Americans. Gone are the modest, middle-class homes and neighborhoods that characterized the sets of most scripted sitcoms of the late 1970s and 1980s. In the reality television world, on shows such as *The Bachelor*, homes are replaced by lavishly furnished mansions. The surroundings of the television shows often contrast sharply with the backgrounds of many minority contestants who see this venue as an opportunity for vertical economic advancement. The women on the shows often confess on camera how being chosen would greatly improve their personal financial situations. The business of doing these reality shows is harmful to television audiences: "In a culture in which young women and people of color often feel they have few options, these shows conflate self-worth with net worth" (Pozner 158). These shows are devoid of the historical conditions of racism and sexism and motivate people to humiliate themselves on global television for a life free of poverty. These intentional sociohistorical blots, coupled with the creative editing, allow the audience to blame the individual on screen for his or her respective dire economic straits, and not the society that produced those straits. While reality television plays upon the anxieties of most Americans, they alleviate any responsibility the hegemony may feel for causing those anxieties through its political and economic policies. In short, reality television makes classism, racism, and sexism fun again. In thirty minutes to one hour, Americans can guiltlessly laugh at the ignorant ramblings of hillbillies and rednecks, the buffoonery of African Americans, or the tawdry antics of housewives in New Jersey. Furthermore, the reality stars get paid modestly for a day's worth of nonunionized labor.

No network captures this sentiment more effectively than the music channel VH1. On January 9, 2003, VH1 introduced a new genre of reality television shows to American audiences with its cheaply produced new show, *The Surreal Life*. The show featured a racially and gender-mixed cast of celebrities past their prime. During the show, a group of celebrities lived together in country musician Glen Campbell's former mansion for two weeks in the Hollywood Hills. The cast members participated in "missions," or group activities, that the cameras captured. These missions were nothing more than outrageous acts that were set up by producers. In fact, one common description of the show reads, "Has been stars share a home and are expected to perform outrageous acts" (Rose and Wood 285). In addition to the "outrageous acts," the cameras also captured their various love trysts, interpersonal relationships, and conflicts. *The Surreal Life* represented a break from the traditional reality television series in that it featured celebrities past their prime instead of young college coeds who whimsically stumble from one episodic mess to another. The series was also one of the first to formally feature cast members of color outside of competition shows. By breaking with the traditional young, white cast, VH1 developed its own formula and captured a niche audience. Audiences rewarded the awful behavior of the middle-aged celebrities on *Surreal Life* so completely that several of the spin-offs developed their own spin-offs. The original show lasted six seasons. VH1's new formula opened the door for African American reality television casts.

Until *Surreal Life* and its spin-offs, most reality television casts were predominantly white, like most American television. African Americans participated only occasionally in competition shows. The history of African Americans in American film and television is one fraught with racial tension and stereotyping. The stereotypes of African Americans presented in most films and television are continuations of the foundational stereotypes that were laid during the bipartite European Enlightenment. Scientific racism and sexism—the other, equally influential development in European philosophical thought and worldview—began slightly before the Enlightenment and only grew stronger in the shadows of the Enlightenment. The same philosophers who wrote eloquent, passionate tracts arguing for individual liberty, democracy, freedom, and the pursuit of property also ascribed to and developed new stereotypes that justified the enslavement of Africans. According to philosophers like Georg Wilhelm Friedrich Hegel, Bartolomeo de las Casas, and Nicholas de Condorcet, African gender customs were inverted: African males were lazy, effeminate, and passive while African women were aggressive, masculine, and dominating. Uncle Toms, coons, bucks, Jezebels, and Mammies were used in Euro-American proslavery arguments then enacted by Euro-American men in blackface on the minstrel stage after slavery as America's most popular form of entertainment. When film technology developed sometime around the early twentieth century, these old stereotypes, in addition to some new ones, were simply transferred to film.[1]

When D. W. Griffith's *The Birth of a Nation* debuted in 1915, it was lauded as a cinematic breakthrough. Yet, its depictions of African American men and women are highly selective and reflective of the stereotypes that were accepted as fact at the time of the film's making. For instance, the film portrays African American women as both the faithful, asexual Mammy who protects the white family against her own people and as a hot pussy, manipulative, seductive Jezebel.[2] In one scene, a Black woman bares her breasts and begs a handsome, white man for intercourse. While Black males are portrayed as criminals and inept leaders, the film introduces a new stereotype: the sexually insatiable Black male brute with a taste for white female flesh. The virginal white woman leaps to her death rather than submit to the clutches of the Black man (really a white man in blackface), and the knights of the Ku Klux Klan ride in to avenge her death. These types of portrayals in *Birth* and films like it justified the sexual harassment and abuse of attractive Black women and the lynching of Black males: "This continued visual presentation also represents the sociopolitical resistance to the Emancipation of the slaves and attempts to restore African Americans to their pre-Emancipation status" (Spencer 20). These images betray the economic and political anxieties of white males who had to share their patriarchal privilege with those they once enslaved. They also reflect "the ruling class's attempts to maintain control of their labor power of the African American through promoting images of that reinforced need for such control" (Spencer 20). Films such as *The Birth of a Nation* portray Euro-American culture as par excellence and Black bodies as ugly, castigated objects that simply have to be restricted and whipped into submission.

In addition to the insatiable Black buck/brute, the hegemonic media developed several other peculiar figures, which survive into the twenty-first century either in their original, horrible forms or as reincarnations. These characters, introduced by white producers and writers, appear only in all-Black casts, thereby creating the illusion of "spontaneous consent" by having Black people play caricatures of themselves. Actually, these roles were slightly better than Mammy and Uncle Tom, but still limited and limiting and the only ones made available to Black actors outside of subservient depictions. I focus on a few: the Pimp, the Sapphire, and the Preacher and how they are recast in reality television. These figures are problematic in that their presentations in film make light of real or imagined areas of continuing intergender cleavages within the African American community for profit. They are also consistent with the misogyny inherent in white supremacist, patriarchal, capitalistic thought. To be clear, "Misogyny is the hatred or disdain of women. It is an ideology that reduces women to objects for men's ownership, use, or abuse. It diminishes women to expendable beings" (Adams and Fuller 939). In addition, these racialized figures relieve members of the dominant culture, even as they create and present them, of any guilt associated with the discriminatory historical and economic conditions that made them possible in the first place by playing upon gender ideals that divide Black men and women. These figures are closely aligned with the racialized misogyny that developed during the plantation era; and "this racialized hatred and sexism has its roots in some of the myths that were used and continue to be used to stereotype and subjugate African American women" (Adams and Fuller 943). While the first two figures are antithetical to European notions of femininity and masculinity, the latter more closely resemble European masculinity models, but they are sexually and/or economically predatory to the Black community, and internalization of these caricatures is destructive to personal relationships between Black men and women.

It is especially important to return to these figures, because the hip hop generation may be unfamiliar with these stereotypes. From the music industry to reality television, these stereotypes are simply repackaged and sold to an eager, unknowing audience. The figures populating reality television are simply extensions of hip hop culture, particularly its music. The Pimp/Sambo, the Sapphire, and the Preacher *all* populate RAP music and videos,[3] and now they also populate reality television shows that feature all-Black casts. T. Denean Sharpley-Whiting defines the hip hop generation as roughly "those born between 1965 and 1984 or more broadly, as the post-civil rights, post-segregation generation" (5). This generation of African Americans suffers from the historical amnesia that plagues most Americans. They are "a generation of Hip-Hop artists who have betrayed and who have been betrayed by their society. They are the children of the ones who forgot to teach them the cultural and historical values that made African Americans symbols of freedom and justice for the entire world" (Asante ix). Because many artists of the hip hop generation are removed from and some are ignorant of the struggle of young Black people for equality in America, they easily internalize then reproduce the images discussed in the previous section through music and now through television consumption. And while the terminology has changed—most people in the hip hop generation hear the name Sapphire or Sambo only in a college-level history, sociology, gender, or film course—the misogynistic ideal remains the same. Today, Sapphire is "represented as the bitch in misogynistic rap, takes the form of money-hungry, scandalous, manipulating, and demanding woman. The bitch is a woman who thinks of no one but herself and is willing to do anything to obtain material possessions" (Adams and Fuller 948). Hip hop artists are currently fascinated with the Pimp and his ability to control his "ho," to paraphrase Snoop Dogg, and the Sambo is now an ignorant Black thug, absentee father who conquers women with his sexual prowess and collects Baby Mamas and children as trophies. Sometimes, the Pimp and the Sambo are one and the same.

Currently, hip hop culture and its music, RAP, create an unhealthy profit-churning alliance in which Black and white men profit from relationship dysfunction and degradation of Black women. More than ever, this type of racialized misogyny is being rewarded monetarily: "Misogynist rap music and the white male dominated patriarchal infrastructure that produces it encourage male contempt and disregard for females" (hooks 62). The Black preacher and the church are no longer hallowed, sacred positions, but are spaces of male domination akin to their secular counterparts. The RAP artist Meek Mill expresses admiration for the ability of preachers to control finances and be served by multiple women in his 2012 single, "Amen." One of the most celebrated figures in hip hop culture is the Pimp-turned-Preacher, Don "Magic" Juan, who pastors Magic World Christian Kingdom Church of the Royal Family in Chicago but occasionally makes television and musical appearances with RAPpers Snoop Dogg and Wiz Khalifa and others while speaking about the lifestyle and wearing the extravagant suits and eyewear of a pimp.

The Pimp became an icon in African American culture and film in the Blaxploitation era. Definitively, "the Black pimp icon is a reactionary image that emerges from the actual prostitution of female bodies that occurs in oppressed communities" (Osayande 57). Though I doubt glorification of sexual exploitation was part of Melvin van Peebles's original idea when he introduced the genre with *Sweet Sweetback's Baadass Song* in 1971, Hollywood certainly latched onto the sexuality portion and exploited it for increased revenue at the box office. The Black pimp as interpreted by Hollywood imagination is a macho, leather-wearing, handsome, financially secure, sexually viable man who is somehow above the law; in some cases, he is the law! He kills many men and sexually satisfies scores of women with the emotions of an iceberg and looks good while doing them both. This figure is also masculine enough to silence Sapphire through psychological manipulation or the threat of or actual use of physical violence. Oddly, the pimp does not pose a threat to white men and certainly does not train his sexual aggression on white women like his Black brute predecessor. The pimps are played only in predominantly Black casts, because a foundation was laid to make it acceptable to portray Black women as whores and prostitutes. With the patronage of Black audiences, Hollywood could safely pimp out and profit from degrading Black people. Currently, the pimp is a misogynistic figure who does not love women, and because the women he hates and exploits are Black women, America at large seems fine with that.

The pimp translates well in the music and reality television world, and one particular man proved to be a positive test case for the pimp's transcendence and durability. One of the more interesting cast members from *Surreal Life* was Flavor Flav. Viewers seemed to respond positively to his buffoonish antics. He received a spin-off, *Strange Love*, featuring a "love affair" with fellow *Surreal Life* cast member Brigitte Neilsen that lasted for three seasons. Ratings skyrocketed as the hip hop generation obsessively consumed the blossoming relationship and "marriage" of the buffoon, Flav, and the Euro-American woman, Brigitte, who was also several inches taller than her beau. Like Jane civilizing Tarzan, she taught him simple things like how to eat from a spoon without biting it. Like Kurtz gone native, the world cringed and collectively gasped while Brigitte kissed Flav's foot. It could not last. Brigitte married a European man, and Flav was left alone once more in the reality television world.

In 2006, Flavor Flav, the world's greatest hype man and member of one of the most aggressively anticolonial RAP groups in America, was given his own reality show, the *Flavor of Love*, on VH1. It was to be a dating show in which the contestants won a shot at love with an aging RAP star who, through his ventures with previous reality shows on VH1, was thought to possess a modicum of star power and a modest amount of money. This concept was not unfamiliar with American audiences: "By the time *Flavor of Love* debuted in 2006, eight seasons of *The Bachelor* had taught viewers what to expect from dating shows: pretty white people, faux sincerity, and the trappings of 'fairytale love'" (Pozner 179–180). In the series premier, Flav proudly announces that he is the "blachelor." Even the setting seems familiar: a huge mansion on stately grounds, immaculately clean and lavishly furnished. A butler or assistant dressed in a nice uniform meets the ladies. So, in every way, the setting resembles other dating shows and is, for the most part, not groundbreaking.

But in walk the characters and the contrast begins. In casting, VH1 deliberately created an all-Black television show that stood in stark contrast to white dating shows. Flav is an aging RAP star whose almost fifty-year-old haggard face betrays the all-night parties, around-the-world concerts, physical fights, and stints in jail. Unlike the quiet, romantic sets of white dating shows, *Flavor of Love* looks like an extended, corporate-backed RAP video in which twenty manipulative women fight for the attention of one man who was fully dressed most of the time. For the price of one man, VH1 received several Black stereotypes. Flav, already a veteran reality show star from previous endeavors on VH1, went into this venture without other quasi-famous cast mates or the members of his RAP group, and it had a profound effect on how he was portrayed: "Politically neutralized without Chuck D by his side, VH1 reduced Flav to a shucking-and-jiving fool. (At one point, he proudly wears a jester's crown.)" (Pozner 182). On camera, Flav is an ignorant thug who cannot remember names, so he renames the girls to suit his memory. He occasionally coons and clowns for the camera and the watching audience by playing basketball on a tennis court in animal print pajamas and making a mockery of his own physical traits by showing a portrait of himself and calling it "fine art." In the news, Flav is an absentee father who took advantage of an insecure younger woman and then left her to care for their children. His jail stints for domestic violence are well documented and widely reported. One of the ladies even confesses that she is aware of his personal demons but believes Flav rehabilitated his image on his previous VH1 reality shows.

Flav, for the most part, seems to relish the attention given him by the women and manages to embody the Sambo and the Pimp simultaneously while the women humiliate themselves in order to gain his attention. First, the environment resembles a harem as the girls surround Flav and join him in unison yelling, "Flavor Flav" at the beginning of most episodes. In addition to sending the women on ridiculous missions, he spends individual time becoming intimately connected—to put it politely—with each woman while he remains relatively idle. In season 2, in an episode called, "She Works Hard for Her Honey," Flav takes the girls to one of his favorite restaurants, M & M Soul Food. Rather than dine with the women, he tells them that their jobs are to work the restaurant as waitresses and cooks. The lady who performs the best job wins a date for the night with him. In this challenge, he is positioned as the Sambo while the Sapphires work to support their "man." When Flav assesses and critiques their skills, he compliments Delicious on her rear end. Furthermore, Flav exploits the women's labor in order to assist one of his friends. Like a pimp he sexually exploits the bodies of the women who work for him while he remains conspicuously out of sight: Flav never dirties himself with these tasks. Instead, he watches and laughs as they perform the menial tasks while he is perched atop a symbol of his elevated economic status—a stretch limousine. The women's arguments are a source of personal entertainment as he chuckles with the male butler or driver. Like a pimp, he occasionally steps between the women to reassert order and male dominance—effectively silencing and controlling his legion of Sapphires.

Film critics and historians argue about the purpose of the Sapphire's invention: "It is argued that the Sapphire construct emerges in an effort to promote intra-racial gender and class antagonisms–a divide and conquer approach" (Spencer 36). Though the Pimp, with his exploitation of Black women's bodies, may have some kind of verisimilitude in respective communities, the Sapphire seems to be without grounding in African American culture. Critics, historians, and sociologists agree that "historical accounts do not support those characteristics as being a real component of the Black woman's attitude or interaction with Black men, which may explain why the wrath of the Sapphire is not projected onto White men in mainstream films" (Spencer 35). There are no personal accounts or formal historical records that show evidence that Black women hold their male partners more accountable for economic peonage or their personal transgressions than their white counterparts. Furthermore, evidence of Black people's internalization of the hegemonically produced Sapphire is manifested in a reactionary Black male stereotype that counters Sapphire and increases the hostility shown in African American heterosexual relationships.

In film, the Sapphire is normally the only person employed in the relationship, supporting the entire family with her wages. She unleashes her anger on the Sambo, who is lazy, trifling, uneducated, lacking ambition, gullible, and apparently allergic to gainful employment. In some aspects, the tense Sapphire–Sambo quarrelsome relationship is reflective of and justification for economic discrimination in larger areas. Black women usually found gainful employment as domestic workers while Black males remained largely unemployed once major wars were over. Sapphire blames her Black husband for the family's dire economic straits, unleashes her fury on her husband, and never targets the real root of their poverty. The dominant culture escapes blame and has a convenient, new stereotype to justify discrimination: the lazy, Black male Sambo. The fact that these characters were played in all-Black films and were produced by Black men sometimes lent veracity to the original Sapphire–Sambo construct.

Sapphire, the loud-mouth, emasculating tyrant, survives and thrives in hip hop culture. In reality television, we see her repeatedly, and she is usually a brown body. The women of *FOL*, the Flavorettes, were mostly Black caricatures of the worst dehumanizing stereotypes ever leveraged at Black women. They stand in stark contrast to white women who populate other dating shows: "Unlike ABC's perky Stepford Wives in training, VH1 seemed to go out of its way to cast women who had worked in strip clubs, porn, and other sex industry jobs—only to frame them as promiscuous, vulgar train wrecks" (Pozner 180). These Black women with horrible dispositions cannot communicate without being aggressive with one another. They demand sexual healing from a man almost twice their age. In addition to frequently highlighting semi-pornographic shots of the girls lavishing Flav with sexual attention in hot tubs and in other places around the house, these ladies perform ridiculous tasks such as cleaning human excrement in the aforementioned episode. After all, Flav needed to know that his woman could keep a clean house. As with the restaurant scene, Flav sits on his hallowed perch of male domination and laughs. He arrives to dinner wearing a gleaming crown of authority; the house is clean, his food is prepared perfectly, and he is refreshed. In scenarios like the ones described above, Flav is clearly the Sambo/Pimp surrounded by a room full of Sapphires.

Perhaps no Black woman in the reality television show embodied the Sapphire and the devious RAP woman more than Tiffany "New York" Pollard: "We heard her moan breathily one minute and rant in irate, Sapphire-esque tirades the next, always in getups that revealed as much of her breast implants as allowed on basic cable" (Pozner 187). In the very first season, New York, like one of the manipulative women of RAPpers' nightmares, began to work her agenda. She randomly targets a woman to aggravate in each episode. She states that her reasoning is to "see if I was powerful enough to twist her mind." After instigating a fight with a fellow cast member during the very first episode, New York triumphantly proclaims, "She got mind screwed by me." Though she manages to have women removed from the show and to sleep with Flav in several seasons, he treats New York as a pimp does: he coldly has sex with her, then discards her in favor of women who seem less aggressive and manipulative.

The producers behind this show took a calculated risk. Mark Cronin (Mindless Entertainment) and Cris Abrego (51 Pictures) "made an intentional choice to give *this particular man* a dating show specifically because he'd reliably act the fool—and then they cast, edited, and framed women of color in ways that intentionally played off deep-seated racial stereotypes" (Pozner 185). They gambled against the historical amnesia Americans tend to suffer from, and they won big. According to Pozner, "They received the highest ratings in their network's history, when nearly 6 million viewers tuned in for *FOL*'s first finale. VH1 broke their own record later that year when 7.5 million people made season 2's finale the number one nonsports telecast on basic cable in 2006" (Pozner 187–188). Cronin and Abrego successfully introduced several stereotypes at once to a new generation of people who would not be familiar with the fight against these stereotypes less than fifty years before. As stated earlier, the hip hop generation is far removed from the days when these stereotypes regularly appeared on daytime television, and they neither witnessed nor have been taught about the various struggles that African American actors and various civil rights organizations, including the National Association for the Advancement of Colored People (NAACP), overcame in order to improve the images of Black people on television and film. The show and its producers casually dismiss the fact that many people's only contact with African Americans is through the television screen and that such portrayals of African Americans could possibly do real damage. Instead, they and millions of African Americans who supported the program through viewing it brushed *FOL* aside as harmless entertainment. The numbers confirmed it: minstrelsy was not only back in vogue, it was downright fun!

Flavor of Love, through the use of a Black male as quasi-Pimp/Sambo who reigns over uncivilized, lower-class women, set a precedent for how

Black women in reality television are portrayed. *FOL*'s numbers demonstrate that Sapphire is not only popular in her new format, but also profitable. Unlike *FOL*, *Real Housewives of Atlanta* (*RHOA*) offers Black audiences a whole host of Sapphires without the Pimp. The women of *RHOA*, though not the lower-class variety of women who appeared on *FOL*, are just as uncouth as New York. The show is one of the highest-rated shows on Bravo. There is also a concurrently running spin-off for the most confrontational, opinionated, vociferous housewife, NeNe Leakes, who just like New York, received her own spin-off on VH1. These shows send the message that no matter how much money a Black woman amasses and no matter how big the house and how immaculate the neighborhood, she just cannot behave. In reality television land, Sapphiric behavior is innate. And no matter how badly she is exploited by men, a Black woman's behavior, so far askew of what is considered normal for white, middle-class, feminine behavior, warrants such exploitation.

Ironically, the Pimp's counterpart in film and other popular culture outlets is the African American Preacher. Historically, the church and its leadership (normally male) are products of the African American community that predates film technology. Cast out of Euro-American churches during the late eighteenth century, the Black church developed autonomously. Though ultimately a product of racism, the Black church and its preacher gained reluctant respect from whites; the preacher was accorded certain privileges in his respective community: "In town after town—even in the Deep South—he was the only black man not referred to as 'George' or 'boy.' He was called 'Rev.' or 'Preacher'" (Hoover 294). Sadly, white American producers did not have to invent the sexism that the Black church practices on screen, and selfish, male chauvinist preachers are not simply figments of their tainted imaginings of Black people. The Black church is sexist, and there is room there for exploitation of the women who support the church.

Like the pimp, the preacher does not depend upon the white supremacist, capitalistic patriarchy for his livelihood, and he enjoys a degree of financial stability even in the leanest of times. Also, like the pimp, the preacher's financial stability is largely dependent upon women: "The degree to which he uses his position selfishly marks the amount of personal privilege and reward he enjoys at the expense of a 'not so well endowed' membership—the majority of which are women" (Hoover 294). Whereas the pimp uses psychological manipulation and violence to control women, the preacher is armed with theology—particularly Pauline scripture. Using 1 Timothy 2:11–15, male preachers effectively keep women relegated to subservient positions within the church while preaching the liberatory nature of Jesus.[4] And it is very effective: "Although an estimated 66–88 percent of Black church congregants are women, men continue to hold the majority leadership roles" (Barnes 373). Once many women feel the urge to spread the good news of the resurrection, they no longer feel welcome in the houses that their time, talents, and offerings built. Michael Eric Dyson declares that these women suffer "ecclesiastical apartheid" (Dyson 142). Many women simply leave their home churches for nondenominational bodies, which may be more accepting of women as authority figures.

Some churches take this doctrine to the extreme, and the irrational nature with which they guard the hallowed throne of Black male privilege sometimes borders a type of gender insanity. Some churches allow Black male teenagers to preach and receive ordination, but they do not allow a woman, no matter her age or status in the community, to put her foot on the pulpit. A woman may approach the sacred male throne only if she is cleaning it or handing the preacher a glass of water or orange juice. Even when Black ministers use their religious convictions to make social change, their sexist theological teachings follow them. For instance, Dr. Martin Luther King Jr. angered several women in the Southern Christian Leadership Conference (SCLC) by downplaying their ideas while using them for support roles. Ella Baker, who was once head of the NAACP in New York and a veteran in the civil rights movement, was underappreciated in the SCLC: "Interviewed for an oral history project at the King Center, she complained that 'those men didn't have any faith in women, none whatsoever. They just thought that women were sex symbols and had no contribution to make'" (Baker qtd. in Ling and Monteith 106). Often younger male ministers were given precedence over more experienced high-ranking women, just like in the church: "Despite their inexperience, the status of the young ministers of SCLC gave them prominent positions in all-male organizations and in local NAACP chapters, but simultaneously deflected them from bridge leadership, except insofar as they linked their local activities to larger state and national campaigns" (Ling and Monteith 107).[5] Like her sisters of the cloth who no longer feel welcome inside God's house once they are called to pastor, Baker exited SCLC to work outside that ministerial, male-dominated organization.

Like the Sambo, the Sapphire, and the Pimp, the figure of the African American Preacher and the church he leads is portrayed often in predominantly Black casts, and the historical Black male sexism that defines the Black church unfortunately follows him on screen. Preachers are often comically portrayed as lustful, back-sliding hypocrites who prey upon lonely Black women. Films like *The Player's Club* and the very popular 1990s television show *Martin* use the characters Dollar Bill, a Chicago pastor who opens a strip club in Baton Rouge, and the Rev. Leon Lonnie Love, a schemer who repeatedly succumbs to the sexual temptations of his flesh, respectively, this way.

Currently, the figure of the Preacher, complete with the Black church's sexism, appears in the reality television world. Oxygen's reality television show, *Preachers of L.A.*, garnered well over two million views with television viewership and Internet streaming combined. It features a predominantly Black cast of male preachers with relatively large congregations in Los Angeles, California. Each week the camera follows these ministerial figures with hopes to humanize pastors: Noel Jones, Clarence McClendon and First Lady Priscilla McClendon, Ron Gibson and First Lady Lavetta, Wayne Chaney and First Lady Myesha Chaney, Deitrick Haddon, and the only white couple, Jay Haizlip and First Lady Christy Haizlip. Before the show's airings, many people questioned the choice of cast members. The show's producers, Holly Carter and Lemuel Plummer, both African American preachers' children, claim they hand-picked these preachers. In an interview posted on Oxygen's website, Carter claims that she simply "wanted to find a way to give a platform to the voice of pastors, and create an opportunity to see them not only as religious leaders, but as fathers and husbands and friends" (Plummer in *Oxygen Blogger*). Both Carter and Plummer claim they chose these specific pastors because they have a global footprint.

The choice of these preachers and the first ladies also seamlessly continues the Black church's reputation of sexism from society to the reality television world. Though sexism is prevalent in the Black church, there are several churches in the Los Angeles area with amazing Black female preachers who could have theoretically been cast for such a groundbreaking show. For instance, Pastor Jean Perez of Ablaze Ministries, who ecstatically proclaimed she has a doctorate degree in "Praying heaven down" during a telephone interview, gained national fame as the pastor who rescued Motown singer Smokey Robinson from drug addiction. One other smaller but growing church around the city is Love, Peace, and Happiness Christian Fellowship Center, with three locations (Downey, Los Angeles, and Rialto). The church is co-pastored by Bishop Leon and his wife, Dr. Jacqueline Martin. The church also runs an eponymous Bible college.

Before the first episode of *Preachers of L.A.* aired, the advertisements for the show caused a much-heated debate on national television and in Black churches across the country. The commercials played to the gender biases of the Black church. Many people wondered why there were no female ministers like Pastors Perez or Martin featured on this new show if the producers claimed that they were out to provide reality television consumers with a groundbreaking view of churches and preachers. During a phone interview, Elder Marshall Hall of New Foundation Christian Center of Detroit, Michigan, explained that "women pastors tend to be more private and not open themselves up to more scrutiny than they are already under immense scrutiny. But, we know Black women have always preached. My former pastor was a woman, an excellent teacher and mentor, and light-years ahead of her time." Many female ministers also concurred with Elder Hall. Some female ministers did say that there may have been some willing women and expressed concern about the ostentatious flourishes of material prosperity seen in the commercials.[6] One female minister proclaimed, "I will not comment on the show until I watch it, but the commercials do concern me. What are they trying to say about Black preachers and the Black church? I may give it a chance." In one commercial, the cameras display the luxury cars and mansions of the preachers while a preacher's voice uses religious rhetoric to justify his lavish lifestyle. Like other reality television shows, the commercials for this show agitate Americans' anxieties about class and income inequality. This particular commercial drew the ire of many people and drove away some potential viewers before the show aired its first episode.

Equally troubling are the producers' and editors' portrayals of the first lady. Within the African American church, the position of first lady, or pastor's wife, is a coveted position, with the term "first lady" being used as a sign of respect. Those ladies in the show who are married to the pastors are shown with first and last names. However, Dominque and Loretta, one engaged to Deitrick Haddon and the other a "friend" of Bishop Jones, respectively, are not given last names—this slight is very telling. Though the first lady is often put upon a pedestal, her high position is but another form of control. Throughout the show, they are not given identities aside from those that come from their husbands—at least the married ladies have that. Because Dominique and Loretta are not married to these men, they are not given any identifying markers other than their first names. Who are these women? Do they have families who gave them surnames before marriage? Though Dominique marries her fiancé, Loretta's portrayal is extremely unsettling. Serving as a "special friend" to Bishop Jones for sixteen years, she is attacked by the other first ladies in the episode "Tea and Sympathy." The bishop insists that the two of them are "friends and nothing more." Viewers never learn anything about this woman other than she owns a restaurant financed in part by Jones and is his special friend. Her portrayal on camera is one of contradictions: "On the one hand, this laywoman is caring and responsible; on the other, she is gullible and irresponsible" (Riggs 47). She is complicit in the gender oppression that dogmatically troubles and cleaves the Black church. Instead of participating in the life of the church as a respected laywoman, she is not a self-actualizing character on the show. She is dependent upon Jones for financial support and is invited to special events only because she is attached to him in some way.

Either through content or presentation, reality shows that feature predominantly Black casts simply re-present age-old stereotypes of African Americans. They are not meant to challenge centuries-old, racist assumptions about African Americans but rather to continue them. Truly groundbreaking television would be those programs that challenge those assumptions and work to force people to reevaluate ideals long accepted as true. Reality television shows in no way perform this function when they feature African Americans. Since the genesis of the majority-Black television cast in *Flavor of Love*, the reality television world has been populated with quasi-Pimps/Sambos and angry, drama-filled Black women, and now exploitative preachers. These shows degrade Black women. They continue the work of white supremacist, capitalist patriarchy ideology in that they continue to bring about the total subjugation of Black women. And because these shows routinely break ratings records, African Americans give the hegemony spontaneous consent for the sake of mindless entertainment and cheap laughs. While African Americans laugh at the latest antics of the current Black reality show characters, someone else from the dominant culture is laughing all the way to the bank.

Notes

1 Donald Bogle's *Toms, Coons, Mulattoes, Mammies, and Bucks* provides a full explanation of these images on film.

2 In her book, *Black Looks: Race and Representation*, bell hooks uses the term "hot pussy" to trace how the dominant culture traditionally has sold Black female sexuality. She uses the figure of Sarah Baartman, known as Hottentot Venus in Europe, a Black woman who was put on display for the "peculiarities" of her gender even after death, to exemplify hegemonic objectification of Black women's bodies.

3 Some say RAP stands for Rhythm and Poetry, Rhythmically Applied Poetry, or Rhythmically Associated Poetry. Although Afrika Bambaata defines this genre of music as hip hop in an interview, Eric B. and Rakim in their song "Follow the Leader" define the genre as Rhythm and Poetry, specifically. For a brief discussion of the rhythmic nature of RAP music, please see the Introduction to *African American Studies: Transdisciplinary Approaches and Implications* by Talmadge Anderson and James Stewart. For this chapter, the acronym RAP will be used.

4 1 Timothy 2:11–15 reads, "[11]Let the woman learn in silence with all subjection. [12]But I suffer not a woman to teach, nor to usurp authority over the man, but to be in silence. [13]For Adam was first formed, then Eve. [14]And Adam was not deceived, but the woman being deceived was in the transgression. [15]Notwithstanding she shall be saved in childbearing, if they continue in faith and charity and holiness with sobriety."

5 Belinda Robnett, in her article "African American Women in the Civil Rights Movement, 1954–1965: Gender, Leadership, and Micromobilization," writes that "within the context of the civil rights movement, African American women operated as 'bridge leaders,' who—through frame bridging, amplification, and transformation—initiated ties between the social movement and the community and between preconfigurative strategies aimed at individual change, identity, and consciousness and political strategies aimed at organizational tactics designed to challenge existing relationships with the state and other societal institutions. . . . The activities of African American women in the civil rights movement provided the bridges necessary to cross boundaries between the personal lives of potential constituents and adherents and the political life of civil rights movement organizations" (1664). In SCLC, by exempting male leaders from the important bridge work, they were spared the day-to-day, hard labor of building a consensus among the people, passing out flyers, and arranging meetings. That support work, which made the movement possible in many areas, was left to women while the more visible positions were given to younger, inexperienced men.

6 For privacy reasons, many of the female pastors I interviewed did not want to be named or identified in this chapter.

Works Cited

Abrego, Chris, and Mark Cronin, creators. *Flavor of Love*. VH1, 2006–2008. Television.

Adams, Terri B., and Douglas B. Fuller. "The Words Have Changed but the Ideology Remains the Same: Misogynistic Lyrics in RAP Music." *Journal of Black Studies* 36.6 (2006): 938–957.

Anderson, Talmadge and James Stewart. *Introduction to African American Studies: Transdisciplinary Approaches and Implications*. Baltimore: Imprint Editions, 2007.

Asante, Molefi K. Foreword. *Murda', Misogyny, and Mayhem: Hip Hop and the Culture of Abnormality in the Urban Community*. By Zoe Spencer. Lanham, MD: U P of Maryland, 2011. ix–x.

Barnes, Sandra L. "Whosever Will Let Her Come: Social Activism and Gender Inclusivity in the Black Church." *Journal for the Scientific Study of Religion* 45.3 (2006): 371–385.

Bogle, Donald. *Toms, Coons, Mulattoes, Mammies, and Bucks: An Interpretive History of Blacks in American Films, Fourth Edition*. New York: Continuum, 1973, 2004.

Carter, Holly, and Lemuel Plummer. Interview by Oxygen network blogger. 7 Oct. 2013. http://www.oxygen.com/shows/preachers-la/blog/qa-preachers-la-producers-holly -carter-lemuel-plummer.

Dyson, Michael Eric. *Know What I Mean? Reflections on Hip Hop*. New York: Basic Civitas Books, 2007.

Flavor of Love. Writ. Chris Abrego, Michelle Brando, Mark Cronin, Kevin Thomas. Dir. Zach Kozek, Alex Palatnik, and Robert Sizemore. VH1, 2006–2008. Television.

Gramsci, Antonio. *Selections from the Prison Notebooks of Antonio Gramsci*. Ed. Quintin Hoare and Geoffrey Nowell Smith. Trans. Quintin Hoare and Geoffrey Nowell Smith. New York: International Publishers, 1971.

Hall, Marshall. Personal interview. 2 Dec. 2013. Telephone.

hooks, bell. *Black Looks: Race and Representation*. New York: Routledge, 1992.

——. *We Real Cool: Black Men and Masculinity*. New York: Routledge, 2003.

Hoover, Theresa. "Black Women and the Churches: Triple Jeopardy." *Black Theology: A Documentary History*. Vol. 1: *1966–1979*. Ed. James H. Cone and Gayraud S. Wilmore. 2nd ed. Maryknoll, NY: Orbis, 1993. 293–303.

Ling, Peter, and Sharon Monteith. "Gender and Generation: Manhood at the Southern Christian Leadership Conference." *Gender and the Civil Rights Movement*. Ed. Peter Ling and Sharon Monteith. New Brunswick, NJ: Rutgers UP, 1999. 101–130.

Madger, Ted. "The Business of American Television in Transition." *Reality TV: Remaking Television Culture*. 2nd edition. Ed. Susan Murray and Laurie Ouellete. New York: New York UP, 2009.

The Master Study Bible. King James Version of the Old and New Testaments. Nashville: Cornerstone Bible Publishers, 2001.

Osayande, Euruare. *Misogyny & the Emcee: Sex, Race, & Hip Hop*. Philadelphia: Machete Media, 2006.

Perez, Jean. Personal interview. 29 Nov. 2013. Telephone.

Plummer, Lemuel, executive producer. *Preachers of L.A.* Oxygen, 2013.

Pozner, Jennifer. *Reality Bites Back: The Troubling Truth about Guilty Pleasure TV*. Berkeley: Seal Press, 2010.

Preachers of L.A. Dir. Calvin Calloway. Oxygen, 2013.

Raphael, Chad. "The Political Economic Origins of Reali-TV." *Reality TV: Remaking Television Culture*. 2nd ed. Ed. Susan Murray and Laurie Ouellete. New York: New York UP, 2009.

Riggs, Marcia Y. *Plenty Good Room: Women versus Male Power in the Black Church*. Cleveland: Pilgrim Press, 2003.

Robnett, Belinda. "African-American Women in the Civil Rights Movement, 1954–1965: Gender, Leadership, and Micromobilization." *American Journal of Sociology* 101.6 (1996): 1661–1693.

Rose, Randall, and Stacey L. Wood. "Paradox and the Consumption of Authenticity through Reality Television." *Journal of Consumer Research* 32.2 (2005): 284–296.

Sharpley-Whiting, T. Denean. *Pimps Up, Ho's Down: Hip Hop's Hold on Young Black Women.* New York: New York UP, 2007.

Spencer, Zoe. *Murda', Misogyny, and Mayhem: Hip Hop and the Culture of Abnormality in the Urban Community.* Lanham, MD: UP of America, 2011.

3

Striving to Dress the Part

· ·

Examining the Absence
of Black Women
in Different Iterations of
Say Yes to the Dress

ALISON D. LIGON

The recent proliferation of wedding-themed reality television shows is intriguing. It reveals much about the continued North American fascination with the commonplace "happily ever after" idyllic ending to a fairy-tale life that is highly coveted and repetitively suggested to girls from the beginnings of their societal consciousnesses. However, despite the growth, popularity, and diversity of recent show offerings—from ceremony and honeymoon competition themed shows to shows that focus on specific aspects of the wedding planning process—one noticeable absence runs through each of these: the presence of women of color, specifically, the image of Black women as prospective brides. Of particular interest are the reality wedding shows that focus on the bride's selection of a wedding dress. One of the most popular shows, the Learning Channel's *Say Yes to the Dress*, has so many spin-offs that it is arguably a subgenre comprised of the aforesaid show and its complements: *Say Yes to the Dress: Randy Knows Best; Say Yes to the Dress: Big Bliss; Say Yes to the Dress: Bridesmaids; Say Yes to the Dress: Unveiled; Say Yes to the Dress: Atlanta*; and *Say Yes to the Dress: The Big Day*. These shows, like those of a similar ilk, capture the incipient humor, drama, and family concerns that are part and parcel of the "realities" of wedding planning shows.

Collectively, these elements make these television formulae beguiling to viewers around the world. Nonetheless, as the wedding theme genre in reality television has morphed into the cash cow of television networks like TLC, Bravo, Oxygen, and WE tv, and the shows themselves focus on diverse representations of women—noticeably white women who vary in age, physical appearance, socioeconomic standing, social circumstance, geographic location, and personal premarital challenges—it is striking that when Black women are presented on these shows, it is almost as if they are enigmatic images, afterthoughts, unicorns in bridal gowns that are just as much absent in their limited presence in this prescribed reality television genre. Also seen in limited numbers are women of color who are members of the bridal salon staffs on the aforementioned reality television shows. These bridal consultants, one may surmise, are much like their Black bridal clients—proverbial flies in the buttermilk. As women, often of darker hues, the Black bridal consultants stand in literal and figurative stark contrast to the brides whom they assist in their searches for dresses. The simultaneous Derrida-influenced presence/absence image of Black brides and bridal consultants, one may find, is evocative of the larger public perceptions and questions about the beauty of the Black female form.[1] Also, these reality bridal shows hint at the historically persistent question of why restorative images of Black women are limited in mainstream media. This essay interrogates some of the questions associated with Black women who, in their axiomatic quest to "say yes to the dress," have become complicit in their own marginalization.

Searching for the Necessary Undergarments, Underpinnings, and Foundations: The (Euphemistic) Pursuit of Modesty and Support in Different Iterations of *Say Yes to the Dress*

Just as women depicted in the array of *Say Yes to the Dress* shows and "real" life determinedly search for the perfect bridal gown—sometimes at the insistent urging of grandmothers, mothers, aunts, friends, and soon-to-be in laws who are in tow at these bridal appointments, these brides are challenged to find the right undergarments that will help their dresses to fit in a flattering, appropriate, and modest manner. Although the dresses chosen by brides vary widely—from silhouettes that range from full-skirted princess and ball gown styles to sleek mermaid and fit and flair styles, to heavily embellished "blinged" crystal- and sequin-encrusted formal frocks, to dress styles that are reminiscent of old Hollywood glamour, and lacy dresses suggestive of romanticized dreams of southern femininity—the search for the right dress as well as suitable bridal undergarments is a cultural carryover from a bygone era. Most noticeably, though, the search for flattering underwear is reflective of the insistence of many female elders— prior to many women's rejection of restrictive undergarments like girdles and hosiery, in the late 1960s and 1970s—that young "respectable" women appear in public spaces with nary a bulge, jiggle, or suggested revelation of any physical protuberance of ample bosom or rear visible for others to see or comment upon. These thoughts and practices of yesteryear differ drastically from present-day norms.

Instead, currently, the natural feminine form unbound by restrictive shapewear is comfortably embraced by legions of women of all ages. Even more revealing is that in the past forty years, public displays of the feminine form sans "good foundation"—once deemed culturally inapt and undignified by many female elders—has now given way from the girdle's strictures, or its modern-day progenitor, Spanx, to a hosiery-free, comfortable ground of near-intergenerational agreement. In fact, the current First Lady of the United States of America, Michelle Obama, is frank about her abandonment of hosiery as daily wear and dons it only out of necessity. Even so, regardless of the past four decades of relaxing fashion tensions existent between women of different generations about the topic of suitable foundation garments to be worn with business attire and formalwear, time has not removed many female elders' desire for social appropriateness to be demonstrated by bridal attendants and the bride on her wedding day. The residual evidence of the foregoing idea is most pronounced during a younger woman's search for a bridal gown with her female elders present. Hence, the search for the modesty-enhancing undergarments to be worn under the bridal gown is simultaneously an act of practicality and is also suggestive of a culturally proscribed rite of passage—the totality of a young woman's transition, at least in the minds of her female elders, into independent womanhood—as the younger woman embraces her impinging roles of wife, prospective mother, and upstanding community member.

These values have not changed much following the 1970s zenith of the women's liberation movement. These points will not be belabored, but they are key considerations that allude to the cultural underpinnings that are loosely stitched into sartorial subtext that frames bridal shows like those in the *Say Yes to the Dress* series.

Whether personal dressing items are procured from the bride's trousseau or purchased in tandem with her bridal gown, there was and remains a certain ceremonial element involved in the identification of the "proper" personal items for a bride to wear under her dress. This ceremony harkens back to times when at the height of femininity, for women of all races and stations in life, keenly reflected puritan expressions of modesty, decorum, and propriety—a nod to a proper upbringing and awareness about how women should present themselves in public spaces. In the present moment, though, this matter is addressed on shows like *Say Yes to the Dress* in a manner that suggests deep intergenerational friction and discord. Often seen on these shows' trailers and highlight reels are the brides' elders staring aghast, through raised, knitted eyebrows and frowning visages at the blushing, brazen brides who boldly present themselves to their families, friends, and the viewing audience in bridal gowns that are either too revealing or not flattering in myriad ways. This incongruous moment alludes to the cultural foundation that suggests a bride will demonstrate, through her choice of a bridal gown and its accouterments, her recognition of societally held views on modesty, femininity, and respectability.

Furthermore, these ideas about femininity and decorousness, for Black women, it seems, have a deeper, historically caustic, acrid beginning: slavery in the Americas. During that era, respect for a woman's humanity, femininity, and social respectability was a rare gift extended to white women of privilege and means, or, if history is generously recollected, limited numbers of women of mixed race parentage who in effect "passed" as white women and were, therefore, accorded limited social privileges. Understandably, it is difficult to examine that forbidding era to find a demonstrative pillar that comfortably buttresses the idea that a connection exists between the inscrutable experiences lived by enslaved Black women and contemporary images of free Black women that are currently seen on reality bridal television shows. Nonetheless, such a connection does exist. It is almost as if many of the naïve, fresh-faced Black brides who in their eager-to-emulate-images-that-they-see-in-mainstream-media are blissfully unaware of the historical and contemporary implications that their presence on these shows, driven by their own volition in these elected spaces—chosen public forums—in fact, suggests. Idyllically, they stand atop elevated platforms in the bridal salons modeling bridal gowns and extending harmless invitations to others, including the individuals who are present during their bridal salon appointments, and, by implied extension, members of the shows' viewing audiences, to comment on how the bridal dresses that they model either complement their physiques or fail to do so.

Such a moment is not an innocent ruse; rather, some may find that because of the inclusion of social media platforms in both the television and online components of the *Say Yes to the Dress* shows—arguably done to create an interactive experience for members of the viewing audiences— creates a space reminiscent of the uninvited public commentary that countless Black slave women were forced to endure as they stood on elevated platforms in slave markets. Spirits broken, heads bowed, and bodies unwillingly revealed on auction blocks in slave markets around the world, slave women of African descent had to bear the stinging lashes of public verbal insults and inquires while their bodies were scrutinized. A powerful visual and symbolic referent known around the world is the image of the South African woman, Saartjie "Sarah" Baartman, whose physiognomy was once ridiculed; in the modern era, her image has been frequently recuperated and reengaged through scholarly discourse.

Or, if one considers a modern comparative example, Pecola Breedlove, the protagonist of Toni Morrison's acclaimed novel *The Bluest Eye*, one may find evidence of the way in which the Black female form has been publicly degraded and reduced to baselessness. Morrison's image of Pecola, a socially scarred, hollow shell of a girl who seeks others' validation and approval during her years coming of age in the 1960s—a time when thoughts about Black women's beauty were not publicly and widely voiced in mainstream contexts. Of such a derided liminal space occupied by Pecola, Morrison writes, "Why, although reviled by others, could this beauty not be taken for granted within this community? Why did it need wide public articulation to exist? These are not clever questions" (xi). In like manner, it is almost as if the awkward images of some young Black brides seen on the *Say Yes to the Dress* cadre of shows are comparable to the aforesaid image struggles of Pecola. Morrison's query in *The Bluest Eye* illuminates Black women's historical and contemporary chafings and contestations about notions of Black feminine beauty. Morrison juxtaposes the social landscape with Pecola's maturation period when positing, "The assertion of racial beauty was not a reaction to be the self-mocking, humorous critique of racial/cultural foibles common in all groups, but against the damaging internalization of assumptions of immutable inferiority originating in the outside gaze" (xi). In like manner, many of the young Black brides on the *Say Yes to the Dress* series are seemingly impervious to recognizing the "immutable inferiority originating in the outside gaze" that is actualized by the realm of television viewers.

One may venture to ask, then, are these young women aware of their personal desires for familial and public praise, validation, and affirmation? In seeking to hear others' articulated recognition of their physical beauty and worth—through the medium of television—is it plausible that many of these women wish to have a few clichéd, fleeting minutes of personal recognition and fame derived from their appearances on the *Say Yes to the Dress* shows? Nonetheless, in so doing, unlike their enslaved foremothers, these free Black women, in choosing to be (re)presented on reality bridal television forums, occupy elected public spaces replete with the pits and snares of social commentary swirling about them. Through their chosen acts, young Black brides who appear on the *Say Yes to the Dress* shows and comparable bridal reality television shows are extending historical trajectory in an unusual near-happenstance manner. Sadly, though equally caustic, callous commentary may be hurled through the Internet and social media outlets at these Black women who elect to share their quests for bridal gowns with countless, nameless faces who view this process on television and online. For many of these Black brides, though, the opportunity to participate in the construction of curative, whole, and humanizing images of Black womanhood in the media exists. Unfortunately, still, some of these uninformed women see their appearances on *Say Yes to the Dress* as mere bridal fashion quests, not opportunities to utilize the television and Internet to present the richness, complexity, and depth of Black women's beauty, embodiment of social graces, and desire to be financially savvy.

For this reason, it is especially distressing to many when young Black women who are featured on reality shows like *Say Yes to the Dress* make unabashed requests for derrière-hugging, cleavage-enhancing, and sometimes tattoo-baring dresses. Even though these may be easily dismissed as innocuous demands made by young women who are seeking to be trend focused and fashionable, it alludes to a point of historical shame, not pride.

These assertions reinscribe the tenuousness of the uneven racial and social terrain that masquerades as a neutral plane: the pursuit of bridal fashion. Although some individuals may have difficulty making this historical leap—and may deem such observations disputatious and far-fetched—a connection arguably exists between the ways in which Black women's bodies in public spaces have been historically objectified and are currently reified through print, television, and electronic media. Reality television, it seems, has created a vacuous space for the reemergence and sustainment of historically troubling images and commentary surrounding women of color, especially Black women, to take root and thrive.

On balance, although many of the young Black women who are featured on shows like *Say Yes to the Dress* appear to have healthy self-concepts, some do not. Even so, all Black brides who are profiled on these bridal shows must be made aware of how they choose to present themselves to a television viewing audience. Such a space is brimming with historically set pitfalls that can entangle individuals in nets laden with the weight of racially and culturally proscribed burdens. For instance, in *Say Yes to the Dress: Atlanta,* episode 18 of season 5, titled "Booty-do's and Ball Gowns," and episode 15 of season 6, titled "Shiny, Happy, Bling!," Jacklyn, an eager, youthful Black bride from Talladega, Alabama, searches in earnest for a bridal gown. During her search for dresses, her mother makes countless references to dress styles that should attractively and effectively minimize her daughter's full rear and midsections—euphemistically described by the family members present at the bridal appointment as "booty-do." On the television show, the mother of the bride emphasizes ad nauseam her personal desire not to see her daughter's fleshy extensions in a bridal gown that is not demure and becoming. Such a humorous sounding term, "booty-do" is expressive shorthand within that family. Their repetitive usage of it causes the bridal salon staff within earshot and, arguably, members of the viewing audience to double over in fits of laughter. Although it is not a sedate reference, "booty-do" is reflective of this family's mindfulness and desire to ensure that their bride-to-be would present herself in a respectable manner on her wedding day.

Such gentle, firm, humorous admonishment of Jacklyn resonates with the temperate indictment that Nthabiseng Motsemme offers in her study of the poetics of dress among young women in South Africa. Although her study is culturally distinct, and not focused on North American bridal trends among Black women, Motsemme's assertion that "sartorial practices [can be] used to liberate black female bodies from their histories of oppression" (12) accurately and effectively describes the possibility for such an enlightened consciousness and discourse to exist surrounding the way that Black women understand fashion—specifically bridal fashion—as an expression of their socially conscious liberating power. Furthermore, Motsemme's contention helps to fashion an argumentative connection between physically and culturally disparate spaces and histories occupied by women in the African diaspora. Within these real and imagined spaces exists the desire for purveyors of popular media to display recuperative images that celebrate the beauty of the Black feminine form in the public domain.

Such a need for restorative (re)imaginings persists when questions of Black women's prospects for marriage—since the 1960s have been consistent deleterious fodder for cultural and economic inquisitors alike.

Romancing the Dress: *Say Yes to the Dress* and the Persistent Question of Black Women's Marriageability

Reality television shows focused on bridal dress selection are at once chronicles of dreams fulfilled for brides to be and are also an inspiration for women who aspire to become brides. Arguably, all iterations of the *Say Yes to the Dress* can be viewed as near-Disney-like sites of escapism through which women can indulge in moments of pleasant diversion that allow them to observe various brides engaged in their individual pursuits of their desired bridal gowns. In his article "Domesticating Politics: Representations of Wives and Mothers in American Reality Television," Jim Brancato acknowledges the uniqueness of this television genre and specifically notes Jennifer Maher's research on women's reality television viewing habits. He astutely observes:

Maher, in an analysis of programming for women on The Learning Channel (e.g., *Wedding Story, A Baby Story*), argues that reality shows often function to "indoctrinate women into traditional gender roles" (49). By presenting a "traditional female life narrative," these shows reproduce traditional roles for female audiences who can vicariously relive important moments, such as getting married or giving birth. Reality TV then, for Maher, can "soothe the pain of the dissimilarity between experience and fantasy by watching another episode that evokes the same romance fantasy and which of course serves to sustain the fantasy." (49)

When considering Maher's and Brancato's observations, one may find that the most challenging question is how the *Say Yes to the Dress* shows offer a "traditional female life narrative," albeit one that is tinged by the particularity of racial differences. Granted, representations of Black women are somewhat limited on the *Say Yes to the Dress* shows, and there are elements of class-based and regional distinctiveness that enable one to further categorize the women seen on these shows. Nevertheless, one persistent question that is hinted at—through Brancato's allusion to opportunities to assuage the "pain of the dissimilarity between experience and fantasy"—is that many of these shows, in presenting a dearth of Black women's images, are accurately reflecting their limited prospects for marriage. Joy Jones's soberly titled opinion editorial, "Marriage Is for White People," published in the spring 2006 in the *Washington Post*, echoes this sentiment. Jones's articulation of the disquieting issue of Black women's dire marital prospects was a seismic moment that caused reverberations among circles of Black women throughout the country. In her essay, Jones poignantly observes:

> I grew up in a time when two-parent families were still the norm, in both
> black and white America. Then, as an adult, I saw divorce become more
> commonplace, then almost a rite of passage. Today it would appear that
> many—particularly in the black community—have dispensed with marriage
> altogether. But as a black woman, I have witnessed the outrage of girlfriends
> when the ex failed to show up for his weekend with the kids, and I've seen the
> disappointment of children who missed having a dad around. Having enjoyed
> a close relationship with my own father, I made a conscious decision that I
> wanted a husband, not a live-in boyfriend and not a "baby's daddy," when it
> came my time to mate and marry. My time never came. For years, I wondered

why not. And then some 12-year-olds [whom I mentored] enlightened me. "Marriage is for white people." (n.p.)

Jones's blunt articulation radically departs from 1960s inception of the modern pathological image of Black womanhood carefully orchestrated within then U.S. Department of Labor secretary Daniel Patrick Moynihan's study, "The Negro Family: The Case for National Action" (infamously known as the "Moynihan Report"). The Moynihan Report set into motion the maelstrom of rhetoric surrounding the economic insufficiency and broken families fashioned out of single, Black female-headed households. Yet an unintended ancillary message that emerged from the Moynihan Report was the idea that Black women are the culpable contemporary laggards in prospects for marriageability because of their generally poor economic state and certain life choices (that is, electing to pursue motherhood outside of a marital union). Although that largely divisive and derided report continues to resonate within certain current public policy circles, and in the mouths of certain political rhetoric pundits, contemporary socioeconomic and cultural studies have documented the realities of changing marriage prospects for Black women. These studies, instead, focus on the varying face of Black America: the emergence of a new so-called Black middle class—whose ranks are overwhelmingly populated by young, single (never married) Black professional women. One examination of this documented trend is Lynda Dickson and Kris Marsh's study, "The Love Jones Cohort: The Face of the Black Middle Class." In it, Dickson and Marsh observe:

> The traditional media presentation of the black middle class has been that of a married couple with children. One might think, for example, of the Huxtable family from *The Cosby Show*. However, the 1990s witnessed a surge of films and television sitcoms that depicted black middle-class characters with quite a different demographic profile. These characters were young (25–44), educated black professionals who had never been married; they were childless and lived alone or with an unmarried partner. Films depicting this new demographic profile include *Love Jones* (1997), *The Brothers* (2001); *Two Can Play That Game* (2001), *Deliver Us from Eva* (2003), and *Something New* (2006). To this list could be added the TV sitcoms *Living Single* (1993–1998), and *Girlfriends* (2000–[2008]). These films and sitcoms are part of a broader social phenomenon that gained increased visibility in media representations since the 1990s.

Drawing from the above-mentioned film, *Love Jones*, Marsh et al. (2007)
define this group as the Love Jones Cohort. (84–85)

To this end, it seems as if many of the young Black brides presented on
the *Say Yes to the Dress* shows who reflect the demographic examined in
Dickson and Marsh's study on the Love Jones Cohort, differ widely from
the residual damaging images of Black women described in the Moynihan Report. Whereas the latter study fueled abysmal statistical claims and
projections that marital prospects for Black women following the Civil
Rights Era were and would remain grim, the former study suggests that
new images of Black women are emerging because of the changing economic and societal landscapes. An overwhelming number of Black brides
profiled on shows like *Say Yes to the Dress* reflect this emerging cohort of
Black womanhood. These salutary images—seen oddly enough in reality
television forums—are images that diametrically oppose those imaginings
of Black women that were constructed during the Moynihan era. Therefore, it appears that reality shows like *Say Yes to the Dress* are responsible for
helping to shift the pendulum toward presenting positive images of Black
women in public spaces that are more attuned to life's "realities." Support
for this notion can be found in Dickson and Marsh's further observation:

> The recent prominence of the Love Jones Cohort in media representations
> of black middle-class life in the United States, combined with the very real
> decline in married-couple households in the black community, invites the
> question: Is the media distorting or reflecting reality? More specifically,
> how representative is the Love Jones Cohort of the black middle class in the
> twenty-first century? Surprisingly, perhaps, given the Love Jones Cohort's
> prominence in the media, existing literature on the black middle class and
> black family has next to nothing to say in response to this question. We are
> interested in determining to what extent the Love Jones Cohort is, in reality, a
> prominent new face of the black middle class. (85)

When considering this posture, it seems plausible that reality shows like
Say Yes to the Dress contribute to the construction of a suitable, reflective
array of images that mirror the lives lived today by many economically
and socially conscious Black women. These questions about marriageability not only usher to the fore questions about how the Black female
form has been historically viewed in public forums, but also hint at the

persistent question of why images of Black women are cast in such a narrow frame of womanhood. Granted, this is a welcome change given the post-Moynihan era orchestrated images of Black women that are rooted in social and economic deficiencies. Nonetheless, these promising images must be handled with care; otherwise, they can be misinterpreted and incorrectly framed by informed and laypersons alike. For instance, when one considers Nicole, an educator and the mother of six-month-old quadruplets (at the time of show's taping) who was featured on *Say Yes to the Dress* season 9, episode 13, titled "Queen for a Day," such imagery may be used to invoke pathological images of unmarried Black women with multiple children made popular during the Moynihan era. Yet in this instance, though, Nicole is a professional woman who is equipped to shoulder the financial responsibilities and demands associated with caring for multiple children.

The complexities of this image must be further considered given assumptions about Nicole's financial affairs that members of the viewing audience may make given her previously described family profile. Yet when she is prompted by the bridal consultant to whom she is assigned, Nicole eagerly requests a Cinderella-style ball gown in the price range of $2,500–$3,000. Giddily, Nicole gushes to her mother and best friends in attendance about her forthcoming wedding in Aruba. This conversation is juxtaposed with her narration of images of the daily toils she faces caring for six young children and two older children. This image is countered by Nicole musing about the attentiveness of the bridal salon staff members who seem to be swirling about her in a nearly syncopated rhythm proffering bridal accessories. Basking in the glow of the bridal staff's attention, Nicole happily chirps, "I feel like a bride. All attention is on me." Indeed, all attention is on Nicole. Even so, for the viewing audience, more attention than she may have wanted is offered. *Say Yes to the Dress*, then, becomes a venue for presenting an unlikely and restorative image of Black femininity that may otherwise have been misrepresented. In fact, Nicole typifies an image of a modern Cinderella whose fairy tale is not a linear, prescribed one. Although her life's trajectory differs greatly from the one described by Joy Jones in her article, "Marriage Is for White People," Nicole's Cinderella-themed fairy-tale ending described on *Say Yes to the Dress* is an alternative one that reflects the modern realities of economically stable Black women who elect to marry after having children.

In considering the Cinderella imagery frequently invoked in shows like *Say Yes to the Dress*, one must consider Sandra Barnes's article that alludes to Collette Dowling's study, *The Cinderella Complex: Women's Hidden Fear of Independence*. In her article, Barnes observes that many women in the United States of America are "socialized from childhood to embrace the role of Cinderella and to anticipate a romantic relationship with Prince Charming" (22). Therefore, it is telling that a frequent refrain of many women—of all races, like Nicole—who seek to find their perfect bridal gowns often reference the image of Cinderella when describing the wedding dresses of their dreams. This reference, then, becomes a signal for the bridal salon consultant to present to the bride for her consideration a formulaic image of femininity, complete with a poufy, crinoline-filled skirt that almost seems to be cut from the puffy cloudlike fabric of little girls' dreams and embellished with shantung and charmeuse silk fabrics that construct many adult women's hopes for living a perfect life—complete with the ultimate, rare appliqué: Prince Charming.

Nicole and Jacklyn represent the "ordinary" Black brides who are featured on the *Say Yes to the Dress* shows who reference Cinderella imagery as a means of articulating their "dream" dresses. Their images as brides contrast with brides who are rarely seen on these shows: financially well-heeled Black brides who have no articulated budgetary constraints. These celebrity brides or, more aptly stated, women who derive their celebrity status from relatives or fiancés often arrive at these reality shows' bridal salons also seeking quintessentially Cinderella-inspired dresses with all of their grandly articulated and clichéd accessories. Unlike the ordinary Black brides who appear on the *Say Yes to the Dress* shows, the Black celebrity brides use these shows as a backdrop to either affirm or highlight their wealth or, in many instances, the wealth that they hope to attain through marriage. Such an example is represented by Crystal, a bride from Texas, featured on the season 9, episode 5 edition of *Say Yes to the Dress* titled "Princess Fantasy." After making her request for two dresses known, the show's announcer interjects that Crystal is "looking for a dress with a price that only real royalty could afford." Therefore, Crystal represents yet another image of Black brides whose existence is made known through shows like *Say Yes to the Dress*. This too, provides an opportunity to create a greater space for representations of Black women of all walks of life who choose to share their journeys toward matrimony on bridal reality television shows. At first blush, it appears as if many Black women who are featured on shows like *Say Yes to the Dress* are focused so intently on their forthcoming nuptials that they are seemingly oblivious to the ways in which they are being depicted by the shows' directors and producers; however, such an assertion would be both uninformed and capricious, for it is widely known that reality shows are in fact scripted and fashioned so that they effectively titillate members of viewing audiences. To this end, Marci Bounds Littlefield asserts:

> Ideas about race and ethnicity are transferred to the public through images and public presentations of racial groups, and until these presentations are filtered and challenged. . . . That is, until minority groups play an active role in self-definition and reject the presentations of minorities by producers who are motivated by the dollar, then media representations will continue to define minority groups. Until African American women and men understand their respective roles in the portrayal of race and are challenged to make different choices, then we will always need public spaces to define and discuss racial issues. (685)

Littlefield's observation is a clarion call, not only to young Black brides-in-waiting who choose to chronicle their searches for wedding gowns through the medium of reality television, but also to those countless Black women whose quests for personal validation and recognition are revolutionary in their own right, but are not televised.[2] In equal measure, Black women of all walks of life must take great care to present complete images of themselves to the wider world that are truly reflective of their matchless worth, beauty, and value. When this is done, only then will Black women effectively dress the part—and embrace all elements of their womanhood and humanity.

Notes

1 This idea is suggestive of twentieth-century philosopher Jacques Derrida's thoughts about ways to expose and subvert binary oppositions that support our dominant ways of thinking. The construct of presence/absence, therefore, suggests a way to frame oppositional arguments.

2 An allusion to musician Gil Scott-Heron's song, "The Revolution Will Not Be Televised." *Flying Dutchman.* 1974. Album.

Works Cited

Barnes, Sandra L. "Romantic and Familial Relationships with Black Males: Implications of the Cinderella Complex and Prince Charming Ideal." *Black Women, Gender + Families* 3.2 (2009): 1–28.

Brancato, Jim. "Domesticating Politics: The Representation of Wives and Mothers in American Reality Television." *Film & History: An Interdisciplinary Journal of Film and Television Studies* 37.2 (2007): 49–56.

Dickson, Lynda, and Kris Marsh. "The Love Jones Cohort: A New Face of the Black Middle Class." *Black Women, Gender + Families* 2.1 (2008): 84–105.

Dowling, Collette. *The Cinderella Complex: Women's Hidden Fear of Independence.* New York: Summit, 1981.

Jones, Joy. "Marriage Is for White People." *Washington Post.* 26 Mar. 2006. Sunday ed.: np.

Littlefield, Marci Bounds. "The Media as a System of Racialization: Exploring Images of African American Women and the New Racism." *American Behavioral Scientist.* 51.5 (2008): 675–685.

Morrison, Toni. *The Bluest Eye.* New York: Vintage, 1970.

Motsemme, Nthabiseng. "Distinguishing Beauty, Creating Distinctions: The Politics and Poetics of Dress among Young Black Women." *Agenda* 57, Urban Culture (2003): 12–19.

"Booty-do's and Ball Gowns." *Say Yes to the Dress: Atlanta.* TLC. Season 5, Episode 18. 2013.

"Princess Fantasy." *Say Yes to the Dress.* TLC. Season 9, Episode 5. 2013.

"Queen for a Day." *Say Yes to the Dress.* TLC. Season 9, Episode 13, 2013.

"Shiny, Happy, Bling!" *Say Yes to the Dress: Atlanta.* TLC. Season 6, Episode 15, 2014.

4

The Semiotics of Fashion and Urban Success in *The Real Housewives of Atlanta*

••••••••••••••••••••••••••

CYNTHIA DAVIS

Whenever African American reality television shows are discussed, in conversation, social media, or in print, the reaction is often negative. Despite the fact that "reality TV is turning countless Black women with a flair for high drama into instant stars with their own spin-offs, cosmetics lines, book deals, and millions of loyal fans" (Amber 84), critics accuse the shows of promoting racial and sexual stereotypes and of setting the race back a hundred years. Antisocial behavior among young women is attributed to the aggression they witness on the shows, while the single-minded pursuit of expensive cars, homes, liquor, clothes, and shoes is deplored by many. Media-savvy actress Diahann Carroll, who starred in the 1968 situation comedy *Julia*, undoubtedly paved the way for Kerry Washington's Olivia Pope in the major network hit *Scandal*. Carroll, however, refuses to watch reality shows, which she deems "a disgrace" (Samuels 62). Although "reality programs starring Black women consistently rank as the highest rated on their respective cable networks" (Amber 85), Phylicia Rashād maintains that these programs portray less diversity than did *The Cosby Show* in the 1980s (Samuels 62). According to Siobhan Smith, the shows are unrealistic in that they utilize a disproportionate number of fair-skinned women and portray Black women more negatively than Black men. In short, critics claim that the programs do not portray affluent, educated Black women as they are: community leaders, philanthropists, churchgoers, entrepreneurs, and devoted wives and mothers.

Surprisingly, given the broad demographic appeal of the African American shows, and their undisputed presence in popular culture, little critical analysis has been published. Over the past five years, popular magazines like *Newsweek* and *Essence* have discussed the programs, but the academy has preserved a dignified silence on the topic. In contrast, several well-researched volumes on Black women in film and television have appeared, such as Donald Bogle's biography of Dorothy Dandridge (1997). Film research is essential because it does reclaim forgotten African American actors, but according to Beretta Smith-Shomade, it sometimes "forwards celebratory, historical, and male-centered assertions" (Smith-Shomade 2). Smith-Shomade's own book, *Shaded Lives: African American Women and Television* (2002), contributes original research on the subject, but few scholars have built on her study, particularly in terms of reality television, even though the author maintains that "African-American women compose an under-addressed population in visual popular culture [in that] they command a substantial amount of coverage" but have "limited access to societal resources and institutions" (Smith-Shomade 1). Neither the *African American Review* nor the *Journal of Black Studies* has addressed the topic, although Siobhan Smith's article on gender representation in BETs *College Hill* appeared in the *Western Journal of Black Studies* in 2013.

Though African American women's reality television shows may appear to have burst into popular consciousness with little contextualization or historical antecedent, one show, *The Real Housewives of Atlanta* (*RHOA*), should be viewed through the lens of an earlier tradition of promoting racial uplift and material success in the African American media. One could explore this thesis in connection with *Ebony* magazine in the 1950s, with its emphasis on race pride and upward mobility, but this chapter specifically views *RHOA* in the context of nineteenth- and twentieth-century fashion magazines for women of color, such as *Ringwood's Afro-American Journal of Fashion* (1891–1894), Josephine St. Pierre Ruffin's *Woman's Era* (1894–97), and Katherine Williams's *Half-Century* (1916–1925). The Chicago magazine *The Bronzeman* (1929–1933), although not exclusively marketed to women, took over *Half-Century's* demographic and resembled the latter, particularly in the publication of fiction by women. While these consumer-oriented publications emphasized fashion, beauty, interior decoration, and entertainment, they also promoted urban acculturation through articles, columns, and short stories that explored the new dilemmas for African American women that were triggered by modern life and the Great Migration. Women now had decisions to make on birth control, relationships, housing, careers, and education, and the magazines helped them to decide.

In fact, Harlem Renaissance writers like Anita Scott Coleman (1890–1960) first published their work in these venues. Coleman, who published eight stories in *Half-Century* between 1919 and 1921, captures the zeitgeist of the Great Migration in her "Peter and Phoebe" stories about a young couple who move up North for a better life, and in her "Bambino Grimke" tales about a trickster figure, "sheik," and itinerant jazz-band leader. Although Coleman addresses discrimination in the "Bambino" stories, she understood her audience and recognized that the mission of these magazines was not to denounce the depredations of racism as did serious journals like Pauline Hopkins's *Colored American* magazine (1900–1909) and W. E. B. Du Bois's *Crisis* (1910–1935). Nor did these publications attempt to uphold rigorous literary and aesthetic standards for the race, as did *Opportunity* (1923–1949). Like her Harlem Renaissance contemporaries, Coleman saved her serious reflections on race and culture for *Opportunity* and the *Crisis*. Du Bois, famously, was uninterested in entertainment; he reproved a reader who complained that the journal was "depressing" with a stern reminder that "the *Crisis* did not try to be funny" (Rooks 7). Similarly, Hopkins modeled her Boston-based magazine on the lofty intellectual tone of the *Atlantic Monthly* (a pro-abolition journal founded in Boston in 1857), and *Scribner's* magazine (1887–1939). The women's magazines, while not as intellectually or aesthetically ambitious as these organs, did oppose, albeit obliquely, racial exclusion and limitations on opportunities for African Americans in the urban North. However, the focus of the magazines, as is the case with *RHOA* today, was on the social activities and consumer goods that define status and success.

The popularity of the magazines was grounded in the avid participation of readers, many of whom still lived in the rural South. Readers shaped the agenda and content of the publications, communicating freely with the editors, expressing their views on stories, fashions, and features. In much of the same way, *RHOA* viewers interact on the Bravo website, responding eagerly to the stars' post-show blogs. Like *RHOA*, the African American women's magazines of fashion and culture "centered on women who were attempting to grow, change, and fully inhabit the cities to which they had recently moved" (Rooks 114). In similar ways, both the magazines and the television show assert the vital presence of African American women in the urban milieu.

Before discussing *The Real Housewives of Atlanta*, or any other reality show, it must be emphasized that no ethnic group in America has a monopoly on behaving badly on television. As actress and activist Holly Robinson Peete points out, "Listen, there are plenty of white women acting a fool on television every night" (Samuels 62). Whether one watches twenty-somethings whose life goals comprise "gym, tan, laundry" (*Jersey Shore*), or the shenanigans of a harem of half-clothed women and an aging rap star (*Flavor of Love*), one can only conclude that the camera brings out the worst in any reality ensemble. Peete maintains, however, that the difference is the balance in the portrayal of white women: "They have shows on the major networks—not just cable and not just reality shows—about them running companies, being great mothers, and having loving relationships" (Samuels 62). Although the network show *Scandal* does feature Kerry Washington as a multidimensional African American character, Peete's assertion still supports Smith-Shomade's claim that in the case of African American women on television, the "contradiction of public visibility and actual disempowerment remains unresolved . . . and unexamined" (1), a situation that the present chapter seeks to explore.

In contrast to these lurid depictions, however, there do exist reality shows about women of various ethnicities that are not exploitative and vulgar, such as *Push Girls* (about four paraplegic women in Los Angeles); *Braxton Family Values* (the five singing Braxton sisters); and *Tia and Tamera* (twin actresses who are wives and mothers), all of which portray ambitious, creative, and balanced women with close, supportive families. But though these shows have achieved good ratings, they cannot compare with "their more conflict-driven competitors. The Braxtons and *Tia and Tamera* both peaked at under a million viewers per episode . . . [while] the episode of *Real Housewives of Atlanta* in which the ladies traveled to South Africa, where they bickered, visited an orphanage and bickered some more, all the while wearing designer heels and full make-up, was watched by almost 4 million people" (Amber 89). Although producers of reality shows understand that, as celebrity lawyer Star Jones puts it, "pitting us against each other is good ratings" (Samuels 62), not all reality television relies on negative behavior to boost numbers. VH1's "Lala's Full Court Wedding" in 2010, a crossover hit watched by a heterogeneous audience, was extremely popular. The family-centered remarriage of NeNe and Greg Leakes in 2013, an extravagant affair at Atlanta's Buckhead Intercontinental Hotel, not only made high ratings, but became a spin-off of *The Real Housewives of Atlanta.*

The Real Housewives of Atlanta, now in its seventh season, is sometimes equated to *Basketball Wives* and *Love & Hip Hop* because of the volatile verbal exchanges on the show; however, it differs significantly from other reality television shows. For example, the women are all community boosters and philanthropists. They visit Boys & Girls Clubs and orphanages, lecture young women on following their dreams, and host elaborate charity events, with varying degrees of success. In fact, since much of *RHOA* involves social disasters, there is much to be learned from the show about how *not* to organize, promote, and host a society fund-raiser. In addition, according to Frances Berwick, president of Bravo Media and the developer of the *Housewives* franchise, "With *Real Housewives of Atlanta* we found a group of women who were actually friends, and one of them happened to be white. We saw their friendship as something fascinating and relatable and the audience agreed" (Samuels 62). *RHOA* has carved out a narrative arc that includes enough conflict to maintain ratings, while it follows a consistent story line about the entrepreneurial achievements, philanthropy, and family relationships of six Atlanta women who may not like each other, but who are educated, articulate, affluent, aspirational, fashionable, and family oriented.

Verbal fireworks are an important element of the show; the women talk constantly with, about, and over each other, and each woman has a distinctive voice. The cast has evolved over six years, and only NeNe Leakes, a professional actress, remains from the first season. Of all the women, NeNe best understands that successful reality television involves timing, pacing, improvisation, consistency of "brand," and ensemble work. NeNe's remarks are mini–comic monologues in which she ranges easily along the linguistic continuum, mixing crisply articulated opinions with impersonations of other cast members and pithy, down-home expressions like "A hit dog always holla." Balancing NeNe's androgynous persona (Kenya accuses her of looking like a drag queen) is tall, willowy, fashion-forward Cynthia, a former runway model and the owner of a modelling and pageant agency. Cynthia's predecessor was Sheree, an aspiring fashion designer who balanced the more aggressive NeNe. Cynthia, like Sheree, seems more averse to conflict than the others, but nevertheless plunges into fraught situations, blissfully oblivious to consequences. Her questionable decisions, such as marriage to Peter, a serial bankrupt, make for lively television. Porsha Stewart, the youngest housewife, comes from a distinguished Atlanta family and is the grand-daughter of civil rights leader Hosea Williams. Porsha's vivacious but naïve persona recalls the zany antics of Lucille Ball. Given her family background, could Porsha really have thought that the Underground Railroad involved real trains? Months later, her *faux pas* still generates viewer comments. The cast also includes Phaedra Parks and Kandi Burruss, both of whom moved to Atlanta twenty years ago and associated with a group of young, rich athletes. The two women also have impressive careers of their own; Phaedra, a prominent entertainment lawyer and a mother of two, is pursuing her mortician's license. She is witty and articulate, with a comedienne's timing, and a distinctly adult sense of humor. Kandi Burruss, outgoing and vivacious, has a successful career as a singer and songwriter (in 1999, she won a Grammy for her song "No Scrubs"), and now owns a bedroom toy business. Kim, the only white character, is no longer on the show, but she is still featured on the *RHOA* blog. Kim generated many volatile encounters among the other women, but despite their frequent conflicts, she and NeNe appear to have maintained an off-camera friendship. One of the newest housewives is Kenya Moore, a former Miss USA. Kenya, like her predecessor Kim, has adversarial relationships with the other women, particularly with NeNe. As was the case with Kim, Kenya does not have NeNe's sharp wit and comic timing, and she inevitably comes off poorly in their skirmishes.

With the exception of Porsha, none of the Atlanta housewives are from the city; all come from smaller Georgia towns or other states. It may well be the narrative of women's urban success, echoing *Sex in the City*, that has made the Atlanta program the most successful in the *Housewives* franchise. The trope of urban success also links *RHOA* to the African American women's magazines. Just as the cast members hold forth on their independence and sophistication, so editors of the magazines were prescriptive, urging photographers like James Van der Zee and the writers of short stories to show that "as the characters define themselves, they desire the opportunity to shop, dress, entertain themselves, and explore freely without the sanction of male approval or support" (Rooks 114). Despite the fictional characters' vaunted independence, however, most stories in the publications end with a happy marriage. Similarly, the *RHOA* ladies, aside from setting out snacks on their granite counters for impromptu get-togethers, rarely cook or perform domestic chores. Only three of the sixth season's six stars are married, and while it seems almost tongue-in-cheek to describe these women as "housewives," the subtext of marriage as an ultimate goal is undeniably present, just as it was in the magazines. Kenya joins the show in season 5 based on the premise that her relationship with her "boyfriend" Walter Jackson would soon lead to an engagement; however, their relationship completely unravels before the end of her first season on the show. Kenya then joins the ranks of the other unmarried "housewives."

Characters in other African American reality programs seem more volatile and less articulate than the Atlanta housewives. Although the women's male consorts did get combative in a recent episode, NeNe insists that physical violence is not a part of the *RHOA* "brand": "We don't fistfight on our show, but you have definitely seen us fighting with words" (Amber 86). The recent fisticuffs of Phaedra's husband at NeNe's "pajama party" was immediately followed by profuse apologies by the stars, both on camera and in their blogs, as if all realized that *RHOA* was treading dangerously close to the vulgarity of other franchises. In avoiding or at least protesting violence, *RHOA* has also avoided boycotts or petitions by irate critics, such as those targeted at *Basketball Wives* and *Love & Hip Hop: Atlanta*. These shows owe their genesis to Jerry Springer, who crafted voyeuristic thrills for the home audience as they watched ordinary people scream and fight on national television.

It is not Jerry Springer but Oprah Winfrey, however, who links *RHOA* and the earlier women's magazines, with her dignified and tasteful but highly interactive and audience-centered environment. Like the magazines, Oprah "validated women's speech, stories, and concerns" (Smith-Shomade 157). Such interaction cannot be underestimated; much of *RHOA*'s appeal stems from the ability of the audience to comment instantaneously, through social media and the Bravo website, on the circular, multistrand plot lines that revisit the same conflicts (NeNe's bossiness;

Cynthia and Peter's financial woes; and Kandi's battles with her mother). After each show, Facebook and Twitter explode with audience reactions to every nuance of the stars' behavior, from arriving late to a party ("Bad manners! No excuse!") to "casting shade" on one another. Dramas are further rehashed on "After Show" specials with *RHOA* executive producer Andy Cohen, who manages to press on every bruise. The stars are paid to blog about each episode, after which viewers respond with comments like: "I love you, Cynthia, you are such a lady," or "Nene, can you be anymore full of yourself?" Though Kenya blogs faithfully, defending and explaining her on-air performances with the intensity of a Monday-morning quarterback, other stars seem to shirk their duties. One fan on the Bravo site praised Kenya's prompt, interactive posts, and wondered why viewers criticized her when she was, after all, doing her job. In contrast, other stars claim to be too busy to blog, and thus avoid backlash and negative feedback from the fans.

Judging from such comments, viewers identify intimately with the housewives. The fact that such affluent and sophisticated women can make, and learn from, social blunders, forges a connection with the audience and generates a shared set of behaviors and values. Thus, the connection of the housewives with their fans is an essential element of the show, and one that recalls the intimate relationship between the readers and editors of early twentieth-century African American women's magazines. For example, in 1916 when *Half-Century* initiated a column called "What They Are Wearing" and published photographs by James Van der Zee of African American models instead of lithographed images of white women, the feature created an avalanche of mail. Readers seemed particularly taken by the fact that "the women pictured represented a variety of heights, skin colors, and weights. They offer wide-ranging options for identification on the part of the magazine's reader" (Rooks 87). With regard to interaction, the peripatetic stars of *RHOA* have, of course, exceeded the limitations of letters to the editor in ladies' magazines; they heighten their accessibility through radio interviews, business ventures (fashion design, funeral planning, and mail-order sex toys), and glamorous girl getaways to Los Angeles and Miami. Fans are consistently treated with respect. On a recent show, Kenya reacts with delight to two young Japanese men waiting politely outside her home for a photograph, and dubs them her "paparazzi." The niece of a colleague of the writer attended Cynthia's modeling school and reports that Cynthia is just as sweet in person as she appears to be on the show, and that she works hard to help the young models achieve their goals. Given six degrees of separation, it is likely that anyone who wishes to do so has connected with at least one of the stars, which is an important element in the show's success. In terms of content, *RHOA* focuses more on a circular process of interacting with the audience and analyzing problems rather than on a linear impetus toward solutions. A similar approach could be seen in Oprah's talk shows, with their "relatively unscripted dialogue . . . [that] juxtapose rather than integrate multiple, heterogeneous, discontinuous elements. Rather than *reconcile*, [Oprah's] shows barely *contain*" [my italics] (Smith-Shomade 152).

Another connection between *Oprah*, the women's magazines, and *RHOA* is that "race, gender, class, and sexuality predominate and provide much of the subject matter" (Smith-Shomade 153). As on *Oprah* and in the magazines, *RHOA* validates the markers of class; the cast members dress, decorate their homes, and entertain in a firmly upper-middle-class but definitively heterosexual milieu. Although the magazines avoided any discussion of sexuality, *RHOA* normalizes conversations about homosexuality, much as Oprah did on her show. Interestingly, *RHOA*'s only gay characters are engaged in service occupations to the stars: doing their hair, advising on their wardrobes, and arranging flowers. Although hairdressers Derek J and Lawrence Washington are invited to social events and even have their own spin-off show, *Fashion Queens*, the cast does not seem to know any prominent Atlanta businessmen or women who are gay. Occasionally, the housewives even tease or gossip about people who may be gay, such as Phaedra's husband, who did some jail time; Kenya's former boyfriend, who was insufficiently enthusiastic in the bedroom; and a longtime female friend of NeNe. Of course, political correctness is not a feature of *RHOA*, or any reality television program, so one must assume that the attitudes displayed on the show are part of a desire for authenticity and to "keep it real."

Like the early women's magazines, Oprah is sometimes criticized because she did not sufficiently privilege race issues on her show, although she certainly did acknowledge and break down racial barriers to social and economic achievement. On *RHOA*, however, a more "postracial" climate is evoked through the absence of any discernible racial tension between the cast and the greater Atlanta community; in fact, the white people on the show, all of whom, like their gay counterparts, occupy subordinate roles as agents, salespeople, lawyers, waiters, and wedding consultants, are flattering and deferential to the show's stars. Meanwhile, the stars themselves are regularly shown dining and drinking cocktails at Atlanta's most fashionable venues, where they receive the warm welcomes accorded favored customers.

Judging from audience comments, viewers are helped to negotiate their own multiethnic, postracial environments as they watch NeNe joke and flirt with waiters in expensive restaurants, and Kenya "twirl" into an exclusive club. In much the same way, the early African American publications helped readers to adapt to social encounters in the urban North. As Rooks points out, these publications offered "the chance to view African American women occupying public spaces, to read about African American female heroines as they negotiated an urban environment that was new to many of the fictional characters, as well as to the stories' readers" (83). As mentioned, Anita Scott Coleman's Phoebe and Peter series "was perfectly tailored for the magazine; readers loved the stories and requested more adventures of upwardly mobile Peter, his pretty country wife, Phoebe, and her feisty best friend, Mayme" (Davis and Mitchell, *Western Echoes*, 25). In "Phoebe and Peter Up North," Peter quickly adapts to urban fashions and insists that Phoebe straighten her hair and wear short skirts. Phoebe refuses, but compromise is reached when Mayme advises her, "No, kiddie, don't straighten your hair. It's already got the wave most of these old Janes around here would die for. Now, Kitten, take it from me . . . always do your hair low. That's your style" (*Western Echoes* 185). Peter falls back in love with his now-fashionable wife, but Phoebe asserts her independence by landing a job in a fancy cake shop, molding elaborate sugar decorations. In "Phoebe Goes to a Lecture" Mayme takes her to a talk on birth control at a fashionable women's club. Phoebe is shocked at the speaker's "horrid" statements, but Mayme remarks that these lectures provide "good food for thought. You've got to go some to refute all that old lady quack's arguments, now don't you?" She explains that she took Phoebe to the lecture "not that I thought you'd enjoy it especially, but . . . you don't need to think other people's thoughts. Think up your own. That's what city life is for" (*Western Echoes* 192). Coleman's stories thus address conflicts of urban/rural values during the Great Migration; they emphasize the advantages of city life in terms of social and economic mobility and suggest compromises that preserve African American cultural authenticity. The characters in the stories are all rural southerners, but they express themselves in proper syntax and vocabulary instead of in stereotyped dialect; this style of dialogue itself suggests how quickly new urban migrants could adopt markers of upward mobility.

Race issues were not foregrounded in the magazines, although a critical white gaze was implied in the many columns urging readers to dress
and furnish their homes tastefully and fashionably. Similarly, race issues
rarely affect the lives of the housewives. The first few seasons of *RHOA*
included Kim, a white Atlantan with a mysterious lover called "Big Papa"
and an improbable blonde hairstyle eventually revealed to be a wig. Kim
seemed to be well integrated into the culture of Black Atlanta; in the segments when the cast members, in elaborate clothes and make-up, comment on the action with jokes and scathing put-downs of one another,
Kim is able to hold her own in "telling lies" and playing the dozens. At
the same time, the other housewives express annoyance with the way Kim
treats her assistant, an African American woman named Sweetie, whose
main responsibility seems to be freshening Kim's cocktails. Kim is also
guilty of the occasional racial faux pas, such as telling the striking Sheree,
with whom she has no resemblance, "You and I look alike. You're kind of
the Black me." Normally, however, the housewives did not inject race into
conversations with Kim, although they trade insults in endlessly creative
ways, abusing one another's taste in men, hairstyles, fashion choices, and
parenting skills. Thus, although race may provide a subtext on the show, in
that Atlanta does appear to be "the city too busy to hate," it rarely overtly
surfaces, however intense the confrontations among the women.

In fact, the ratings-boosting interactions among the cast provide another
link to *Oprah* because the *RHOA* audience, like Oprah's fans over the
years, enjoys "the catharsis of confrontation" (Smith-Shomade 154). Such
drama propels other shows like Donald Trump's 2011 *Celebrity Apprentice*
in which NeNe accused attorney Star Jones of being "bossy, manipulative,
and conniving" (Samuels 62). Jones took it in stride, telling an interviewer
that it is up to the stars to know how to handle ratings-building conflict,
and disclosing that when she goes on television she always has a plan,
which is to promote her own projects. NeNe seems to have learned from
the more media-savvy Jones, for she now often announces on *RHOA* that
she is "very smart" and "very strategic" in everything she does.

In addition to facilitating catharsis, *Oprah's* real accomplishment
was to encourage all women to demonstrate self-help, agency, authority,
and the American ethos of hard work, while she validated their preoccupation with home, health, beauty, and fashion as markers of upward
mobility, a formula that defines *RHOA* today. In this way, both *Oprah*
and *RHOA* are twenty-first-century descendants of the impetus toward

racial uplift and material success originally manifested by the African American women's magazines and clubs that appeared in the nineteenth century. As Rodger Streitmatter points out, "It was from the women's club movement that a national communication network evolved, linking African-American women across the country" (61). When the women's clubs could not satisfy the desire for interaction within the race, there was an upsurge in magazine publishing directed toward African American women readers; between 1891 and 1950, there were eight magazines specifically marketed to Black women (Rooks 4). In these venues, "concerns, issues and narrative strategies . . . were transformed by the experience of urbanization with its attendant emphasis on consumerism" (Rooks 2). In 1894, Josephine St. Pierre Ruffin, the aristocratic Bostonian and social activist, launched a magazine called *Woman's Era* (1894–1897), named after the national club she founded with the same name. Her first editorial declared that "the stumbling block in the way of even the most cultured colored woman is the narrowness of her environment. . . . It is to help strengthen this class and to achieve a better understanding among all classes that this little venture is sent on its mission" (Ruffin 8). Although married to a prominent Boston judge, and herself a mother, Ruffin ensured that "one specific feminist theme threaded through the newspaper was that a woman should not limit herself to the narrow identity of wife and mother" (Streitmatter 64). Although, in retrospect, Boston's much-lauded racial inclusivity seems misplaced, Ruffin's social milieu considered itself immune from discrimination. At the same time, Ruffin campaigned strenuously for full economic and social integration of African American women of all classes, at one point declaring that "the exclusion of colored women and girls from nearly all places of respectable employment is due mostly to the meanness of white women" (Streitmatter 67). Could Ruffin view *The Real Housewives of Atlanta* today, she might well be shocked by the stars' lack of decorum, but she certainly would have lauded the broad social and economic opportunities that these African American women have created for themselves.

Ruffin, a member of the group W. E. B. Du Bois called "the talented tenth," had a very definite idea of the demographic for her magazine: on the one hand, she hoped to attract women exactly like herself who, along with affluence, education, and distinguished lineage, felt a sense of *noblesse oblige* to less privileged women of color. The masthead of her magazine, with its stated intention to appeal to "women of the refined and educated classes," does appear, in retrospect, to be rather elitist. This impression is reinforced by the society columns for which Ruffin recruited prominent women from all over the country as reporters; the African American community was thus linked nationally by reports from as far afield as California, Texas, and Louisiana that described weddings, parties, professional honors, and accolades, and celebrated the acceptance of African American students to prestigious colleges. The magazine also attracted subscribers with features on high-end fashion, food, entertaining, culture, and the arts. Ruffin understood that "an understanding of fashion was an essential element of urban migration . . . [since] fashion marked both migratory and class status" (Rooks 88). Advertisers in Ruffin's magazine appealed to a leisured population, and included a Boston shop that sold "prepared icing" for one's fancy teacakes. A *couturier* announced the creation of a "walking dress" for twenty-three dollars, which would certainly have exceeded the budgets of frugal Bostonians of any ethnicity. In the same way, the red-soled Louboutin shoes and designer frocks worn by the *RHOA* cast are out of reach of most women, yet in watching the show, everyone can aspire to the fantasy of ownership.

During Ruffin's time, magazines like her *Woman's Era* and the mainstream *Ladies' Home Journal* (founded 1883) were highly aspirational. These publications, while ostensibly directed toward an affluent audience, really sought to instruct recent arrivals to urban areas from Europe and the rural South in the customs and values of middle-class American life. Ruffin's subscribers might not all have been able to attend the Boston Symphony or to summer on Martha's Vineyard, but they could still learn from the behavior of socialites while vicariously enjoying the social and economic advances of the race. Ruffin's journalism thus "enhanced the pride and confidence of thousands of her black sisters" in much the same way that Oprah and *RHOA* would do a century later (Streitmatter 62). *Woman's Era* folded in 1897, unable to match the revenue of the "slick" national magazines that competed for Black readers by advertising in race periodicals; in vain, Ruffin urged her readers to support a journal that published and promoted the writing of African American women rather than one, like *Ladies' Home Journal*, that did not. This was brought home years later when a novel by Dorothy West, the daughter of one of Ruffin's friends, was first accepted and then rejected by *Ladies' Home Journal*, on the grounds that it might offend white southern readers (Davis and Mitchell, *Literary Sisters* 118).

Although Ruffin's journal was short-lived, she certainly planted the seed for other aspiring African American women journalists throughout the country. Pauline Hopkins, also from Boston, was a friend of Josephine St. Pierre Ruffin and the secretary of Ruffin's Woman's Era Club. In 1901, Hopkins founded the *Colored American Magazine*. The masthead proclaims that the venture is "Devoted to literature, science, music, art, religion, facts, fiction, and the traditions of the Negro." Although "the *Colored American* afforded Hopkins a nationwide audience, largely of women and an ideal forum in which to combine her political and literary passions," not to mention a venue for her novels and short stories that might otherwise have gone unpublished, it was not a magazine devoted to consumerism and fashion (*Literary Sisters* 60). A few years later, another women's magazine, *The Half-Century Magazine for the Colored Home and Homemaker* (1916–1925), was launched in Chicago and underwritten by a wealthy businessman and lawyer, Anthony Overton (Fultz 100). Overton, who eventually owned a bank and an insurance company, was honored by the National Association for the Advancement of Colored People (NAACP) as well as the Spingarn and Harmon Foundations for his work as an African American entrepreneur. On the South Side of Chicago, Overton built a modern factory to house his Hygienic Manufacturing Company, from which he produced and sold a line of perfumes, face powders, and lipsticks for women of color under the trade name "High Brown." Realizing that he needed a venue to promote his products, Overton enlisted the elegant and entrepreneurial Katherine Williams and made her editor-in-chief of a magazine that he called *Half-Century*, a title that referenced the fifty years since Emancipation.

Like Pauline Hopkins, Williams was a political activist; she was a member of the Alpha Suffrage Club, established by Ida Bell Wells-Barnett, which helped elect the first African American alderman in Chicago, Oscar DePriest. But Williams was also interested in fashion and beauty, and was determined to make a success of her magazine. She eschewed an intellectual or "high-brow" tone, and also avoided the race politics of the *Crisis* (1910) or *The Messenger* (1917). Instead, she focused on the uplift and entertainment of ordinary women; the magazine comprised "short fiction, biographical sketches, serialized novels, editorials, columns on etiquette, domestic science, urban life, and fashion" (Rooks 71). It would appear that Williams knew what she was doing. According to writer Dorothy West, many middle-class families in northern cities like her own did not subscribe to *Crisis* for fear that the graphic stories about lynching and other depredations would discourage the children in whom they wanted to instill confidence and optimism. Williams was also a good businesswoman. She shared with her readers the costs and challenges of running a magazine to discourage them from sharing instead of buying copies, and argued persuasively that there were eight reasons why women should subscribe:

1. To conduct your home more easily and more cheaply
2. To dress smartly at the lowest cost
3. To read the best stories by the leading Colored writers
4. To bring up and train your children better
5. To see our own beautiful women depicted in the latest and smartest costumes
6. To know the most novel ideas for entertaining
7. To be a leader in the social life of your community
8. To keep in touch with all that is newest and most vital in women's interests, inside and outside the home. (Rooks 71)

As an incentive to subscribers, Williams added a personal shopper to the magazine staff who, at no charge, would purchase items in the Chicago stores. This service appealed not only to rural readers far from shops, but also to those in states where discriminatory practices discouraged African American customers (Rooks 76). The personal shopper, the enthusiastic letters from readers, and the chatty columns full of fashion advice endeared readers to the magazine and built a sense of shared community and values. If one removes the references to thrift and budgeting, never concerns of the Atlanta Housewives, Williams's values are exactly those espoused on *RHOA*: fashion, entertaining, interior decorating, self-improvement, family relationships, and community leadership.

Williams's audience, though not the affluent African American reader targeted by Josephine Ruffin, was broader, her goals were more realistic, and her venture was more successful: she directed her magazine toward "newly arrived migrants to urban areas, whom she believed ill-equipped to the demands of living in such a new and different environment" (Rooks 72). Even the fiction was carefully calibrated to the magazine's intention to "prepare Afro-American women for a place in urban social landscapes" (Rooks 4). James Weldon Johnson's novel *The Autobiography of an*

Ex-Colored Man, with its frank treatment of the urban milieu and racial passing, was serialized in *Half-Century* magazine between 1919 and 1920.

In the 1920s, Harlem Renaissance writer Anita Scott Coleman published two stories in *The Bronzeman*, another Chicago magazine, published by Robert Cole, president of the African-American Metropolitan Mutual Assurance Company. Although not specifically targeted to women, *The Bronzeman* "featured light fiction, gossip, sports [and] fashion" designed to inform and interest subscribers who aspired to Chicago's urban sophistication (Weems 6). Coleman's witty tales about Bambino Grimke, the leader and pianist of the Ginger Blues Band, appealed to the magazine's readers with precise description of Jazz Age fashions in hair, clothes, slang, and music, all of which Coleman would have observed near her home in Los Angeles, around the jazz clubs on Central Avenue. Bambino is the quintessential young man on the prowl or "sheik," as inspired by Rudolph Valentino: "Not a feature askew. His skin smooth as satin, cream-colored, and glistening with health and tonsorial perfection. His hair . . . if ever 'twas kinky, the hair-dresser's magic has stolen the kink. His eyes . . . simply dazzling orbs" (*Western Echoes* 119). But the light-hearted Bambino stories contain a serious subtext: most of his schemes involve the provision of jobs and decent accommodation for his itinerant jazz band, not an easy task in a period of racism and discrimination. In terms of his music, Bambino must also contend with "learned white folks" wondering "Who created jazz?" Determining that "jazz is too much of a coup to concede to their dark brethren," white culture decides that "such exponents of the art as Bambino have caught the knack of jazzing things up a bit through downright apeishness, or when better disposed . . . an aptness at mimicry" (*Western Echoes* 118). Although the dialogue employs Jazz Age expressions, Coleman's characters speak along a linguistic continuum, ranging from highly formal English to vernacular slang. Bambino's elegant letter to his boarding house landlord, requesting "tender sincerest regret at taking French leave . . . [since] important business forced my hurried departure," contrasts with the "down home" language he employs with his fellow musicians. The syntax of the stories is accessible to recent emigrants from the rural South, while it models educational and cultural heights to which the recent arrival might aspire.

Thus, although they did critique race issues and discrimination in their own way, magazines such as *Half-Century* and *The Bronzeman* were frankly consumerist and aspirational, and focused on fashion, hair, make-up, food, cocktails, dance steps, music, entertaining, etiquette, and interior decoration. Even the fiction in these venues was designed to show the reader how to succeed in the more secular, urban, materialistic, consumerist, racially heterogeneous northern culture. New developments in the rotogravure process permitted lavish illustrations of the clothing and accessories of debutantes and leaders of African American society throughout the United States, such as those who appeared in important newspapers like the *Pittsburgh Courier* and reached a pinnacle in the lush color photographs in *Ebony*. One of the most important accomplishments of these venues was to show that that the African American woman no longer needed to "fit herself... into constructs and ideologies designed for white American women" (Rooks 150).

In comparing these magazines to *The Real Housewives of Atlanta*, contextual commonalities are immediately apparent. In the short fiction, "the women are generally new to urban environments, self-affirmed, and described in ways aimed at highlighting their intellect and character, as opposed to their sexuality or desire for marriage" (Rooks 117). Similarly, all of the housewives save one are migrants to Atlanta from less glamorous rural or suburban locations. They are nothing if not self-affirmed; the show's structure allows each woman ample time in the "confessional" segments to tout her own impeccable taste, business acumen, social skills, independence, and ambition. Though the stars spend hours in hair salons and spas, and lots of money on clothes and shoes, they do not flaunt their sexuality. Men figure prominently on the show, but none of the stars has ever been depicted as unfaithful. The rare bedroom scene is filmed with utmost propriety, and even the women's elaborate beauty routines seem designed to impress each another rather than men. In the magazine stories, men also feature prominently; they are usually "respectable and hard-working but harbor character traits that keep them from reaching their full potential... even within the context of marriage" (Rooks 117). On the sixth season of the show, only three of the six women are married, while all of the men, including NeNe's husband, the financially successful Greg, have character issues (selfishness, fecklessness, infidelity, laziness, lack of impulse control) that preclude satisfactory relationships with their partners.

In both *RHOA* and the African American women's fashion magazines, marriage to successful, stable men is presented as the ultimate goal, yet women are also portrayed as capable of creating their own opportunities for uplift and advancement in a competitive, postracial urban environment. In addition, they are shown as devoted mothers, attentive if not always compliant daughters, faithful wives, honest and hard-working businesspeople, and active participants in the community. Their gleeful materialism and the pro-liferation of Louboutin shoes on the show simply reflect the same American values depicted in commercials, films, and other television shows. Although not all of the African American reality television shows can claim these same qualities, or can be contextualized within the tradition of women's maga-zines of aspiration and uplift, *The Real Housewives of Atlanta* does provide models for women of all ethnicities as they negotiate self-actualization amid the stresses and conflicts of contemporary American life.

Works Cited

Amber, Jeanine. "Real World." *Essence* (January 2013): 84–89.

Bogle, Donald. *Dorothy Dandridge.* New York: Amistad, 1997.

Davis, Cynthia, and Verner D. Mitchell. *Literary Sisters: Dorothy West and Her Circle, A Biography of the Harlem Renaissance.* New Brunswick, NJ: Rutgers UP, 2012.

———. *Western Echoes of the Harlem Renaissance: The Life and Writings of Anita Scott Cole-man.* Norman: U of Oklahoma P, 2008.

Fultz, Michael. "'The Morning Cometh': African-American Periodicals, Education, and the Black Middle Class, 1900–1930." *Journal of Negro History* 80.3 (Summer 1995): 97–112.

Rooks, Noliwe M. *Ladies' Pages: African American Women's Magazines and the Culture that Made Them.* New Brunswick, NJ: Rutgers UP, 2004.

Ruffin, Josephine St. Pierre. "Editorial." *Woman's Era* Mar. 1894. 8.

Samuels, Allison. "Reality TV Trashes Black Women." *Newsweek* 1 May 2011, 62.

Smith, Siobhan. "And Still More Drama: A Comparison of the Portrayals of African-American Women and African-American Men on BET's *College Hill.*" *Western Journal of Black Studies* 37.1 (2013): 39–49.

Smith-Shomade, Beretta E. *Shaded Lives: African American Women and Television.* New Brunswick, NJ: Rutgers UP, 2002.

Streitmatter, Rodger. *Raising Her Voice: African-American Women Journalists Who Changed History.* Lexington: U P of Kentucky, 1994.

Weems, Robert E., Jr. "Robert A. Cole and the Metropolitan Funeral System Association: A Profile of a Civic-Minded African-American Businessman." *Journal of Negro History* 78.1 (Winter 1993): 1–15.

5

Homes without Walls, Families without Boundaries

• •

How Family Participation
in Reality Television Affects
Children's Development

DETRIS HONORA ADELABU

Television has become the primary storyteller for many young children, telling "most of the stories to most of the people, most of the time" (Signorielli 321). For many American children, television is their window to the world, shaping what they believe to be true about the world around them. With children viewing, on average, more than three hours of television a day, television has become a primary cultural socializer for children of all ages and across every ethnic and economic group (Rideout et al.; Roberts and Foehr; Signorielli). Children who are often in the early stages of learning about culture, society, and the many people around them receive some of their first messages regarding self and other via television. Studies show that television sends a powerful message to children regarding what it means to be of a particular gender, ethnicity, socioeconomic status, or sexual orientation, often perpetuating commonly held societal stereotypes regarding what it means to be a member of a particular group (Asamen and Berry; Berry and Asamen; Graves 2008; Berry 2003; Huston et al.; Signorielli; Smith; Tyree).

Of particular concern regarding the media is the television image of African Americans. Disguised as entertainment, television communicates to children worldwide what they should think about African Americans, often contributing to widespread denigration of what it means to be a person of African descent living in America (Asamen and Berry; Dates and Stroman; Van Erva). Reporter John Stossel, in a mini-experiment designed to examine school-age children's ideas about race, showed a group of children two pictures, one of distinguished Harvard professor Roland Fryer, an African American male, and the other of Oklahoma City bomber Timothy McVeigh, a white male. Children were then asked to share what they thought about each person. One of the children indicated to the group that Timothy McVeigh looked angry, yet students overwhelmingly choose Timothy McVeigh as the nicer guy and as the guy who was most likely a teacher. Distinguished professor Roland Fryer was relegated to the role of criminal and basketball player, images of the African American male commonly portrayed in the media (ABC News).

However, while much is known about the impact of television on children's beliefs and attitudes in general, less is known about its impact on children whose families are prominently displayed on television, particularly through reality television. This chapter addresses what can happen when the protective boundaries of home and family are removed to publicly broadcast the private lives of parents and children. In particular, the chapter examines the role of reality television in dismantling the image of the African American family and how this dismantling has potential to affect the development of children, in general, and children of reality parents in particular. Focus is placed on *The Real Housewives of Atlanta*, *Basketball Wives*, and *Hollywood Exes*. The chapter begins with a discussion of the impact of reality television on the image of the African American mother and family and goes on to explore the impact of these images on children's development.

Assassinating the Image of the African American Family

The Cosby Show told the story of the Huxtable family, an upper-middle-income African American family headed by a doctor and a lawyer raising five children in Brooklyn, New York. The show painted an ideal image of a healthy functioning African American family, not because of the family's income or dual-parent structure but because the Huxtables provided a model for how a family unit could coexist in an atmosphere of dignity and respect. What made the Huxtables ideal was their ability to effectively communicate, to positively address conflict, and to love and trust. Emotionally and psychologically healthy homes as portrayed by the Huxtable family build socially, emotionally, and psychologically competent children (Baumrind; Milevsky et al.; Steinberg and Silk). Healthy functioning homes, homes that convey warmth and effective communication, build children who are autonomous, self-confident, and socially competent. These homes build children who are generally well liked by peers and adults and who tend to be socially conscious (Baumrind; Rothrauff et al.; Steinberg and Silk). The consequences of growing up in an emotionally healthy home environment are long term, with children having been raised in emotionally healthy homes reporting a greater sense of overall psychological well-being across the life span when compared to children who were raised in less healthy functioning homes (Baumrind; Rothrauff et al.). Similarly, African American families portrayed as less affluent than the Huxtables, like the Evans family of *Good Times* and the Winslow family of *Family Matters*, also provide a positive image of what a healthy, functioning African American family can look like. Together, *The Cosby Show, Good Times*, and *Family Matters* suggest that African American families function in healthy ways regardless of family income or educational attainment.

Reality television shows such as *The Real Housewives of Atlanta* and *Basketball Wives* assassinate the image of a healthy, functioning African American family to paint the African American family as one in perpetual conflict and plagued by anger, volatility, and distrust. Violence on *Basketball Wives* became so pervasive that it led to a national petition to have the show removed from television. Through the use of commonly held stereotypes of African Americans, the media and African American reality parents co-construct and perpetuate negative images of the African American family. Though the images portrayed in these reality shows are not a divergence from historical stereotypical television images of the

African American family (Berry and Asaman; Comer), reality television depicts the image as all too real, leading viewers to believe that what they see on television is an unscripted, real window into the day-to-day lived experiences of the African American woman and her family—thus providing viewers with their "first real window" into the life of "the" African American family. Although viewers were aware that the Huxtable family of *The Cosby Show* was fictitious, the documentary style filming of reality shows leads viewers to believe that what they see is authentic and perhaps representative of the broader African American family. Cultivation theory suggests that "over time, exposure to the themes in television content shifts viewers' social perceptions toward the television version of reality, regardless of the accuracy or precision of that content" (Gerbner qtd. in Greenberg and Mastro 76).

Children are not the only ones to believe what they see on television. A 2013 study of frequent viewers of reality television found that adult viewers tend to believe that what they see on television is representative of real-world behavioral patterns among everyday individuals (Riddle and De Simone). In a similar study, researchers found that after watching just one episode of the reality show *The Biggest Loser*, viewers reported more negative feelings toward overweight individuals and attributed weight issues to individuals' lack of personal control (Domoff et al.). The stereotypical images of African American women and families portrayed on reality television may similarly perpetuate negative societal views of African Americans.

One could argue that reality television focused on white women and their families such as *The Real Housewives of Beverly Hills* or *of New Jersey* paint a similarly negative picture of the American family, and perhaps this is true. However, there are far more white Americans on television and therefore more opportunities for white Americans to counter the negative images garnered by the white women of reality television. Limited positive media images of African Americans coupled with the fact that Americans are a mostly residentially segregated society—segregated by race and class—limit the opportunity for children and adults to encounter counternarratives to the negative images of African American families as viewed on reality television. Children do not get to see enough counter-images on television depicting emotionally healthy African American families (Berry; Dates and Stroman; Graves 1993). They do not get to see on television how emotionally healthy African American families can disagree without yelling, storming out of a room, or ripping off one's shoe to "beat the shit out of" one another. On reality television, children see mothers threaten to "drag that 'ho" or to "fucking drag you in this bitch." They see adults needing rules like "You can't get out of your seat," because getting out of one's seat during a disagreement can lead to a physical altercation, as in the highly publicized pajama party turned brawl on *The Real Housewives of Atlanta*. In *The Triumph of Reality TV: The Revolution in American Television*, Leigh H. Edwards writes, "Reality programs proffer their own take on how best to approach family and the very viability of that social unit in America today" (5). Reality TV's version of family life is often one that is damaged.

Americans tend to live in isolated "cultural zones" oblivious to the lives of "other"—other ethnicities, other socioeconomic groups, other sexual orientations—beyond what is viewed on television. Studies show that when given opportunity to relocate, to possibly integrate ourselves with "other" we move even closer to those who mirror our physical appearance, our perceptions, and our beliefs (Brooks). These segregation patterns mean that for many, the image of the African American family as portrayed on reality television is "the image" of African American families. This argument is not to place the entire plight of the scorned image of the African American family on the shoulders of African American–based reality shows, but to say that until there are more diverse images of African American families represented on television, the reality families currently represented may want to consider their impact on the image of the broader African American community.

In addition to assassinating the image of the African American family, reality television goes straight for the jugular in its attack on the image of African American mothers. Reality television hypes historical gender role stereotypes of the African American mother as a dominant, controlling wife and mother in ongoing conflict with her friends and partner—whining, complaining, gossiping, and frustrated. The African American father is painted as violent, neglectful, or oppressed. Taken together, African American– based reality shows depict an image of African American parents as individuals who "do not care about serious matters, are frivolous and irresponsible" (Allen 156). These shows provide an image of parents who are more concerned about gossip, hanging out, and about other people's marriages and businesses than about their own.

Gainfully Employed Housewives: No More Weezy Jefferson

The Jeffersons told the story of George and Louise "Weezy" Jefferson, an African American couple who through hard work and sacrifice built a successful chain of dry cleaning stores. George was an outspoken entrepreneur, known for his sexist and prejudicial ideologies. Weezy Jefferson was the dedicated housewife who managed the household and was deeply committed to community. Weezy fits the image of a housewife. However, the working women, mostly working mothers, of reality television, such as *The Real Housewives of Atlanta*, do not. Weezy was a housewife who would not have even been considered a stay-at-home mom because for much of *The Jeffersons*, her only child was in college or married. The women of *The Real Housewives of Atlanta* are gainfully employed lawyers, entertainers, and business owners, making the title *housewives* a misnomer; although for some, their only responsibility appears to be reality cast member, as they appear to have no children, spouse, or career. Therefore, at the very least, the women of *The Real Housewives of Atlanta* can be referred to as working moms or mommypreneurs, not because there is dishonor in being identified as a housewife but because these women are working mothers.

So why do the working mothers of *The Real Housewives of Atlanta* choose to downplay their roles as mothers and as professionals for the sake of entertainment? Why do they allow their businesses to function as poorly positioned product placements flanked between catfights and tirades? What message does it send to their children regarding the ability to balance home and family? What message does it send regarding women? Jennifer Pozner suggests that bashing women's intellectual capacity is at the heart of realty television, that "women's intellectual inferiority is among reality TV's basest notions" (108). She goes on to assert that what reality television teaches us about women is that "women are stupid" and that "women are incompetent at work and failures at home" (97). According to Pozner, the more incompetent the women, the more popular they tend to become on reality television. Of concern is what appears to be a lack of attention shown toward work and family among the working mothers of reality television. The working mothers of *The Real Housewives of Atlanta* seem able to drop everything at any moment to travel, party, or lunch. Rarely is there mention of who will manage their business or look after their children while the working mothers are off on their next excursion. In the real world, balancing home and work is a major source of stress for working mothers (Davis, Sloan, and Tang; Heintz-Knowles). However, the image presented on *The Real Housewives of Atlanta* is one in which work and family rarely come into conflict. Heintz-Knowles suggest that television's representation of work and family as "separate spheres that rarely intersect is not only a misrepresentation of the lives of most adults, but it can send a powerful message to viewers struggling with these collisions" (197), implying that there must be something wrong with real-world working mothers that they cannot seem to do it all.

Similarly, the women of *Basketball Wives* and *Hollywood Exes* have chosen to be known as "the wife of" instead of as women with their own identities. The women of *Hollywood Exes*, for example, seem to bond first around a common understanding of what it means to be "in the shadows" of their ex-husbands' careers and seem to strengthen their bond through a shared identity as "the wife of." For example, in an episode of *Hollywood Exes*, Andrea Kelly, the ex-wife of famous musician R-Kelly, shares what it was like being married to a famous spouse and shares her desire for "lifting the veil to see what's on the other side." Andrea, like the fellow ex-wives, shares a desire for personal accomplishment and a personal identity, suggesting that the women see value in stepping out of their husband's shadow. However, their mere presence on a show that is, after all, titled *Hollywood Exes*, suggests the women continue to gain relevance from having been married to X than for their own success or personal identity.

Reality television tends to frame women and mothers on reality television as "ladies of means, leisure and indulgent patronage" (Chocano 1), downplaying women's strengths, skills, and abilities. Cumulatively, less positive images of women and mothers on reality television contribute to a cultural hegemony of women as less serious minded and less competent individuals—an image that does not bode well for women and mothers who continue to fight for gender equity in the home and workplace, or for children who observe the stereotypical images of women and mothers portrayed on reality television. The following section discusses how the behaviors exhibited by reality parents can affect children's development.

Like Parents, Like Children: What Happens When People in Glass Houses Throw Stones

As early as infancy, children look to parents for guidance and reassurance regarding how to respond in situations. By age one, an infant will take a quick glance at a parent's facial expressions to determine how to proceed in a situation. This quick read of a parent's expression, known as social referencing, gives the child confidence and a sense of how to approach a situation (Baldwin; Berger). This social referencing is evident during infancy and can follow us into adulthood. Just consider, for example, how often adults use their parents as a point of reference regarding how to navigate a particular situation. As many adults can attest, although reluctantly, there are some things adults continue to do just like mom or just like dad throughout the life span. Simply stated, parents have tremendous influence over their children, whether they recognize it or not. When researchers asked a group of children to name the most influential person in their lives, many named a parent (Rosenthal and Kobak). Parents influence children's attitudes in such areas as learning, eating habits, participation in physical activity, identity development, and behaviors toward others (Hill et al.; Joe and Davis; Keller and Whiston; Lee, Daniels, and Daniel; Mitchell et al.; Phares, Steinberg, and Thompson; Stack et al.). In fact, parents influence their children's behaviors right down to something as simple as a child's choice of body fragrances. In a 2012 study of adolescents, researchers found that teenagers' choice of cologne was influenced by the type of cologne worn by their parents (Yoo, Jacob, and Baier). So, how might the behaviors of African American reality parents influence their children's behaviors? What might the children of reality parents see if they took a quick glance at their parents in order to gauge how to proceed in a situation?[1] What happens when a child's social reference is flawed—when children look to mom or dad for guidance only to find mom and dad behaving badly? The women of reality television, in some cases, are coparenting and at times costarring with their partners to project a certain image of self and family. Therefore, the mothers and fathers of reality television share responsibility for the potentially negative impact of their on-screen behavior, hence the shift from discussing reality mothers to discussing reality parents. Parenting is a shared responsibility; reality mothers should not hold sole responsibility for the impact of choosing to involve the family in reality television.

For the sake of entertainment, children of reality parents get a front-row seat to view mom and dad behaving badly. A glance at mom or dad often provides the children of reality parents with an image of parents in ongoing conflict with friends and partners. Children see their social reference fighting, cursing, and degrading others on national television, providing children with messages regarding what it means to be a friend and partner, and what it means to effectively handle conflict. For instance, friendships, generally defined by engagement "in mutual companionship, support and intimacy," tend to buffer us from stress and to enhance our overall happiness (Berger; Santrock 303). By age ten most children know how to be a good friend (Rose and Asher). To children being a good friend means being supportive and kind. To children, friends are peers with whom they laugh and have fun (Berger). The parents of reality television can take a lesson from young children regarding friendships; the friendships modeled by reality parents are a far stretch from the stress-buffering friendships that tend to bring joy and laughter. Friendship patterns on reality television appear to model a game of musical chairs—friends one minute and enemies the next. As one housewife yelled to another during a friendship break-up, "You don't know how to be a fucking friend." The friendships of reality television give new meaning to the cliché "With friends like these, who needs enemies?" Friendship models shown by reality parents teach children that friendships are about competition, not companionship—are bought, not earned. They show a model of friendship that is stressful and in ongoing conflict.

Studies show a connection between the externalizing behavior of parents as displayed on reality television and the aggressiveness of their children. Negative behavioral patterns like those exhibited toward friends on reality television are significantly associated with children's aggression, with mothers' behavior having a stronger impact on a child's aggressiveness than fathers'—a word of caution to the housewives, ex-wives, and basketball wives of reality television (Wahl and Metzner) Further, there is evidence of continuity in aggressiveness from childhood through adulthood. Older children who engaged in aggressiveness were found to have been exposed and prone to aggressive behavior as young children (Alink et al.; Cummings; Huesmann, Dubow, and Boxer; Tremblay, Hartup, and Archer).

Reality parents are not just in conflict with friends; they are also engaged in marital/partner conflict regarding serious issues like infidelity and child support to less serious issues like he said/she said drama. Regardless of the seriousness of the issue, it seems their attempts to handle conflict go from zero to sixty in minutes. A casual lunch can become a yelling match. Such conflicts when handled well can serve as a catalyst for learning among children. Children can potentially learn to handle conflict respectfully through reconciliation and compromise (Cummings et al.). However, when parental conflict escalates to yelling, verbal assaults, or walking away, children learn that the louder voice prevails and that avoidance is an effective means to handling conflict. Marital conflict like that observed by the children of reality parents has long been connected to maladjustment issues among children because it serves as a "significant source of adversity and risk for adjustment problems for children" (Cummings 63). Children from homes with heightened family conflict are at risk for both negative internalizing, such as depression, and externalizing, such as acting out, behaviors (Katz and Gottman).

Positive parent–child relationships are known to buffer the negative effects of exposure to parental discord. However, the structure of reality television limits the opportunity to view ongoing positive parent–child relationships because children appear in one episode of these reality shows and disappear for extended periods of time. The pattern observed regarding the appearance of children is possibly due to parents' attempt to shield their children from the impact of reality television, a positive judgment call on the part of reality parents. However, the pattern suggests that children are dispensable, around only when necessary and are not significant to the day-to-day functioning of a family.

So a glance at Mom or Dad behaving badly sends children the message that parents' observed behavior is acceptable and endorsed by their parents. After all, parents are their children's first teachers and role models—the homeschoolers, the early purveyors of values, beliefs, and practices regarding right and wrong. As Cynthia Bailey's ex, Leon Robinson, stated in an episode of *The Real Housewives of Atlanta*, "I'm your daddy, it's my job to take care of you." Robinson is on target regarding his responsibility as a parent; unfortunately it is rare to see reality parents engaged in such intimate moments with their children.

Mothers Molding Shaky Identities

Growing up means making mistakes—it means hitting bumps in the road and attempting to bounce back, it means finding a sense of place and a sense of self within the context of home, school, community. But what happens when a family's bumps in the road are exposed for all to see, when reality television makes a mockery of children, their families, and their families' dysfunction? What happens to that child's sense of self? How might the identity, the sense of self formed by the children of reality parents, be shaped by the image of their parents on reality television?

Parents have an important influence on how children come to see themselves. Children's understanding of self—their identities—depends in part on parental support and guidance and on family dynamics and communication patterns (Erikson). Parental practices contribute to the "cultivation of a child's values, beliefs, dreams, and expectations, which shape the adult identity a child will carry" forward in life (Huntemann and Morgan 306). For African American children, developing a personal identity is inextricably connected to their development of an ethnic identity, defined by feelings of affiliation, belonging, and connectedness toward one's ethnic/cultural group (Phinney 1990, 1992; Phinney and Nakayama 1992). When African American parents work to encourage a positive ethnic identity in their children, there are positive long-term social, psychological, and behavioral outcomes. A positive ethnic identity is associated with overall positive well-being, academic achievement, positive mental health, heightened self-esteem, and fewer behavioral issues (Chapell and Overton; Chavous et al.; Perry; Smith et al.).

If African American children are to "construct a strong, positive, and stable self-identity, then they must be able to incorporate into that sense of self a positively valued ethnic identity" (Phinney and Rosenthal 145), leading one to question how the ethnic identity of the children of reality television might be informed by television images of their parents behaving badly. Studies show that African American children who observe negative images of African Americans on television tend to be more ambivalent regarding their ethnic identity and tend to have a less positive self-concept (Berry; Huntemann and Morgan). Nina Huntemann and Michael Morgan suggest that observing the repeated devaluing of one's ethnic group on television can lead to three potential outcomes for children: (1) children may come to feel that it is undesirable to be a member of their own ethnic group, (2) children may attempt to deny ownership in their ethnic group by attempting to change their appearance, or (3) children may reject media images and feel a greater sense of connection to their community (317). It would be interesting to examine whether watching negative images of members of one's own ethnic group is intensified when the individuals on television are one's parents. Studies show that African Americans tend to watch African American–based television programs with a strong sense of identification (Greenberg). Therefore, it could be that reality parents are reinforcing an affirmation of self, a personal identity, in their children that affirms historical stereotypical media images of African Americans. That is, reality parents may be co-conspirators with the media in the hijacking of their children's positive view of self as individuals and as African Americans.

Conclusion

Reality television is growing in popularity, particularly among young viewers. The current generation is growing up with reality television as a primary cultural socializer, socializing young children, in the case of *The Real Housewives of Atlanta*, *Hollywood Exes*, and *Basketball Wives*, about the African American woman and her family. Unfortunately, many images portrayed in reality television paint a negative picture of African Americans and contribute to a cultural hegemony of African American women and their families as families engaged in ongoing conflict in which children are not central to the day-to-day functioning of the family. With limited images of African Americans on television, images projected by reality television have potential to become "the image" of African Americans. "What is still missing after 50 years of portrayals is the emergence of a variety of images that is sustained overtime" (Dates and Stroman 223) and that is accurate. Until television reaches a level of accuracy in representing the diversity of African Americans, reality television as currently formatted does little to maintain or elevate the positive image of African Americans. Further, these shows have potential to harm not only the current generation but also generations to come. What individuals watch on television moves from fantasy to reality becoming real in the minds of viewers. The shift from fantasy to reality means that not only might viewers watch reality television and come to expect African Americans to behave as observed on television, but also young African American viewers may also come to believe that the behaviors they observe on television are the behaviors they are to emulate. As a result, African American reality parents may be unknowingly shaping the identity development of not only their own children, but of the children of many other African American families.

Note

1 The children of reality parents range in age. Some are old enough to view their parents on television, while others may hear about their parents from friends. Of course, given the pervasiveness of the Internet, young children will have future access. Regardless of the child's age or the child's direct/indirect access to reality television, their parents' behavior has potential impact.

Works Cited

ABC News. "Race and Sex: What We Think but Can't Say." *20/20*. 15 Nov. 2006.

Alink, Lenneke R. A., Judi Mesman, Jantien van Zeijl, Mirjam N. Stolk, Femmie Juffer, Hans M. Koot, Marian J. Bakermans-Kranenburg, and Marinus H. van IJzendoorn. "The Early Childhood Aggression Curve: Development of Physical Aggression in 10- to 50-Month-Old Children." *Child Development* 77.4 (2006): 954–66.

Allen, Richard. "Conceptual Models of an African American Belief System: A Program of Research." *Children and Television Images in a Changing Sociocultural World.* Ed. Gordon Berry and Jay Keiko Asamen. Thousand Island, CA: Sage, 1993. 155–76.

Asamen, Joy Keiko, and Berry Gordon. "Television, Children, and Multicultural Awareness: Comprehending the Medium in a Complex Multimedia Society." *Handbook of Children and the Media.* Ed. Dorothy Singer and Jerome Singer. Thousand Island, CA: Sage, 2012. 363–77.

Baldwin, Dare A. "Interpersonal Understanding Fuels Knowledge Acquisition." *Current Directions in Psychological Science* (Wiley-Blackwell) 9.2 (2000): 40–45. Academic Search Premier.

Baumrind, Diana. "The Influence of Parenting Styles on Adolescent Competence and Substance Use." *Journal of Early Adolescence* 11 (1991): 56–95.

Berger, Kathleen Stassen. *The Developing Person Through the Lifespan.* New York: Worth, 2008.

Berry, Gordon. "Developing Children and Multicultural Attitudes: The Systematic Psychosocial Influences of Television Portrayals in a Multimedia Society." *Cultural Diversity and Ethnic Minority Psychology* (2003): 360–66.

———. "Public Television Programming and the Changing Cultural Landscape." *Children and Television Images in a Changing Sociocultural World.* Ed. Gordon Berry and Joy Keiko Asamen. Newbury Park, CA: Sage, 1993. 291–95.

Berry, Gordon, and Asamen, Joy Keiko, ed. *Children and Television Images in a Changing Sociocultural World.* Newbury Park, CA: Sage, 1993.

Brooks, David. *"On Paradise Drive": How We Live Now (and Always Have) in the Future Tense.* New York: Simon and Schuster.

Chapell, Mark S., and Willis F. Overton. "Development of Logical Reasoning in the Context of Parental Style and Test Anxiety." *Merrill-Palmer Quarterly* 44.2 (1998): 141.

Chavous, Tabbye M., Debra Hilkene Bernat, Karen Schmeelk-Cone, Cleopatra H. Caldwell, Laura Kohn-Wood, and Marc A. Zimmerman. "Racial Identity and Academic Attainment among African American Adolescents." *Child Development* 74.4 (2003): 1076–90.

Chocano, Carina. "Housewives, Rebranded." *New York Times* 18 Nov. 2011.

Comer, James. "The Importance of Television Images of Black Families." *Black Families and the Medium of Television*. Ed. Anthony Jackson. Ann Arbor, MI: Bush Program in Child Development and Social Policy, 1982.

Cummings, E. Mark. "Children Exposed to Marital Conflict and Violence: Conceptual and Theoretical Directions." *Children Exposed to Marital Violence: Theory, Research, and Applied Issues*. Ed. George Holden, Robert Geffner, and Ernest Jouriles. Washington, DC: American Psychological Association, 1998. 55–93.

Cummings, E. Mark, Marcie C. Goeke-Morey, and Lauren M. Papp. "Children's Responses to Everyday Marital Conflict Tactics in the Home." *Child Development* 74.6 (2003): 1918–29.

Dates, Jannette, and Carolyn Stroman. "Portrayals of Families of Color on Television." *Television and the American Family*. Ed. Jennings Bryant and J. Alison Bryant. Mahwah, NJ: Lawrence Erlbaum, 2001. 207–78.

Davis, Cindy, Melissa Sloan, and Catherine Tang. "Role Occupancy, Quality, and Psychological Distress among Caucasian and African American Women." *Affilia: Journal of Women and Social Work* 26.1 (2011): 72–82.

Domoff, Sarah E., Nova G. Hinman, Afton M. Koball, Amy Storfer-Isser, Victoria L. Carhart, Kyoung D. Baik, and Robert A. Carels. "The Effects of Reality Television on Weight Bias: An Examination of *The Biggest Loser*." *Obesity* 20.5 (2012): 993–98.

Edwards, Leigh H. *The Triumph of Reality TV: The Revolution in American Television*. Santa Barbara, CA: Praeger, 2013.

Erikson, Eric. *Identity: Youth and Crisis*. New York: W. W. Norton, 1968.

Gerbner, George, Larry Gross, Michael Morgan, and Nancy Signorelli. "Growing Up with Television: Cultivation Processes." *Media Effects: Advances in Theory and Research*. Ed. Jennings Bryant and Dolf Zillmann. 2nd ed. Mahwah, NJ: Lawrence Erlbaum, 2002. 43–67.

Gottman, John Mordechai, and Robert Wayne Levenson. "A Two-Factor Model for Predicting When a Couple Will Divorce: Exploratory Analyses Using 14-Year Longitudinal Data." *Family Process* 41.1 (2002): 83.

Graves, Sherryl Browne. "Children's Television Programming and the Development of Multicultural Attitudes." *The Sage Handbook of Child Development, Multiculturalism, and Media*. Ed. Joy Keiko Asamen and Gordon Berry. Thousand Oaks, CA: Sage, 2008. 213–32.

———. "Television, the Portrayal of African Americans, and the Development of Children's Attitudes." *Children and Television Images in a Changing Sociocultural World*. Ed. Gordon Berry and Joy Keiko Asamen. Newbury Park, CA: Sage, 1993. 179–90.

Greenberg, Bradley. "Minorities in the Mass Media." *Perspectives on Media Effects*. Ed. Jennings Bryant and Dolf Zillmann. Hillsdale, NJ: Lawrence Erlbaum, 1986. 165–88.

Greenberg, Bradley, and Dana Mastro. "Children, Race, Ethnicity, and Media." *The Handbook of Children, Media, and Development*. Ed. Sandra Calvert and Barbara Wilson. Oxford: Blackwell, 2011. 74–97.

Heintz-Knowles, Katharine. "Balancing Acts: Work-Family Issues on Prime-Time TV." *Television and the American Family*. Ed. Jennings Bryant and J. Alison Bryant. Mahwah, NJ: Lawrence Erlbaum, 2001. 177–206.

Hill, Nancy E., Lea Bromell, Diana F. Tyson, and Roxane Flint. "Developmental Commentary: Ecological Perspectives on Parental Influences during Adolescence." *Journal of Clinical Child and Adolescent Psychology* 36.3 (2007): 367–77.

Huesmann, L. Rowell, Eric F. Dubow, and Paul Boxer. "Continuity of Aggression from Childhood to Early Adulthood as a Predictor of Life Outcomes: Implications for the Adolescent-Limited and Life-Course-Persistent Models." *Aggressive Behavior* 35.2 (2009): 136–49.

Huntemann, Nina, and Michael Morgan. "Media and Identity Development." *Handbook of Children and the Media*. Ed. Dorothy Singer and Jerome Singer. Thousand Island, CA: Sage, 2012. 303–19.

Huston, Aletha C., David S. Bickham, June H. Lee, and John C. Wright. "From Attention to Comprehension: How Children Watch and Learn from Television." *Children and Television: Fifty Years of Research*. Ed. Noma Pecoro, John P. Murray, and Ellen Ann Wartella. Mahwah, NJ: Lawrence Erlbaum Associates, 2007. 41–63.

Joe, Emanique M., and James Earl Davis. "Parental Influence, School Readiness, and Early Academic Achievement of African American Boys." *Journal of Negro Education* 78.3 (2009): 260–76.

Katz, Lynn F., and John M. Gottman. "Patterns of Marital Conflict Predict Children's Internalizing and Externalizing Behaviors." *Developmental Psychology* 29.6 (1993): 940–50.

Keller, Briana K., and Susan C. Whiston. "The Role of Parental Influences on Young Adolescents' Career Development." *Journal of Career Assessment* 16.2 (2008): 198–217.

Lee, Sang Min, M. Harry Daniels, and Daniel B. Kissinger. "Parental Influences on Adolescent Adjustment: Parenting Styles versus Parenting Practices." *Family Journal: Counseling and Therapy for Couples and Families* 14.3 (2006): 253–59.

Milevsky, A., M. Schlechter, S. Netter, and D. Keehn. "Maternal and Paternal Parenting Styles in Adolescents: Associations with Self-esteem, Depression, and Life-satisfaction." *Journal of Child and Family Studies* 16.1 (Feb. 2007): 39–47.

Mitchell, Jessica, Helen Skouteris, Marita McCabe, Lina A. Ricciardelli, Jeannette Milgrom, Louise A. Baur, Matthew Fuller-Tyszkiewicz, and Genevieve Dwyer. "Physical Activity in Young Children: A Systematic Review of Parental Influences." *Early Child Development and Care* 182.11 (2012): 1411–37.

Pendry, Patricia, Alexa M. Carr, Lauren M. Papp, and Josh Antles. "Child Presence during Psychologically Aggressive Interparental Conflict: Implications for Internalizing and Externalizing Behavior." *Family Relations* 62.5 (2013): 755–67.

Perry, Theresa. "Up from the Parched Earth: Toward a Theory of African American Achievement." *Young, Gifted, and Black: Promoting High Achievement among African-American Students*. Ed. Theresa Perry, Claude Steele, and Asa Hillard. Boston: Beacon Press, 2003. 1–108.

Phares, Vicky, Ari R. Steinberg, and J. Kevin Thompson. "Gender Differences in Peer and Parental Influences: Body Image Disturbance, Self-Worth, and Psychological Functioning in Preadolescent Children." *Journal of Youth and Adolescence* 33.5 (2004): 421–29.

Phinney, Jean S. "Ethnic Identity in Adolescents and Adults: Review of Research." *Psychological Bulletin* 108.3 (1990): 499–514.

———. "The Multigroup Ethnic Identity Measure: A New Scale for Use with Diverse Groups." *Journal of Adolescent Research* 7.2 (1992): 156–76. ERIC.

Phinney, Jean S., and Stephanie Nakayama. "Parental Influences on Ethnic Identity Formation in Adolescents." (1991): ERIC.

Phinney, Jean S., and Doreen A. Rosenthal. "Ethnic Identity in Adolescence: Process, Context, and Outcome." *Adolescent Identity Formation*. Thousand Oaks, CA: Sage Publications, 1992. 145–72.

Pozner, Jennifer. *Reality Bites Back: The Troubling Truth about Guilty Pleasure TV*. Berkeley, CA: Seal, 2010.

Riddle, Karyn, and J. J. De Simone. "A Snooki Effect? An Exploration of the Surveillance Subgenre of Reality TV and Viewers' Beliefs about the 'Real' Real World." *Psychology of Popular Media Culture* 2.4 (2013): 237–50.

Rideout, V. J., U. Foehr, and D. Roberts. "Generation M2: Media in the Lives of 8 to 18 Year Olds." Menlo Park, CA: Henry J. Kaiser Foundation, 2010.

Roberts, Donald, and Ulla Foehr. *Kids and Media in America: Patterns of Use at the Millennium*. New York: Cambridge University Press, 2004.

Rose, Amanda J., and Steven R. Asher. "Children's Goals and Strategies in Response to Conflicts within a Friendship." (1997): ERIC.

Rosenthal, Natalie L., and Roger Kobak. "Assessing Adolescents' Attachment Hierarchies: Differences across Developmental Periods and Associations with Individual Adaptation." *Journal of Research on Adolescence* (Wiley-Blackwell) 20.3 (2010): 678–706.

Rothrauff, Tanja C., Teresa M. Cooney, and Jeong Shin An. "Remembered Parenting Styles and Adjustment in Middle and Late Adulthood." *Journals of Gerontology*: Series B: *Psychological Sciences and Social Sciences* 64B.1 (2009): 137–46.

Santrock, John. *Adolescence*. New York: McGraw-Hill, 2012.

Signorielli, Nancy. "Television's Gender Role Images and Contribution to Stereotyping: Past, Present, Future." *Handbook of Children and the Media*. Ed. Dorothy Singer and Jerome Singer. Thousand Island, CA: Sage, 2012. 321–39.

Smith, Emilie Phillips, Katrina Walker, Laurie Fields, Craig C. Brookins, and Robert C. Seay. "Ethnic Identity and Its Relationship to Self-Esteem, Perceived Efficacy, and Prosocial Attitudes in Early Adolescence." *Journal of Adolescence* 22.6 (1999): 867–80.

Smith, Siobhan. "And Still More Drama!: A Comparison of the Portrayals of African-American Women and African-American Men on BET's *College Hill*." *Western Journal of Black Studies* 37.1 (2013): 39–49.

Stack, Dale M., Lisa A. Serbin, Leah N. Enns, Paula L. Ruttle, and Lindsey Barrieau. "Parental Effects on Children's Emotional Development Over Time and across Generations." *Infants and Young Children* 23.1 (2010): 52–69.

Steinberg, Laurence, and Jennifer S. Silk. "Parenting Adolescents." *Handbook of Parenting*, Vol. 1: *Children and Parenting*. 2nd ed. Mahwah, NJ: Lawrence Erlbaum, 2002. 103–33.

Tremblay, Richard E., Willard W. Hartup, and John Archer. *Developmental Origins of Aggression*. New York: Guilford Press, 2005.

Tyree, Tia. "African American Stereotypes in Reality Television." *Howard Journal of Communications* 22.4 (2011): 394–413.

Van Evra, Judith. *Television and Child Development*. Mahwah, NJ: Lawrence Erlbaum, 1998.

Wahl, Klaus, and Cornelia Metzner. "Parental Influences on the Prevalence and Development of Child Aggressiveness." *Journal of Child and Family Studies* 21.2 (2012): 344–55.

Yoo, Jeong-Ju, John Jacob, and Margaret Baier. "Adolescent Boys' Grooming Product Use and Perceived Health Risks: An Exploration of Parental Influence." *Health Education Journal* 71.3 (2012): 299–308.

6

**Where Is Clair Huxtable
When You Need Her?**

• •

The Desperate Search for
Positive Media Images of
African American Women
in the Age of Reality TV

MONICA FLIPPIN WYNN

For most of us, a few stolen hours in front of the television are one of the few guilty pleasures we allow ourselves in our busy schedules. Whether we catch it on a first network run or taped and stored for later or on a portable device, we look forward to our time to catch up on a favorite show. However, one needs only to shuffle through the massive number of network television and cable programming offerings to sigh and to wistfully yearn for the good old days of television. As I navigate my remote up and down the dial, I am consistently confused and frustrated with the paltry choices available in the current television programming.

Research conducted by Nielsen asserts that African Americans watch 37 percent more television than other groups and that Black women tend to be heavier viewers than their male counterparts (15). Historically, much of the content has consistently "warped, distorted and bastardized representations of African American life" (Sims et al. 142). Shelia Crump Johnson, once part owner of Black Entertainment Television (BET) with her husband Robert Johnson, is unhappy with the status of programming for African Americans, especially on BET. She states, "I just really wish—and not just BET but a lot television programming—that they would stop lowering the bar so far just so they can get eyeballs to the screen" (Graves). She acknowledges the need to pay the bills, but adds, "There has got to be some responsibility" (Graves). In addition, the consistent negative depictions of African Americans can indeed have a negative consequence on their self-esteem and self-identity, but the negative television portrayals have continued to be a daily menu item on the television cafeteria buffet. Recently, television viewers have been inundated with negative depictions of Black women camouflaged by modern-day versions of the same stereotypical images: the Mammy, the Jezebel, and the Sapphire that African Americans have fought so defiantly to annihilate more than four decades ago. Media insider Tom Burrell, interviewed by Jenée Desmond-Harris for *The Root,* stated, "When you do communications programming that distracts and anesthetizes people, you are taking them out of the game" (qtd. in Desmond-Harris).

The Cosby Show was a landmark in presenting a positive representation of an African American family to mainstream audiences when it was urgently needed. Many critics have suggested the show was not realistic; however, it did provide a balance of representations. There was enough room in the landscape of African American realities for both a James and Florida Evans from *Good Times* and a Cliff and Clair Huxtable from *The Cosby Show.* Thinking of the character Clair Huxtable leads one to a visual of a vibrant and inspiring image of the African American woman. Clair Huxtable, portrayed effortlessly by Phylicia Rashād, came into American homes for years and made women, especially Black women, feel proud. She was funny, intelligent, and sexy. She was a role model for positive self-esteem and identity to women in general, but Black women were elated because she belonged to us; we took ownership.

The portrayal of Clair Huxtable was not consistent with the demeaning depiction of the Mammy, Jezebel, or the Sapphire and it appeared that the fictionalized portrayal of Clair Huxtable would in fact begin to mirror and represent the wonderfully diverse, colorful and amazing lives of Black women (Bogle 9; Pouissant 72). For African American women, positive characterizations and associations as a group work toward positive self-concept and images of themselves. Lewin argued that it was necessary for individuals to have a strong sense of belonging or group identification to establish a sense of well-being (qtd. in Phinney 501). However, if the group is held in low accord by the dominant group in society, then it could affect the group's social identity (Phinney 501–502). The continuous onslaught of unconstructive television depictions of African American women evokes a boatload of consequences for African American women and society as a whole.

Not much has changed, and the depictions of African American women continue to be more overtly negative throughout the spectrum of reality television. Essence Atkins, an African American actress, explains, "We are challenged to try and get different kinds of images out there besides the stereotypes and besides the ones that we are seeing portrayed on reality TV" (qtd. in Croom). In fact, she continues, "reality television has extreme versions and extreme caricatures of personalities and that is not the totality of who we are. Our struggle is really to find ways and find mediums that will host other images besides these" (qtd. in Croom). The overall argument is not that the current reality programming should all be obliterated because people are different and need choices. However, there are so many different versions of African American women, characteristics, life stories, and all of those versions should be presented and available to the viewing audiences. The biggest issue is the lack of balance.

A survey on the media images of Black women conducted by *Essence* magazine, in tandem with research consultants Added Value Cheskin, with more than 1,200 respondents, found that the "the images [of Black women] encountered on a regular basis on TV, in social media, in music videos and other outlets are overwhelmingly negative and fall into categories that make us cringe—Gold diggers, Modern Jezebels, Baby Mamas, Uneducated Sisters, Ratchet Women, Angry Black Women, Mean Black Girls, Unhealthy Black Women and Black Barbies" (Walton). Nowhere is this more evident than in the current onslaught of reality television. Robert Kilborn defines reality television as "the attempt to simulate such real-life events through various forms of dramatized reconstruction [and] the incorporation of this material, in a suitably edited form into an attractively packaged television programme which can be promoted on the strength of its 'reality' credentials" (423). Steven Reiss and James Wiltz suggest one reason America is fascinated with this thriving television genre is the audience's preoccupation with status and celebrity. They write, "The message of reality television is that ordinary people can become so important that millions will watch them," and many hope that possibility may come true for them (Reiss and Wiltz). Reality programs have made it easy to dream of success and making audiences feel connected. In the essay "Why People Watch Reality TV," Reiss and Wiltz write:

> People who are motivated by status have an above average need to feel self-important. Reality television may gratify this psychological need in two ways. One possibility is that viewers feel they are more important (have higher status) than the ordinary people portrayed on reality television shows. The idea that these are "real" people gives psychological significance to the viewers' perceptions of superiority—it may not matter much if a storyline is realistic, so long as the characters are ordinary people. Further, the message of reality television—that millions of people are interested in watching real life experiences of ordinary people—implies that ordinary people are important. Ordinary people can watch the shows, see people like themselves, and fantasize that they could gain celebrity status by being on television. (373–374)

Viewers often believe they are similar to the cast members on *Love and Hip-Hop* or *Marrying the Game* or some other reality show. They feel connected because they see these scripted lives as mirroring their own lives. The audiences take more with them than the images that are depicted; sometimes they salvage optimism and success for themselves.

Michelle Conlin argues that reality television can be designated as network crack, in that it is "fast, cheap, and addictive." Whatever one deems to call this type of programming, it has rehashed persistent concerns about televised images of Black women and how these images influence a perceived reality. For the most part, reality programming has drastically changed the backdrop and unconstructively usurped the representations of Black women. The images have been completely festooned with portrayals of loud, earsplitting, neck-bobbing, booty-shaking, gold-digging, morally reprehensible, stagnant characterizations of Black women. Allison Samuels concurred in a piece written in *Newsweek*, "From Oxygen's *Bad Girls* to Bravo's *Real Housewives* franchise, the small screen is awash with black females who roll their eyes, bob their heads, snap their fingers, talk trash, and otherwise reinforce the ugly stereotype of the 'angry black woman'" (Samuels, "Reality TV Trashes Black Women?"). The television viewing experience has become a minefield. Kimora Lee Simmons, star of the canceled *Life in the Fab Lane*, is not a fan of the current slate of reality programming. Simmons maintains, "I think the state of reality TV is going down the tubes. I'm not proud of it and I'm not proud of how women are depicted. I'm not proud of how when you turn on the TV, you are fighting and scratching and cursing at your mum and you are naked" (Sarie). On her reality program, Kimora was portrayed as a self-defined diva and businesswoman who seemed to work hard on her show and tried desperately, despite the opulence, to lovingly raise her two girls and son.

Now, there are some reality shows out that attempt to provide positive characterizations of African American women, their lives, and their reality, but as Sil Lai Abrams suggests, "The formulaic presentation of Black women on TV is lucrative. The numbers are in and the people have spoken." The television fare that depicts "dysfunctional relationships and lifestyles," says Abrams, "are the programs that are grabbing the audiences." Allison Samuels adds that this "angry black woman" stereotype brought about in large part by NeNe Leakes from *The Real Housewives of Atlanta* (*RHOA*) "fuels the reality-TV genre" (qtd. in Arceneaux). The major problem with all of this is that the reality programming broadcast day in and day out has one flavor, negative. There is not really a menu of contrasting options or representations available to choose from, so these negative depictions are the images that are most often associated with Black women. Shaunie O'Neal, creator and executive producer of *Basketball Wives*, argues that there should be more than one kind of image depicted on reality television for Black women. O'Neal states, "I'm not saying we have to create shows that only paint a pretty picture about who we are, but there should be a balance and most of all some integrity to the shows we create." Balance in the images that are produced that represent women of color is needed. In fact, we need a reality television Clair Huxtable to balance out the NeNes.

There are a number of reality TV shows that are taking a different approach to representation and really working to provide positive portrayals of African American women. Where and on what channel can they be found? In doing this research, there were a few programs that, initially, I wanted to avoid because of the characters and the general impressions I had of the content and the characters. What I found from the experience was that if I opened myself up to the general message and themes of the shows, I saw that there are some very positive representations of Black women on reality television. There are women of color who are making dynamic choices, taking care of families, showing entrepreneurial shrewdness, and doing what needs to be done. *Tiny and Toya, T.I. and Tiny: The Family Hustle, Tia and Tamera, Welcome to Sweetie Pie's,* and *Raising Whitley* are all shows that demonstrate the wonderful array of diversity in African American women. These programs provide a balance to the negative depictions audiences seem to clamor for in today's crowded reality television landscape.

My Contrition: Hooked on the Love

The search for positive images of African American women on reality television began as my own personal expedition. I needed to pay penance. The deluge of available mediocre programming and word of mouth from my impressionable summer school students provided the hype and the impetus into my short love affair with reality television. Sure, I had watched a few episodes of *Real World*, but I quickly became frustrated by the characters and the redundant scenarios, so I just stopped watching. Nor was I was moved to consider *Survivor* or any other show that involved watching people concoct devious plots for survival—I personally had enough of that in real-time academia. Yet little did I suspect that once I began to follow the antics of Hoops, Flavor Flav, and New York on the ridiculously stereotypical and deliciously naughty *Flavor of Love* that I would be hooked. Despite the stereotypes, the crude sexual and homophobic humor, the moral ineptitude, and the backlash the show received from industry and academic critics, I continued my guilty pleasure, and I did not share with anyone my secret pleasure for watching Flav give out the watches at the end of the show, or the fights that were bound to happen before the end of each episode. Farai Chideya stated that the "VH1 show, *Flavor of Love,* had enchanted and disenchanted a whole bevy of viewers." And according to Dawn Turner Trice of the *Chicago Tribune*, "The show's ratings revealed that by the fourth week of the first season, *Flavor of Love* had beaten ESPN's Monday Night football, making it the highest rated show among African American households," so it seems I was in good company, and a good number of people were also hooked on the same nonsense.

As I sat and watched the degradation of the female contestants and the staged battles between Hoopz and Goldie, I frankly enjoyed the escapism, the pure insanity of the antics, and the primping and posturing by Flavor Flav. Turner Trice interviewed Juanita Crear-Price, a sixty-year-old African American social psychologist who also found the show to be quite addictive. Crear-Price said, "She innocently watched the first episode out of sheer curiosity and ended up—making it appointment TV" (qtd. in Turner Trice). Crear-Price also claimed that she watched the show because it was "great theater, filled with suspense and drama and colorful characters" (qtd. in Turner Trice). It was interesting to note that an accomplished older Black woman would find Flavor Flav appointment television. It does suggest that it is just that: entertainment, nothing more; however, the issue is that these images tend to be the majority of images depicted for African American portrayals. Some find it difficult to decipher real from fantasy.

I watched the two seasons and then moved over to *I Love New York*, a spin-off of the *Flavor of Love* reality show, but I consistently felt like I was a Judas and needed to hand in my race card. In an interview with Rhonesha Byng, Sil Lai Abrams, a contributing writer for *Ebony* and *The Grio*, observed that women from all walks of life find themselves being drawn to the "ratchetness" available in reality programming (Abrams). Abrams also found it distressing that so many women who label themselves as "Black feminists or womanists gleefully support the degradation of their sister(s)" (Abrams). The biggest dilemma, of course, is that more reality programs are being developed, and for the most part networks are not offering an array of different depictions for African American women; instead, these new offerings remain consistent with what is already being produced. Mark Anthony Neal argued that the success of shows like *The Flavor of Love* has raised concerns about the "images of black folk that circulate in mainstream media," but he adds that viewers must be careful who they aim their contempt at for the dearth in available programming choices (qtd. in Chideya). The changes will not come unless audiences decide that there are changes that need to be made. Neal cautions, "As a community, we must stop simply complaining about programming we dislike or find offensive and start being more activist minded in our exchanges with mainstream media, including boycotting their programming and more importantly, the advertisers who largely underwrite such programming" (qtd. in Chideya). Sil Lai Abrams acknowledges that if audiences do not begin to "create or demand them" the "existing depictions will demote the positive landscape of African American women's identities and contributions and that could destroy us" (Abrams). Yet, in doing research for this chapter, I found that there are and have been some positive choices in reality programming out there, but unfortunately audiences do not flock to these shows in large numbers, and unfortunately in this business, ratings equal survival. Many of the shows that provide some diversity in the representations of Black women may disappear after one season without having the chance to garner an audience. And to be frank, some of the positive reality programs that I investigated for this research had not crossed my television viewing radar until I consciously went looking for them. Perhaps this is because they are for the most part absent of drama-laden activities, and most of these shows are rarely discussed or reviewed in mainstream media.

Tiny and Toya

As I went searching for positive reality fare, I initially thought that I was going to have to watch every reality program ensconced within the hundreds of cable and broadcast networks; I was not optimistic. Besides, all of the media experts had alleged there was nothing good in reality television, yet after much research and review both the *Tiny and Toya* reality show and *T.I. and Tiny: The Family Hustle* revealed themselves to be serious contenders in producing positive reality content and incorporating strong characterizations of African American women rarely seen in reality television.

Tameka "Tiny" Cottle is a platinum-selling recording artist and a founding member of the '90s girl group Xscape; however, she landed this reality gig because she was the then-fiancée (married in 2011) of rapper T.I. (Clifford Harris). It is interesting to note, a fellow member of the group Xscape, Kandi Burruss, has also found solace in reality television on *The Real Housewives of Atlanta*. Nevertheless, as Dre Cummings points out, Tiny was not a gold digger as some have assumed. In fact, Kristal Brent Zook suggested in an online article on reality television and images of African American women, "*Tiny and Toya*, like *Basketball Wives* and *Real Housewives of Atlanta*, featured ex-girlfriends and wives trying to make names for themselves on the heels of relationships with famous men." But, in actuality, Tiny already had a Grammy, and initially had more money, fame, and royalties coming in from her previous hits and songwriting than did T.I., so her relationship may have been instrumental in landing this show, but she had already demonstrated herself to be a capable, strong, and self-motivated young Black woman. In addition, Antonia (Toya) Carter is the former wife of best-selling rapper Lil Wayne (Dewayne Michael Carter Jr.). Toya married young and was looking for ways to build relationships and stability for herself and her daughter with Lil Wayne.

The series was first broadcast in 2009 on BET. Dre Cummings echoed my aforementioned sentiment: "I was apprehensive at first that the *Tiny and Toya* show would only enforce the stereotypes that Black women often fall victim to in the media, especially the baby mama, gold digger persona." But after watching the first episode and moving past some of the ill-mannered elements, the show seemed to have promise. I was excited to review the next several episodes. Cummings stated that he found the "openness and willingness to share the intimate aspects of their lives, good and bad, especially refreshing." The immediate draw for Tiny and Toya's reality show was the connection it would provide to the popular rappers. The show's debut drew more than 3 million viewers, the highest series debut for a reality program in BET's history. Rodney Ho explains that in the first episodes, Tiny and Toya "both came across as grounded women. And the first episode was not salacious, ostentatious, or ridiculous. Rather, it showed two women struggling with issues such as how to deal with a man going to jail (Tiny), how to handle a mom who has drug problems (Toya), and how to break out from the shadows of two famous stars (both)" (Radio and TV Talk with Rodney).

In the next several episodes of the first season, the audience is introduced to Tiny's and Toya's families. Family and structure were important to both of these women, and it was evident throughout these episodes. The audience watched as Tiny and T.I. prepared for his impending prison sentence, and she revealed her confusion and anxiety in having to stand tall for the family in his absence. These episodes also introduced other family members, including Tiny's father, who suffered from Alzheimer's, and her mother, who had the main responsibility of his care. Viewers also became acquainted with Toya's family, which included her mother, who had real substance addiction issues, and a brother who had served ten years in the prison system and had recently been released—real-life situations.

Tiny and Toya are not the traditional figures one might think to associate as positive African American women, and definitely not Clair Huxtable, but there are some similarities. It was depicted that Clair Huxtable loved her family, wanted her children to be functional members of society, had her own career, and had a wonderful sense of humor. Those same attributes are depicted in Tiny and Toya. This reality show exudes substance, relationships are key, and at the end of the day, they are trying to navigate through the terrain of their lives the best they know how. Ayanna Guyhto suggests, "The unscripted rawness strangely intrigues the viewer. Even though these ladies are at best a little rough around the edges." Their rough edges and imperfections endear them to the audience because of the portrayal of their authentic selves, often said to be missing from *The Cosby Show*. Michael Arceneaux argues, "With episodes centered around opening a business, fighting Alzheimer's disease, and raising children, the show wasn't exactly *Amos 'n Andy*. Moreover, perhaps their Southern twangs and lack of pedigree couldn't bypass the 'talented tenth' definition of positivity, but overall the theme of the series was progression" (Arceneaux). This popular show was cancelled after two seasons, and Toya Carter went on to do another reality show that was also soon cancelled. Tiny can be seen currently in *T.I and Tiny: The Family Hustle* and *Tiny Tonight* on VH1.

T.I. and Tiny: The Family Hustle

When describing this popular reality program seen on VH1, Rachel Miller-Bradshaw said that *T.I and Tiny: The Family Hustle* "displays the lives of a hip hop Brady Bunch. The show is positive displaying a couple's love for each other while successfully raising children, some from previous relationships." *T.I. and Tiny: The Family Hustle* premièred on VH1 in December 2011, and its debut averaged approximately 4.3 million viewers with its prime demographic of adults ages 18–49 (Gorman). The popular family reality show is in its fourth season and consistently dominates its ratings timeslot (Gorman). Kelly Smith Beaty contends the show portrays how an African American family goes about its day-to-day life and interestingly also provides a flashback to viewers' childhoods. In this way, the show can be considered pioneering as it speaks to an entirely new generation about handling the daily grind and hustle of living life (Smith Beaty). T.I and Tiny are making a name for themselves as the new professional couple, balancing professional careers and family.

Not only is this bustling family compared to the iconic Brady Bunch, but also during a recent photo shoot and interview with *In Touch Weekly* magazine, it was suggested that *T.I. and Tiny: The Family Hustle* could be compared to the beloved Huxtable clan: "Interestingly, Tip Harris opined that it was flattering but he believes there are some distinct differences in the two families, in that the Huxtables were fictional, older, and more conservative than the Harris family bunch, but he believes they share a sense of unity, strength, and prominence" (*In Touch*). Lucette Jefferson took the Huxtable–Harris comparisons one step further in an article in the *Huffington Post* and created a comparison list to briefly compare and contrast the Huxtable and Harris families. She argues that the couples share a deep love and are professionals at the top of their respective games. There are some distinctive differences between the families, but what both of these television families do have in common, regardless of the external trappings, is a positive representation of family, home, love, and the daily ambition to get it all right.

Although Tiny shares billing with her husband, popular rapper T.I., the show provides a platform in which Tiny again demonstrates some very positive representations of African American women. On the online website, *Hello Beautiful*, Tiny was characterized as a "ride or die chick." In other words, she supports T.I. no matter the circumstance. This support is apparent throughout the four seasons; Tiny consistently demonstrates her loyalty, respect, and genuine love for her husband, despite claims of consistent infidelity and the rumblings of an outside child, she remains devoted.

Smith Beaty points out that "Tiny's soft and nurturing manner evokes memories of the many moms that I've met throughout my life, who above all things put the happiness and wholeness of their families." The show does demonstrate Tiny's dedication to her family, but she also maintains a healthy relationship with an assortment of girlfriends and continues her own grind by managing a girl singing group, OMG Girlz, and creating and developing her own fashion brand, Pretty Hustle. Tiny demonstrates that she is a savvy businesswoman with entrepreneurial and leadership skills. It is important that she support her husband and her family, but it is also important that she maintain her own dreams and objectives. Tiny is definitely a different package than Clair Huxtable, but she offers a diverse insight and image of the talents, ambitions, and family commitments of African American women. If one is searching for Clair Huxtable, Tiny Cottle is a 2015 version and it can be argued that she is also a more relatable version for viewers today.

Tia and Tamera

On the top of everyone's list of reality shows that provide positive images and portrayals of African American women is the *Tia and Tamera* reality show, originally broadcast on the Style Network in 2011, then moved to the E network, and was cancelled in early 2014. Most remember these twin dynamos from their popular show, *Sister, Sister,* where they played twins who had been separated at birth and found each other as teenagers. These two young ladies are charming, intelligent, and funny, and definitely have in the last three seasons provided positive, strong representations of African American women. The series premiered in August 2011, and Kenya Byrd comments, "Even though there were no cat fights, drink-tossing, messy public divorces or scandalous infidelities, the *Tia and Tamera* show managed to debut to the highest ratings in the history of the Style Network."

In the first few episodes of the series, viewers discovered where and what the young ladies had been up to since they were last seen on *Sister, Sister.* They had attended and graduated college, traveled internationally, gotten married, and started families. But most intriguing for the audience was that they had grown up into successful, well-rounded, attractive, witty, passionate, and determined young African American women who have consistently demonstrated that Black women are multitalented and diverse and that one set of images does not accurately define the many different dimensions of African American women (Robinson). During the show's first season, Tamera gets married and Tia prepares for her first child. Sibling disappointment, frustration, and how these two young ladies are carving out their own separate lives are featured. In the wedding episode, the issue of racism is explored honestly and intently. Tamera's husband, Adam Housley, is a white reporter with Fox News. When their engagement photos are leaked onto the Internet, Tamera is distressed by the racist and hurtful comments that people make about her and her future husband. In an interview in *TheyBF.com*, Tamera explains, "I was just shocked that some people still feel that way. It's 2011! They did a poll recently and 83% of Americans are OK with interracial relationships. I never expected that kind of negative response to us" (Natasha). Tamera concluded that "the fact of the matter is—if you have 99.9% who see it with positivity, you're gonna have that .1% who don't. My husband had the best response to that on the show. He said 'That's not our issue. That's their issue. So they can deal with that'"

(Natasha). The episode gave the audience an opportunity to see their honest reaction to the hurtful things that are said about them or placed on the Internet. It also provided viewers with the chance to see Tamera's humanity and appreciation for the diversity in her life and how she decided to handle a difficult subject—without any fanfare or the quintessential drama.

In a supportive environment, Tia and Tamera are making their mark and consciously or unconsciously becoming role models for another generation. Tia's decision to adopt a healthy vegan lifestyle shows the importance of taking care of oneself and getting and staying healthy. Tamera struggles living in Napa, California, when her work and family are in L.A. Her struggle is one to which many young women can relate. How she handles her husband's attitude and finds alternative ways to juggle it all and make it work is definitely positive and helpful for young women, especially those who find themselves in similar situations. She works through difficult situations but illustrates for viewers that marriage, like anything, requires commitment and compromise to be successful.

When Tia Mowry-Hardict was asked about her reality show in the online magazine *Vibe Vixen* and specifically how it is different from the current slate of reality programs such as *Basketball Wives* and *The Real Housewives of Atlanta,* she responded:

> I haven't seen *Basketball Wives*, but I heard about it. I am huge fan of *The Real Housewives of Atlanta*, but I just think that Tamera and I have a different take on these reality shows. I remember when we were pitching our show to different networks, many of them didn't want to pick it up because they felt we didn't have enough conflict. My sister and I were like, "we aren't those type of people," so it's all about us being positive role models. (qtd. in McGloster)

Tia and Tamera have consistently provided fresh and innovative programming choices. In today's culture of head butting and group skirmishes, their reality show provided a different, more positive option. Although their show was recently cancelled, both women continue to be involved with programming options that shine brightly for African American women.

Welcome to Sweetie Pie's

The network owned and operated by Oprah Winfrey (OWN) recently underwent a major overhaul to focus more on original programming. Allison Samuels discussed the recent changes in an article written for the *Daily Beast*. She observed that "in an era when positive images of women of color still lag considerably behind women of other races and when reality shows do little more than highlight decades-old stereotypes of African-American women, Winfrey's revamped version of OWN is now a much needed leveling field in the land of television. It's a one-stop shop for stories most mainstream networks, cable or otherwise would not think of airing" (Samuels, "Why Oprah"). They are developing shows that highlight authentic African American lives, not celebrity-influenced drama-fests that offer little opportunity to relate for the average African American woman. On the current schedule, OWN includes reality programs about raising sextuplets, *The McGees*; redemption, *Iyanla: Fix My Life* starring Iyanla Vanzant; celebrity lives, *Life with La Toya* starring La Toya Jackson; entrepreneurship and family, *Welcome to Sweetie Pie's* with Robbie Montgomery; and single parenting and adoption, *Raising Whitley* featuring Kym Whitley. *Welcome to Sweetie Pie's* and *Raising Whitley* both feature distinctive African American women characters.

Welcome to Sweetie Pie's, according to the OWN website, is a reality show that focuses on the life of a former Ike and Tina Ikette, Robbie Montgomery. When Montgomery's singing options disappeared and she had a child to raise, she decided to concentrate on her other talent: cooking. In 1996, she opened her first restaurant in St. Louis, called Sweetie Pie's, which specializes in home-cooked soul food entrees served up in an open cafeteria/buffet style. There are now three different Sweetie Pie's locations (Garcia). The show centers on interacting with the people who work at Sweetie Pie's and the customers. In the first episode, the main characters are introduced, including Robbie's only son, Tim, who is the manager of the main location, his girlfriend of several years who gets pregnant, Robbie's nephew Charles, who is always looking for a reason not to work, and various other family members and friends. In this reality show, Robbie is in complete control; nothing happens that she does not know about. She greets customers, inspects the premises, makes sure enough food has been prepared, listens to employee and family problems, and continues to look for ways to improve and extend her business.

Robbie uses old-school discipline and common sense in how she handles the various issues that arise at Sweetie Pie's. She can be seen in several episodes lashing out at her nephew for messing up and trying to weasel out of doing any work. Yet, you also see throughout the series, she wants Charles to take responsibility and to do well, so her reproach is to make sure he does not fall by the wayside. In the very first episode, her son Tim is looking to purchase his longtime girlfriend an engagement ring, and he asks Robbie for a few thousand dollars to accomplish his goal. Robbie quickly responds by telling Tim "if he can't afford it, he doesn't need it and he must be living above his means." So, Tim is left to his own devices and has to pawn his beloved Rolex to get his girlfriend the ring. Working it out for himself is a lesson he needed to have and is a shrewd testament to Robbie's role as a businesswoman and as a mother (Pisani). In future episodes, the relationship between Tim and Robbie becomes difficult and toxic to a conducive business working relationship, although, part of the intrigue for this reality show is the dialogue and the intense interactions between Robbie and Tim (Garcia). Yet, the mood on the set and the negative effects the interactions were having on the overall business required a visit from life coach Iyanla Vanzant to calm the waters between mother and son (Garcia). The show is a realistic representation of relationships between parents and their grown children and figuring out how to make it work (Garcia). Both Robbie and Tim have to figure out how to navigate their business and personal relationships. After the intervention, Robbie concludes, "I don't have to like his ways of doing things" (qtd. in Garcia), but they do have to find a way to work together for the sake of the family business. Life coach Vanzant is also a mainstay on the OWN network, where her specialty is bringing people together and opening closed and toxic lines of communication. Her show provides another perspective to African American women and the ways in which they handle conflict. *Welcome to Sweetie Pie's* recently began its fifth season, and Robbie has seen her business grow as a result of the reality show audience and because the food is good and the prices are reasonable. There is still occasional drama on *Welcome to Sweetie Pie's*, but what the audience witnesses in this reality show is a down-to-earth business operating in an urban city, providing jobs for the community, and as Samuels sums it up in the *Daily Beast*, "The general theme is a view of a loving mother and smart businesswoman working to make a better life for her family" ("Why Oprah"). According to recent figures, OWN is doing something right, because recent numbers, according to Peter Hamilton, "suggest a 55% increase in serving its target market, of African American women." *Welcome to Sweetie Pie's* is the network's most profitable nonfiction programming content, although it is suggested that the recent shows created by Tyler Perry have also added to the sudden increase in favorability.

Raising Whitley

Kym Whitley has appeared as an actress in several television sitcoms and popular movies over the past two decades. She is most famously known as Uncle's Elroy's supersexed girlfriend Suga on the second installment of the popular *Friday* movie trilogy, starring Chris Tucker and Ice Cube. This show is pleasantly surprising due to its life lessons, diversity, and the gathering of folk devoted to help with raising Whitley's son. Whitley can be tasteless at times, and many of the episodes had explicit meanings within most of the scenes. Her character is funny, honest, and not afraid to let the audience know that she is flying without a parachute as she navigates this new journey of raising her adopted son. Whitley becomes an immediate mother when a young mentee of hers has a baby and designates Kym as the guardian. Whitley admits, "Joshua was the gift [I] had never asked for" (Huffington Post). Although Whitley does not advocate single motherhood, she impressively provides a platform for single-mother experience and advocates for adoption in the Black community. So, the foundation of the show follows Whitley and her endearing cast of friends (her village) and family as they steer the uncharted waters of raising a child in the Internet age (Samuels, "Why Oprah"). The show has some honest moments that are truly touching and ripe for social media. The episodes are infused with Whitley's humor and charm, exemplifying the importance of blended families, older mothers, and the necessity for outside help when rearing a child today. Whitley says it best when she indicates what she wants viewers to get from this reality show: "I want to help single parents figure that out, and know they don't have to do it all on their own, that it's okay to ask for help. If they need to, they can build their own village. Their village doesn't have to be eight people. It can be two people, whatever it is that they need. I really hope that this show inspires people. I'd also like it to take away the stigma of adoption and that adopted people are special" (Whitley qtd. in

St. Vil). Like Tiny, Tia and Tamera, and Robbie Montgomery, Whitley is a devoted mother who provides a positive representation of Black women.

Positive Images Revealed

Some could say that the title for this chapter, "Where Is Clair Huxtable When You Need Her?," was doomed from the start, not because she could not be found, but because reality television is a different type of content than situation comedies, and *The Cosby Show* was in its heyday more than twenty years ago. Maybe the real objective should have been to realize that there are positive representations of African American women available, and that there are various possibilities. Looking for just one option and type was a set-up from the beginning. Audiences must be willing to step out of their comfort zones and to take a chance on different and varied viewing experiences. Black viewers must be advocates of the positive programming that is being created. No one is suggesting that people completely turn away from their favorites all at once, but watching diverse programming increases the ratings of these shows and it illustrates to producers and networks that African American women cannot all be defined with one template. Michael Archeneaux poignantly observed the following: "When it comes to black women on reality TV, it's not an issue of wanting more than just snaps, shouts, and shade. More is already there. The question is: are you watching it?" Are you?

Works Cited

Abrams, Sil Lai. "Reality TV and the Changing Image of the African-American 'Leading Lady.'" *Grio* 31 Mar. 2013.

Acklin, Barbara, and Eugene Record. "Have You Seen Her." Brunswick Records, 1970. *MetroLyrics* 28 Dec. 2013.

Arceneaux, Michael. "Root: Positive Images of Black Women Exist on TV." *National Public Radio* 12 May 2011.

Bogle, Donald. *Toms, Coons, Mulattoes, Mammies & Bucks: An Interpretive History of Blacks in American Films.* New York: Roundhouse Publishing, 1994.

Boylorn, Robin M. "As Seen on TV: An Autoethnographic Reflection on Race and Reality Television." *Critical Studies in Media Communication* 25 (2008): 413–433.

Byng, Rhonesha. "Sil Lai Abrams Dishes Out a Digital Reality Check to Change the Image of Black Women on TV." *Madame Noire* 23 Oct. 2013.

Byrd, Kenya N. "Double Exposure: Tia & Tamera Mowry." *Black Enterprise* 29 Aug. 2011.

Chideya, Farai. "Skin Color, Stereotypes, and 'Flavor of Love.'" *NPR.ORG.* Host. Farai Chideya and Commentator Marc Anthony Neal. 1 Dec. 2006.

Conlin, Michelle. "America's Reality—TV Addiction." *Bloomberg Businessweek* 29 Jan. 2003.

Croom, Tene.' "Essence Atkins Blasts Sensationalism on Reality Shows." *EURweb Original Content* 13 Mar. 2013.

Cummings, Dre. "TNT—Tiny N Toya Are Dynamite." *Hip Hop Law.Com: Where the Hip Hop Nation Meets Critical Legal Theory* 14 July 2009.

Desmond Harris, Jenée. "Scandal Exploits Black Women's Images?" *The Root* 13 Oct. 2012.

"Five Reasons We Love *T.I & Tiny: The Family Hustle.*" *Hello Beautiful* 6 Dec. 2011.

Garcia, Courtney. "Soul Food Gets Spicer with the Return of Welcome to Sweetie Pie's." *Grio* 29 July 2013.

Gorman, Bill. "VH1 Debuts Another Hit Series With 'T.I. & Tiny: The Family Hustle.'" *The Blog* 6 Dec. 2011.

Graves, Lloyd. "Shelia Johnson Slams BET." *Daily Beast* 4 Apr. 2010.

Guyhto, Ayanna. "Tiny & Toya: Hip-Hop Party Girls or Southern Fried Angels?" *Yahoo Voices* 12 July 2009.

Hamilton, Peter. "U.S. Non-Fiction Networks: Who's Hot? Oprah's OWN Is the Hottest of Them All." Real Screen Workshop. *DocumentaryTelevision.Com* 2 Dec. 2013.

Ho, Rodney. "Tiny & Toya Interviews about BET show." *Radio & TV Talk with Rodney Ho* 7 July 2009.

Jackson, Derrick. K. "A March on Too Much Television." *Boston Globe* 2 Nov. 2005.

Jefferson, Lucette. "T.I. Family 'The Cosby Show' Photo: When You Think of the Huxtables, Do You Also Think of the Rapper's Family?" *Huff Post Black Voices* 22 Oct. 2012.

Kilborn, Robert. "How Real Can You Get?" *European Journal of Communication* (1994).

"Kym Whitley on Raising Son Joshua: He Was a Gift I Never Asked For." *Huffington Post,* 17 Apr. 2013.

McGloster, Nikki. "Tia Mowry Approaches New Horizons." *Vibe Video Vixen* 29 May 2012.

Miller-Bradshaw, Rachel. "Reality TV—Please Let Us Get Our House in Order." *KultureKritic* 30 Dec. 2013.

Natasha. "Exclusive Interview: Tamera Mowry-Housley Dishes on Advice for Brides, Interracial Dating Haters, & Why She Chose Celibacy." *TheyBF.com* 3 Oct. 2011.

O'Neal, Shaunie. "Commentary: Negative Portrayals of Black Women on Reality TV." *CNN* 11 July 2011.

Phinney, Jean S. "Ethnic Identity in Adolescents and Adults: Review of Research." *Psychological Bulletin* 108 (1990): 499–514.

Pisani, Joseph. "Reality TV's New Stars: Small Businesses." *Long Island Newsday.Com* 12 May 2013.

Poussaint, Alvin. "The Huxtables: Fact or Fantasy." *Ebony* Oct. 1988: 72–74.

"Rapper T.I. Family Photo Shoot: We're the Hip-Hop Huxtables." *In Touch Weekly.Com* 10 Oct. 2012.

Reiss, Steven, and James Wiltz. "Why America Loves Reality TV." *Psychology Today* 1 Sept. 2001.

———. "Why People Watch Reality TV." *Media Psychology* 6.4 (2004): 363–78.

Robinson, Phoebe. "Tia and Tamera Dish about Their TV Show, Motherhood, and Taking Over the World." *Obsessed Glamour.Com.* 7 July 2013.

Samuels, Allison. "Reality TV Trashes Black Women?" *Newsweek* 1 May 2011.

———. "Why Oprah Winfrey's New Shows Are Working for OWN." *Daily Beast* 13 June 2013.

Sarie. "Is Kimora's Life in Fab Lane Coming to a Halt?" *Black Celebrity Kids* 17 Nov. 2011.

Sims, Brian Carey, Zakiya Toms, Jessica Cannady, and Jovan Shumpert. "Coding Cosby: Racial Identity Themes on Television." *American Journal of Media Psychology* 3 (2010): 141–55.

Smith Beaty, Kelly. "T.I. & Tiny and The Obama's Usher in National Black Family Month." *The Blog—Huffington Post BlackVoices* 7 Sept. 2012.

St. Vil, Christine. "Interview: Kym Whitley Discusses New Show 'Raising Whitley' on OWN." *Black and Married with Kids* 13 Apr. 2013.

Turner Trice, Dawn. "*Flavor of Love* Tastes Like Insult to Girls, Women." *Chicago Tribune* 27 Nov. 2006.

Walton, Dawnie. "*Essence*'s Images Study: Bonus Insights." *Essence.Com* 7 Oct. 2013.

Whiting, Susan, Cloves Campbell, and Cheryl Pearson-McNeil. "Resilient, Receptive, and Relevant: The African-American Consumer." Diverse Intelligence Insights Series. Sept. 2013.

"Why T.I. Thinks Tiny Is Beautiful?" *Hello Beautiful* 5 Dec. 2011.

Zook, Kristal Brent. "Has Reality TV Become Black Women's Enemy?" *The Root* 24 May 2010.

7

Questions of Quality and Class

• •

Perceptions of Hierarchy in
African American Family–
Focused Reality TV Shows

PRESELFANNIE E.
WHITFIELD McDANIELS

In his article "The Case for Reality TV: What the Snobs Don't Understand," Michael Hirschorn writes, "The current boom may be a product of the changing economics of the television business, but reality TV is also the liveliest genre on the set right now. It has engaged hot-button cultural issues—class, sex, race—that respectable television, including the august *CBS Evening News*, rarely touches" (1). Published in the *Atlantic* in 2007, this article sought to connect reality TV shows with the genre of documentary (even when a bit too scripted); it sought to make the case that some reality TV shows exhibit the hard work put into them, are worth watching, and can be intellectually engaging. If nothing else, the case was made for the hierarchy in reality TV based on quality of programming. Hirschorn goes on to comment that the professional focus on reality TV shows has enhanced the creativity of its even more respected ancestor-counterpart: "For all the snobbism in the doc community, reality TV has actually contributed to the recent boom in documentary filmmaking. The most successful docs of recent vintage have broken through in part by drawing heavily from reality television's bag of tricks, dropping the form's canonical insistence on pure observation" (2). Of course, Hirschorn has his own reasons for defending the reality TV genres. He is the "executive vice president of original programming and production for VH1 and has produced many of that cable channel's reality programs" (Atlantic Monthly Group 138). The position from which he projects his argument makes Hirschorn's analysis questionable; however, I cannot help but see the merit in his argument and be inspired to examine it from my own perspectives.

So like Hirschorn, I approach the chosen topic from my different positions: via my occupation and as a viewer. As a college-level teaching academic and one who examines popular culture and how it intersects with the literature, writing, and research that I teach, I must connect with my students and colleagues on many levels. Because reality TV is, according to Hirschorn, "the liveliest genre on the set right now," current shows come up in my conversations with students and other academics. As I have gathered from many conversations with my academic colleagues, it seems that one, as an academic, must first choose to admit to being a reality TV watcher; then, one must find her or his level of comfortable confession about what one watches. Of course, this is not a problem for those who research popular cultural themes and such; they can just claim it all as a work hazard.

Interestingly enough, my watching admission has been the opaquely clear high road, and I readily state: There are really only a few shows that I watch. *Tia and Tamera* and *The Sheards* are my only must-see shows. Most of the rest, I just really can't handle. For me, in this role of a scholarly examiner of popular culture, my own personal viewing sentiments clearly indicate a perceived notion of a certain existent hierarchy in reality TV programming. By perceived hierarchy, I am referring to the fact that certain shows, because of whom they feature and those persons' reputations in the "real world," are considered to be more positive watching experiences than the shows that feature less popular people or those who are considered non-role-model material. Further, because of my own viewing preferences, which are directly connected to my academic research areas of African American and U.S. women's literary family dynamics, I am compelled to explore that perceived hierarchy in African American family–focused reality TV shows.

My Confession

In order to begin an exploration of this hierarchy in African American family–focused reality TV shows, I begin with a confession of sorts. I was once greatly ridiculed by academic colleagues, nonacademic friends, church members, and family members for publicly acknowledging that I was absolutely drawn to watching *Being Bobby Brown*, an earlier reality show that filmed January–June 2004 and aired in 2005 (IMDb). The show featured the more-than–dramatic family dynamics of singer Bobby Brown, music superstar Whitney Houston, their young daughter Bobbi Kristina Brown, and members of Bobby Brown's family, especially his brother Tommy, who also produced the show and later produced Tyra Banks's talk show. I reiterate that I was ridiculed for admitting to being a viewer, not necessarily for the act of watching. I heard criticism like the following: "How can you say that out loud? You have a PhD and you are watching that trash?" The show was referred to by many as trash because it displayed the couple in obvious impaired states, using profanity and arguing, and seemingly neglecting their daughter. I further admit that the ridicule affected my viewing habits of reality TV shows from that point on and even greatly affected my public discussions of what reality TV shows I was watching, as well. However, I do see more clearly now that many in the African American community saw the airing of the show as another way of destroying the reputation of the beloved Whitney Houston, who was once considered a serious African American woman role model, successful model, pop music superstar, and serious businesswoman. She had succeeded outside of African American culture, and her fame was international. By the time the reality TV show aired, though, evidence of serious drug use had already taken its toll and was continuing to rip apart the role-model image of Houston on a daily basis. Her case was a sore spot for the African American community, both as a public debacle for Houston herself and as a source of personal sadness for Black people.

The show was characterized as Bobby Brown's further financial exploitation of Whitney's troubled life. He was most often characterized as the "bad guy" in Whitney's very public fall from superstardom. Her fall was taken personally by the world, African American and not, because the public had fallen in love with Whitney on TV and movie screens, and now those same screens were destroying the image they had aided in crafting. However, in later interviews after Houston had successfully completed her final rehabilitation stint, she did characterize her choices as her own and attempted to dismiss some of the blame that was being dealt toward her husband for getting her into the drug scene. Her statement made sense, then, as Brown was known to be a hard drinker and was never really characterized as a hard drug user. My admission to watching her demise on the reality TV show was perceived as actively participating in her "tearing down." This accusation was significant as it related to African American images, because I only received this criticism from African Americans. But, I chose only to discuss it with African Americans, as well. To do otherwise seemed like race betrayal. However, perceptions of reality TV shows have changed much in the eight years since *Being Bobby Brown* aired.

Such a serious indictment on me as a viewer of that show speaks volumes about how certain segments of the African American community feel about shows that portray African American life in the reality TV genre. Those segments of people are divided by educational attainment, socioeconomic levels, and generation/age divisions, and the perceived hierarchy in the quality of shows seems to be strongly related to a similar societal hierarchy in the viewers themselves. Of course, this is not a new discovery; academics have for many decades explored this hierarchy in the history of the African American community as a direct result of the slave era–structure in the United States and its continuing effects on the family dynamics in the community. This type of analysis is directly tied to the concept of respectability politics in African American studies. Kali Gross asserts:

> Claiming respectability through manners and morality furnished an avenue
> for African Americans to assert the will and agency to redefine themselves
> outside the prevailing racist discourses. Although many deployed the politics
> of respectability as a form of resistance, its ideological nature constituted a
> deliberate concession to mainstream societal values. The self-imposed adher-
> ence to respectability that permeated African American women's lives, as well
> as African American culture, also later impacted African American activism
> and the course of scholarship in African American Studies. This strict adher-
> ence to what is socially deemed "respectable" has resulted in African American

scholars' confining their scholarship on African Americans to often the most "heroic," and the most successful attributes in African American culture; it has also resulted in the proliferation of analyses.(n.p.)

My examination of hierarchy in African American reality TV shows and viewers' consumption of the images does not seek to defy respectability politics, but I also do not allow its restrictions to deter me from examining the negative images as well as the positive images.

Allow me to return to the dividing segments in the community for a moment. For example, there is the reality TV friend-focused series *The Real Housewives of Atlanta*, which premiered August 7, 2008, on the Bravo network and is currently in its seventh very successful season. This African American reality show has become the source of an imperative debate within the African American community; values, money, violence, and image as portrayed on this show have become hot topics in magazines and on TV and radio talk shows. In most cases, grave comparisons are made to the other shows in the *Real Housewives* franchise that do not feature a predominantly African American cast and also do not have nearly the number of viewers. The *Atlanta* series garnered more than 3 million viewers for its past two season premieres (Nededog). The debate within the African American community must include, though, the differing opinions of the show across generation/age divisions, educational attainment, and socioeconomic levels. For example, the show is mostly viewed by adults between the ages of twenty-five and fifty-four, "with 1.9 million viewers in that demo," in particular (Nededog). Hierarchy or not, this show is making serious money, and as such usually renders negative critics powerless and eventually voiceless. But, of course, African American critics cannot fundamentally cease their negative critiques of the show, because as a community, they were most likely taught that there is something basically wrong about "putting your business in the streets" or in the public eye, in this case.

The Hierarchy

The rejection of reality TV is common. Hirschorn argues, "The resistance to reality TV ultimately comes down to snobbery, usually of the generational variety. People under 30, in my experience, tend to embrace this programming; they're happy to be entertained, never mind the purity of conception" (2). This may be true for many reality TV shows, but demographic research shows that African American family reality TV shows are consumed by African American women viewers over thirty on a consistent basis. He continues, "As an unapologetic producer of reality shows, I'm obviously biased, but I also know that any genre that provokes such howls of protest is doing something interesting" (2). Those howls of protest are also displayed quite fervently in the African American community when discussing which shows project positive and negative images of African Americans as individuals, families, and representatives of the race. This issue has become a substantial one as race theorists continue to examine the fact that African American positive images have been on a steady decline in the entertainment business; they are continuously searching for the second coming of *The Cosby Show* in TV viewing.

And whether one acknowledges this criticism or not, racial undertones certainly exist in reality TV programming just as they do in the television genres of talk shows, sitcoms, and dramas. Not only in the reality genre of family-focused shows is this issue a problem, but it is also a problem in the competitive reality TV shows. For example, there is yet to be an African American focus character on *The Bachelor* or *The Bachelorette*, and shows like *Flavor of Love* and *For the Love of Ray J* are considered "raunchy" versions of the mainstream *Bachelor* show. Some suggest that reality TV cannot be taken seriously and that too much emphasis is placed on these shows; however, the fact that the reality TV genres are steadily growing keeps that emphasis from fading away. At least one commentary on the "realness" and importance of reality TV shows is quite entertaining; that commentary is provided by a (not-so-real)ity show.

Famed comedian Kevin Hart's fake reality show *Real Husbands of Hollywood* premiered January 15, 2013, on the BET network, as a spoof of the *Real Housewives* shows. The following was written on the day the show premiered on BET: "What happens when you get a bunch of pampered Hollywood husbands in a room, marinate them in their own inflated egos and beer, and let them vent about their pet peeves? Well, someone else will have to do that show. In the meantime, though, comedian Kevin Hart is bringing the 'realest fakest reality show' in history to BET tonight with the debut of his hilarious *Real Husbands of Hollywood*" (Kaufman). Hart comments on the mission of the show: "'Our job is to make fun of the *Basketball Wives of L.A., The Real Housewives of Orange County*. You're seeing a bunch of fake drama. It's all drama between a bunch of men who act like women,' says series creator Kevin Hart of the fake fighting on his new BET series" (Kaufman n.p.). Whether attempting to or not, the show's parallels to negative critiques of the "real" reality TV shows keep right on coming: "The *Los Angeles Times* not[es] that the stars all play themselves as 'unremarkable, petty, confused, obsessive, argumentative and rarely bothered with actual work'" (Kaufman). Despite these negative and hilariously "fake" portrayals of African Americans in reality TV shows, some shows have managed to break the traditional reality TV mold, especially in the area of family-focused reality shows. *Tia & Tamera*, *The Sheards*, *Braxton Family Values*, and *T.I. and Tiny* are examples of shows that have projected mostly positive images of the African American family in their own different ways, while still garnering successful ratings as they take their respective places in the upper levels of the viewing hierarchy of reality TV shows. The next sections covering these four reality shows provide information on how the shows have been received by the critics and the viewing audience. The section following these four shows focuses on four of their counterparts, *Keeping Up with the Kardashians*, *The Tequila Sisters*, *Here Comes Honey Boo Boo*, and *Duck Dynasty*.

Good Clean Fun

Tia and Tamera Mowry established their claim to fame with the sitcom *Sister, Sister* in the 1990s. They established a lasting fan base that they have been able to maintain and reclaim in the viewing audience of their family-focused reality show, *Tia & Tamera* on the Style network. The show's syndicated episodes currently air on the Oxygen network. Robert Seidman records the following on the viewer numbers for the premiere of the reality show:

> Los Angeles, CA, August 9, 2011—The debut of Style Network's new docu-series *Tia & Tamera* on Monday at 9:00 P.M. delivered the network's most-watched series launch in its history, averaging 757,000 total viewers. Combined with the encore airing at 10:00 P.M., the series delivered nearly 1.5 million total viewers on Monday night. The premiere at 9:00 P.M. also ranks as Style's most-watched series launch ever among women 18–49 (357,000) and women 18–34 (203,000), and the second most-watched Style telecast overall in both key demos. (Seidman n.p.)

Of course, reestablishing a viewing public for a TV series takes on a whole new meaning in this age of technological advancements, much different from the 1990s audience for *Sister, Sister*, which still airs in syndication.

Like the show that brought them instant fame as teenagers, their self-titled television reality show *Tia & Tamera* projects the quintessential picture of the wholesome and tight-knit African American family. The name of their production company, Good Clean Fun, says it all. Viewers returned to watching the sisters again because they expected the same quality programming from the Mowry family that they had experienced in the past. Interestingly, the reality show has not only exposed viewers to the sisters' family lives as wives, mothers, and friends, but it has also featured their career struggles as they relate to entrepreneurship in new business ventures as partners and in searching for their next television roles as individual actors. By almost everyone's standards, the reality show has been a great positive success; however, it has been announced that the show will no longer air, despite its reception from the watching public. As a viewer, I was disappointed that the show might be leaving the air for good; however, I didn't feel any great sadness for the sisters because I had been privy to the fact, as a viewer, that they were moving on to exciting new acting jobs.

Critics situate the show high on the hierarchy of quality programming: "'*Tia & Tamera* exemplify what the Style brand is all about—they're optimistic, inspiring, passionate, dynamic and incredibly fun,' said Salaam Coleman Smith, President, The Style Network. 'It's fantastic that Style viewers have embraced this new series as they join Tia and Tamera on this intimate journey filled with major life transformations'" (Seidman). Although the show has received great reviews, the twins have found it very different to receive the viewers' reactions to their real-life events instead of critiques of characters that they portray in a television drama or sitcom. On the positives and negatives of the show, Tamera Mowry-Housley says, "'Doing a reality show, you're open for the world to see. People are open to judge, and you're open to judging. As an actress, they're judging your talent; they're judging how you play your role. Whereas this, they're judging you as a human being. Fortunately, with our show, we have more positive than negative'" (O'Hare). Tamera also discusses the negatives of having one's life under a microscope; she experienced the hurtful sting of negative comments about her interracial marriage and her biracial son on the Internet, so much so that her angered husband took to the Web to defend his wife and their family. She also chose to expose and to react to some of those negative comments on the show itself.

Church Family and Church Folk

Some members of the Church of God in Christ (COGIC) denominational family have not agreed with the Sheard family's decision to enter the TV reality show genre at all. They have feared that anything negative that surfaces about the family may be an irreparable stain on the COGIC denomination itself: The show "stars Gospel icon Karen Clark Sheard, part of the legendary Clark Sisters, her husband Bishop J. Drew, a mega church pastor in the Motor City and their children, Stellar Award winner and Grammy-nominated gospel songstress Kierra Sheard and producer J. Drew Sheard [II]" (Hearn). *The Sheards* premiered April 7, 2013, on the BET network. A robust viewing audience considers it good family programming and quality gospel programming:

> BET continues to remain in the forefront of quality gospel programming. The series premiere of *The Sheards* captured an audience of 1.2 million viewers, according to the Nielsen Company. When viewership is combined with the 11 P.M. encore, the episode attracted almost 2 million total viewers. This makes *The Sheards* the #1 Sunday cable reality series telecast in its 10 P.M. time-slot this year among adult women 18+ and a top 3 Sunday cable reality series debut for 2013 among total viewers. (Hearn n.p.)

J. Drew Sheard II comments on how the show was created:

> "The opportunity was presented to me by one of my good friends who worked in the TV entertainment business. It's actually a guy that I've known for a long time," Sheard told [*Christian Post*]. "He (said) you know it would be dope if we could do a reality show on some Christians but yet they're still normal people and they do normal things. . . . I got my whole family together, my mom, my dad and Kiki. I asked them 'how would y'all feel about us doing a reality show?' They were like 'man, it would be great.'" (Thomasos n.p.)

By far, the series' biggest focus is on Kierra and her brother, and the breakout star of the series is J. Drew II.

The show has also been a public platform for documenting J. Drew II's struggle with his faith and his life decisions: "Although Sheard said he recalls truly developing his relationship with God, reading his Bible and tuning into church sermons more around the age of 18, a preview of *The Sheards* shows that the 23-year-old struggles with trying to balance his life in and out of the church community" (Thomasos). In an interview, not featured on the show, he maintains his statement of faith:

> "I really believe that when it comes to the whole being a Christian or being a true man of God it's all about the time that you spend with God outside of church. Don't get me wrong, going to church is a great thing. It all ties into being a Christian as well," the Sheard son told [*Christian Post*]. "To kind of still be a believer and not really care too much about the stuff that goes on in church I just continue to pray to God outside of church and read my Bible and seek God. I believe that he's with me. . . . No matter what I do I just feel his presence with me." (Thomasos n.p.)

Despite these sentiments, J. Drew II's off-the-air move to secular music as a producer and as an artist and his seemingly budding relationship with "video vixen" Deelishis have been fuel for the media frenzy that now surrounds the family as a result of the reality show. These are prime examples of the unwanted attention that a reality show can bring to one's "real" life, regardless of what one chooses not to air. This type of portrayal of any scandalous behavior is what members of the COGIC denomination feared most with the airing of the show.

Even worse than the COGIC members could have imagined has been the public speculation of longtime rumors of Bishop J. Drew's infidelity and the show's exposure of Karen Clark Sheard's past life-threatening surgical experience in order to lose weight. Or perhaps, these revelations are just what they fearfully imagined and why they spoke out against the airing of the show. After all, the promotion of the show was predicated on the fact that the Sheards would present the picture of a "good" Black family, built on trusting the Lord in their everyday lives. Of course, no one expected a perfect picture, but maybe they did envision a family that would triumph over evil, like the Bible says. The show was presented as one that would be high on the hierarchy of reality TV programming, but the family material that has not been aired threatens the image created by the show itself and threatens to destroy its intended hierarchal position.

Singing Sibling Rivalry

Braxton Family Values premiered April 12, 2011, on WE tv and documents the family lives of Grammy Award–winning performer Toni Braxton and her four younger sisters: Traci, Towanda, Trina, and Tamar, and the family's matriarch, Evelyn. Their assigned on-screen names and roles are as follows: Toni-the-Superstar, Traci-the-Wild-Card, Towanda-the-Responsible-One, Trina-the-Party Girl, and Tamar-the-Diva. *Braxton Family Values* is often a sparring stage for the five Braxton sisters. The show, at its best, is a battleground for serious sibling rivalry. Although it is obvious that these sisters love each other fiercely, as is evidenced in their apologetic making-up scenes with their mother at the helm, it is definitely the explosiveness of their relating to one another that fuels their solid fan base. This show features profane dinner table arguments, little-sister rehearsal tantrums, a serial cheating husband, a busy music mogul husband, a criticized stay-at-home dad, revived music careers, a spokesperson for autism and lupus, and divorce announcements, including the Braxton matriarch and patriarch who are also divorced. Common Sense Media, an online media-rating tool for concerned parents, recommends that the viewer's age for the show be fourteen-plus.

The success of the show has led to the promotion of two other projects: "Toni Braxton and her family have already proved they can bring in the monster ratings with *Braxton Family Values*, their hit reality show for WEtv. Now the Braxtons are turning their eyes toward syndication with their own daytime talk show" (Shuter). And, breakout series star sister Tamar comments on her spin-off reality show *Tamar and Vince*, which features her marriage with popular music manager Vince Herbert: "The only con is a lot of people might not agree how Vince and I conduct our relationship. We work together every single day; we're together all the time. We're pretty much velcro. And he manages me, so it's a lot. The way we decide to communicate and what works for us, a lot of people won't agree with that" (Williams n.p.) Even though viewers express disdain for Tamar's antics, she has used her success on the show to gain a new role on the daytime talk show *The Real*, which also features Tamera Mowry-Housley.

Even if viewers "love to hate" Tamar's behavior, they consistently tune in to watch her and her sisters in their continually dramatic interactions on

Braxton Family Values. Until the debut of the show, most viewers really felt only "acquainted" with Toni Braxton. She was the superstar whose life's ups and downs had been in the public light for years, but her sisters were only known as her background singers. So, in essence, with Toni's decision to launch the show with her sisters, she has relaunched her own singing career and orchestrated the present successful entertainment/business careers of her sisters as well. Before then, they had been living only in her public shadow and apparently craving much more of the limelight. She enabled the viewing public to meet her sisters, and they have been embraced. Even though their dramatic squabbles are most times "over the top," their genuine love for each other always seems to come shining through, making their family image much more positive than negative, keeping this show situated on the positive side of the hierarchy in reality TV.

Family Ties in *The Family Hustle*

The reality television viewing audience had embraced Tameka "Tiny" Cottle-Harris before she joined her husband, famed rapper T.I. Harris, on their current family-focused reality show. In fact, *T.I. and Tiny: The Family Hustle* should be considered a spin-off of the successful friends and family reality show *Tiny and Toya*, because Tiny had already introduced herself and her family to the reality TV viewing world, with occasional appearances by her husband, T.I. *Tiny and Toya* featured Tiny, also known for her success as a singer and songwriter of the R&B group Xscape, and her close friend Antonia "Toya" Wright, the ex-wife of music rap star Lil' Wayne. Via their show, the friends shared their single-parenting ups and down with the viewers as Tiny was left to head the family during T.I.'s prison term. They also emerge as strong daughters who aid their parents and siblings when needed and as women struggling to find careers that fit their new "grown women" personalities. In both series, Tiny's genuine role as doting mother is obvious, and her maintenance of the family structure is undeniable. In the very first episode of the family-focused show, T.I. establishes his motto as patriarch of the Harris family: "God, family, hustle . . . in that order" of importance (*T.I. and Tiny: The Family Hustle*). Common Sense Media assigns thirteen-plus as the viewer age for this reality show. Interestingly, the viewers' embracement of the show has led to some unrest with those who make up T.I.'s music management team. It has been rumored that they believe the softer side of T.I. as a father and husband shown on the reality show may be having a negative impact on his hard-edged image as a rapper—what a testament to the positivity of the public image projected by the show.

The public sentiment of viewers of the show has been overwhelmingly positive. The fourteen-year relationship of this couple has made many viewers fall in love with them and their family of a combined six children. The ultimate testament of how this show is situated on the perceived hierarchy of reality TV is the fact that the Harris family has been dubbed by some as the "Hip Hop Huxtables," comparing the show to *The Cosby Show* sitcom, which starred the Huxtable family, the ultimate representation in positive family portrayals on television and considered the number one show in all of African American television history. Of course, there are many critics who say that the two are not comparable in any way, and just recently the collision of reality TV image and real life threatened to destroy the positive image that the Harris family has garnered via *The Family Hustle*, as rumors of T.I.'s possible infidelity and an illegitimate child have surfaced. In reaction, fans are using social media to discuss their fears about the rumors as they wait for the outcome and hope that their favorite couple will stay together.

The Counterparts

Reflective of the small number of mainstream television shows that feature a majority African American cast, African American–dominated shows in the reality TV genres are also few in number. However, regardless of the plethora of non–African-American-focused reality shows, hierarchy exists in the quality of these counterparts, as well, especially in the genre of family-focused shows. The long-running *Keeping Up with the Kardashians*, which premiered October 14, 2007, on E! network, is still bringing in solid ratings. Common Sense Media says the following about the show:

> Just when you thought it *might* be safe to channel surf, E! unleashed *Keeping Up with the Kardashians*, yet another mindless reality series about a privileged family clamoring for their 15 minutes of televised fame. As far as families go, the Kardashians are kind of like the Brady Bunch on crack.... For diehard fans of reality TV, *Keeping Up with the Kardashians* is a fine way to while away

30 minutes. But it's a terrible show to watch with young children. At best, they'll be exposed to binge drinking, stripper poles, and rampant materialism. At worst, they may start emulating what they see. (Common Sense n.p.)

Even if often criticized negatively for their lavish lifestyle, esoteric values, and fame seeking, the Kardashian–Jenner family has most definitely maintained its viewing audience over the years. The breakout star, Kim Kardashian, receives the bulk of the criticism and the media attention. She is often accused of being talentless and creating her fame because of her many orchestrated associations with "real" famous people. Unlike African Americans featured in reality TV shows, Kardashian's behavior is not analyzed via respectability politics. Unlike African Americans, portrayals of whites are not as scrutinized. Kim Kardashian does not have to serve as a representative for her race because most images on television are of whites, establishing a significant number of positive white images.

On a different note, *The Tequila Sisters*, a new series, which premiered December 10, 2013, on the TVGuide network, provides another opportunity to observe possible racial undertones in the reality TV genre, as it chronicles the family life of another minority family, but not an African American one. In the *New York Daily News*, Zaydra Rivera writes about this new show: "The *Tequila Sisters* may be yet another reality TV show detailing the lives of a wealthy family in Southern California, but they are anything but typical. The new half-hour series, debuting Dec. 10 on the TV Guide Network, focuses on the life of the Marins, a Mexican family who came from nothing and are now living in luxury in Orange County" (Rivera n.p.). The family patriarch made his fortune in the tequila business and supports his four twenty-something daughters' very "lavish lifestyle" (Rivera). The Marin family matriarch, like Ethel Braxton of *Braxton Family Values*, provides a sounding board for her daughters and keeps them as focused as she possibly can. In addition, the show documents those living hyphenated existences in the United States. In the Marins' case, that is living a hyphenated existence: "The primary challenge for the Marin sisters, who are first-generation [Mexican American], is finding a balance between the American culture they were raised in and the Mexican roots deeply embedded in their parents' values. Although all four girls are in their 20s, their father Bill has a hard time letting go and would rather see them live at home until they're married" (Rivera). Such a desire displays for the viewers a positive look at their ethnic cultural values.

Unlike the positive reception for the matriarchs of the Braxton and Marin families, June Shannon, the mother in *Here Comes Honey Boo Boo*, rarely receives much positive feedback. This family-focused reality show premiered August 8, 2012, on the Learning Channel (TLC). Even though it is probably one of the most negatively critiqued shows on TV, *Here Comes Honey Boo Boo* still has its supporters. *Kennebunk Post* staff writer Tracy Orzel opens her article with the following embracement of diversity:

Many Americans will argue TLC's reality series—*Here Comes Honey Boo Boo* is a blemish on the face of civilized society. To others—like me—the show is an unapologetic snapshot of this great country. . . . As far as I can tell, the biggest gripe people have about the show is it makes Americans look dumb. Well . . . some Americans are. According to a report from [the] educational firm Pearson, the United States placed 17th out of 40 developed countries in quality of education. (Orzel n.p.)

Orzel goes on to congratulate the seven-year-old for her insightfulness, as well:

Honey Boo Boo's thoughts on homosexuality? "Everybody's a little gay." The pageant princess has since been nominated for a Gay and Lesbian Alliance Against Defamation (GLADD) Media award. In a statement, GLADD President Herndon Graddick said the nominees "enlighten and entertain, but also reflect a new American landscape where a growing majority accept and value their LGBT family, colleagues and friends." (Orzel n.p.)

Orzel also cites the following negative critique of the show within her defense article: "*Forbes* contributor Helaine Olen compared the show to dwarf tossing and chastised those who tuned in for 'participating in the destruction of what is left of the American working class'" (Orzel). TLC recently canceled the show once evidence surfaced that Shannon was having a relationship with a registered child molester.

Duck Dynasty premiered March 21, 2012, on the A&E network and became an instant hit. In his very opinionated and obviously angry article, the *Washington Times'* John Hurt writes the following about the currently racially and religiously controversial *Duck Dynasty* clan, so popular now that they have reached the status of being featured on Barbara Walters's annual *Most Fascinating People* series for 2013:

> The great thing about America and the genuinely promising thing about the onslaught of modern technology is the stunning degree to which the elite's long-held monopoly on media and culture is shattered. The barbarians are at the gate and can no longer be kept out. . . . Those barbarians, of course, come in the form of "Duck Dynasty." It has been such a joy in recent weeks to watch how this sleeper of a TV show has sneaked past all the palace guards and become the single most popular program in cable history. (Hurt n.p.)

Of course, the religious beliefs for which this clan is touted are the same religious beliefs that slave owners embraced as they gathered around their own family dinner tables to pray, too.

The recent controversy concerning the racially and sexually discriminatory beliefs of the family patriarch was serious fodder for the media frenzy for a while, but eventually the financial and contractual matters of the family show triumphed over the public outcry against his politics. In addition, there were as many supporters of the show and the patriarch to speak his mind as there were protesters. So, they are still on the air and still bringing in more than decent viewing numbers. Like the Kardashians, bad behavior bars the *Duck Dynasty* crew from the positive hierarchy of reality TV, but it does not keep their popularity down. Dissimilar to the criticism of the African American shows that do not register on the positive hierarchy, there is no real concern about how such images found in *Keeping Up with the Kardashians* and *Duck Dynasty* will affect the white community.

Lasting Images

African American reality TV shows like *Tia & Tamera* and *The Sheards* house the best of intentions when displaying positive images and quality programming, even if they are not always successful. There are also shows that seemingly seek to purely let the public in to see what's "real" and the positive aspects come shining through, like *Braxton Family Values* and *T.I. and Tiny*, despite the fact that real life comes crashing through in an attempt to destroy the media image created. It is more than evident that positive African American images in the US media are scarce. All a viewer needs to do is turn on the local nightly news in any moderately sized city with a modicum of an African American population in order to see images of young African American males being handcuffed and dragged away to jail for some crime. Positive images of African Americans on the television and film screens become necessary motivators for the youth in our communities, who are most often untutored consumers of media images. We must continue to critique the negative images portrayed in television programming, including the reality TV shows cropping up daily across the genres, as these images are much more dire for our community. In addition, we must support the positive images that we see and agree to demand their presence when they are obviously absent. This need is especially urgent in light of the affects they have on younger viewers. Recent research shows that TV viewing lowers self-esteem in African American boys at an alarming rate and girls (both African American and white) at a moderate rate. However, white boys seem to be either unaffected by their viewing or get some type of ego boost from seeing the powerful images of white men as they are portrayed in television (*Week* Staff). Even the research says that African American positive images are crucial to the future of our community.

Works Cited

Atlantic Monthly Group (Michael Hirschorn). "Reality TV Has Value." *Popular Culture.* Ed. David Haugen and Susan Musser. Farmington Hills, MI: Greenhaven, 2011. 138–143.

Common Sense Media. *Braxton Family Values.* 2013. https://www.commonsensemedia.org/tv-reviews/braxton-family-values.

———. *Keeping Up with the Kardashians.* 2013. https://www.commonsensemedia.org/tv-reviews/keeping-up-with-the-kardashians.

———. *T.I. and Tiny: The Family Hustle.* 2013. https://www.commonsensemedia.org/tv-reviews/ti-and-tiny-the-family-hustle.

Gross, Kali N. "Examining the Politics of Respectability in African American Studies." *Almanac* 43.28 (1 Apr. 1997). http://www.upenn.edu/almanac/v43/n28/benchmark.html.

Hearn, Sarah. "*The Sheards* Debut as Top Cable Reality Show." *D C Gospel Music Examiner* 9 Apr. 2013. http://www.examiner.com/article/the-sheards-debut-as-top-cable-reality-show.

Hirschorn, Michael. "The Case for Reality TV: What the Snobs Don't Understand." *Atlantic* 1 May 2007. http://www.theatlantic.com/magazine/archive/2007/05/the-case-for-reality-tv/305791/.

Hurt, John. "The Boo-Boo of *Here Comes Honey Boo Boo.*" *Washington Times* 27 Aug. 2013. http://www.washingtontimes.com/news/2013/aug/27/the-boo-boo-of-here-comes-honey-boo-boo/?page=all.

IMDb. *Being Bobby Brown.* http://www.imdb.com/title/tt0429311/.

Kaufman, Gil. "Kevin Hart Promises *Real Husbands of Hollywood* Is 'Realest Fakest Reality Show.'" *MTV News* 15 Jan. 2013. http://www.mtv.com/news/1700238/kevin-hart-real-husbands-of-hollywood/.

Nededog, Jethro. "*Real Housewives of Atlanta* Scores Highest-Rated Season Premiere." *The Wrap Covering Hollywood* 5 Nov. 2013. http://www.thewrap.com/real-housewives-atlanta-scores-highest-rated-season-premiere/.

O'Hare, Kate. "*Tia & Tamera:* Pregnant Tamera Mowry-Housley Deals with Critics, Declares Belly Off-Limits." *Zap2It* 10 Oct. 2012. http://www.zap2it.com/blogs/tia_tamera_pregnant_tamera_mowry-housley_deals_with_critics_declares_belly_off-limits-2012-10.

Orzel, Tracy. "Honey Boo Boo: The (Un)American Dream." *Kennebunk Post* 25 Jan. 2013. http://post.mainelymediallc.com/news/2013-01-25/Community/Honey_Boo_Boo_The_unAmerican_Dream.html.

Rivera, Zaydra. "*Tequila Sisters* Chronicles Upscale Mexican-American Family." *New York Daily News* 5 Dec. 2013. http://www.nydailynews.com/entertainment/tv-movies/tequila-sisters-chronicles-upscale-mexican-american-family-article-1.1538478.

Seidman, Robert. "*Tia & Tamera* Shatters Records Delivering Most-Watched Series Premiere Ever for Style." *TV by the Numbers on Zap2It* 9 Aug. 2011. http://tvbythenumbers.zap2it.com/2011/08/09/tia-tamera-shatters-records-delivering-most-watched-series-premiere-ever-for-style/100056/

Shuter, Rob J. (Naughty but Nice Rob). "Toni Braxton Talk Show: Singer and Family Pitching New TV Series." *HuffPost Celebrity* 8 Nov. 2012. http://www.huffingtonpost.com/2012/11/08/tony-braxton-talk-show_n_2094007.html.

Thomasos, Christine. "*The Sheards* Exclusive: J. Drew Sheard II Opens Up about Pressure from 'Church People.'" *Christian Post* 8 April 2013. http://www.christianpost.com/news/the-sheards-exclusive-j-drew-sheard-ii-opens-up-about-pressure-from-church-people-93371/.

Week Staff. "How TV Lowers Self-esteem in Kids . . . Except for White Boys." *The Week* 31 May 2012. http://theweek.com/articles/475043/tv-lowers-selfesteem-kids-except-white-boys%7D.

Williams, Brennan. "*Tamar & Vince:* Tamar Braxton Opens Up on New Show and Becoming a Mother." *HuffPost Black Voices* 21 Sept. 2012. http://www.huffingtonpost.com/2012/09/20/tamar-vince-tamar-braxton-new-show-becoming-a-mother_n_1901880.html.

8

Contemplating
Basketball Wives

. . . .

A Critique of Racism, Sexism,
and Income-Level Disparity

SHARON LYNETTE JONES

In the opening sequence of the VH1 television show *Basketball Wives*, the stars of this reality series pose provocatively in body-hugging clothing next to trophies while the names of the women appear across the screen introducing them to the viewers of the program. Their well-groomed hairstyles, fashionable clothing, and impeccable make-up present them as upwardly mobile, sexy, and glamorous women. The sequence allows viewers to gaze upon the stars of this famous and infamous show. The audience gains access to the lives of many women who are or who have been romantically involved with professional basketball players. The program, which is in its fifth season, presents a side of the athletic world that many viewers were not privy to before this program aired. Though on the surface *Basketball Wives* may appear to be groundbreaking in its representations of professional basketball by shifting the focus away from the lives of the male athletes and toward the lives of their female current or ex-mates, children, and their families, the depiction of African American females on *Basketball Wives* simultaneously condemns and promotes racism, sexism, and income-level disparity in episodes of the show. *Basketball Wives* fails to convincingly and strongly present an extensive critique of oppressive forces that African American women face in America because of the racist, sexist, and economic stereotypes on the program. Unfortunately, the show, which had the potential for promoting, encouraging, and facilitating a meaningful dialogue and discussion on important issues, has proven to trivialize the lives of its subjects, and by extension, the lives of other women who may be facing similar experiences.

Basketball Wives contains stereotypes that reflect historical misrepresentations and oversimplifications rooted in biases against African American women. These depictions can best be viewed within the context of feminist, cultural, and historical approaches to analyzing the role of African American women in television programs. The depiction of African American women in popular culture and American society is a subject that has continued to gain more scholarly attention in articles and books because of heightened awareness of these issues. Using feminist, cultural, and historical approaches, this chapter draws upon the works of scholars such as Patricia Hill Collins in *Black Feminist Thought: Knowledge, Consciousness, and the Politics of Empowerment*; Charisse Jones and Kumea Shorter-Gooden in *Shifting: The Double Lives of Black Women in America*; and Tia Tyree in the article "African American Stereotypes in Reality Television" for a discussion of the stereotyping depictions of African American women historically and in popular culture as a means of laying the groundwork for exploring these representations in *Basketball Wives*. Although the texts by Collins, Jones and Shorter-Gooden, and Tyree do not explore the show *Basketball Wives* specifically, their ideas on representations of Black females can be applied to an analysis and study of the show. Furthermore, this analysis of *Basketball Wives* demonstrates how the depictions of Black females on the show present a setback for Black females in America rather than an advance in achieving and enjoying equal rights and treatments in the United States.

Collins's *Black Feminist Thought: Knowledge, Consciousness, and the Politics of Empowerment* identifies representations of African American females within American society. These include a loyal female employed as a laborer engaging in household work (71), a matriarchal female who dominates males (73–74), a female receiving governmental funding for subsistence (77), and a female involved in sexual activities (77). Collins's recognition of these depictions indicates how Black females have been viewed within the context of American culture. She argues that these Black female representations illustrate "racial" and gendered as well as economical discrimination (78).

Likewise, in their highly informative study of Black females, Jones and Shorter-Gooden provide information about historical and contemporary views and perspectives on Black females, including those grounded in truth and those grounded in false and misguided ideas related to racial identity, gender roles, and status. Jones and Shorter-Gooden point out, "While most people of color, and African Americans in particular, are perceived through a distorted lens, Black women are routinely defined by a specific set of grotesque caricatures that are reductive, inaccurate, and unfair" (3). They identify several prevalent stereotypes of Black females, and these stereotypical depictions can be identified as the idea of Black females symbolizing inferiority, being unaffected by hardships, lacking womanly attributes, engaging with unlawful activities, and libidinous (11–12).

The topic of how African Americans are represented in television is an important area of academic inquiry. In the article "African American Stereotypes in Reality Television," Tyree provides a useful analysis about depictions of Black females. Tyree's argument proves to be instructive and applicable to an understanding of the show because her examples of depictions also appear in *Basketball Wives*. She argues that "the reality of reality television is that the programming is not real" (395). She continues, "Ultimately, when taking into account the impact of stereotypes in the United States and the power of television to reproduce them, it is important to see how reality television fits within society" (395). Despite the fact that Tyree's article does not discuss *Basketball Wives*, the article does contend that these types of television shows are important for analysis. Tyree states, "In essence, television and reality television programming, in particular, can be an informational tool for audiences to gauge who they are, who others are in their society as well as what is or is not socially acceptable behavior" (397). In the case of *Basketball Wives*, on VH1, the viewers gain exposure to a show that presents stereotypes of Black females that simultaneously support and condemn racism, sexism, and income-level disparity. Like Jones and Shorter-Gooden, Tyree identifies stereotyping depictions of Black females that can be applied to *Basketball Wives*. The most relevant include being maternal, domineering, libidinous, destitute, mad, or materialistic (Tyree 398). According to Tyree, a maternal Black female possesses a large body size, behaves deferentially with others, and engages in domestic household work for whites (398). A domineering Black female, Tyree claims, possesses a matriarchal role while criticizing men she has mated with in her life (398). Tyree suggests that a libidinous female can be described as engaging in sexually intimate acts for materialistic reasons (398). Tyree asserts that a destitute female remains unemployed while receiving governmental funding (398). A mad African American female demonstrates a personality that reflects "the angry Black woman" personality (398). Tyree warns, "If these African American stereotypes are present in reality television shows, they can have an impact on both African Americans and others" (399). Tyree's commentary demonstrates the importance of how and why scholars must be vigilant in this type of research in order to identify depictions of stereotyping in popular culture that endorse racism, sexism, and income-level disparity. In turn, if scholars identify and critique the programs that endorse these ideas, then it is possible that viewers will demand and support alternative representations that challenge the depictions so prevalent on shows such as *Basketball Wives*.

The show features a memorable cast of characters who occasionally defy, but who mostly support and reinforce, racial, sexual, and economic stereotypes of African American women. The fifth season, which aired on VH1, features Black women such as Shaunie O'Neal, Shaquille O'Neal's former spouse, a mother and "producer" for the program ("*Basketball Wives* Shaunie O'Neal"); Tami Roman, a parent involved in entrepreneurial activity ("*Basketball Wives* Tami Roman"); and Tasha Marbury, who also has entrepreneurial experience and a notable spouse ("*Basketball Wives* Tasha Marbury Seasons 5"). Roman is divorced from Kenny Anderson, who played basketball professionally (Manuel-Logan). According to the program *Basketball Wives*, Marbury's spouse (Stephon Marbury) maintains an active schedule, and Marbury is described as "a veteran basketball wife" on a VH1 website ("*Basketball Wives* Tasha Marbury Seasons 5"). Other women on the fifth season include Evelyn Lozada, who has "Puerto Rican" heritage ("*Basketball Wives* 4 Cast Evelyn Lozada"); her identities include being a former mate of Antoine Walker, a parent, and an entrepreneur ("*Basketball Wives* 4 Cast Evelyn Lozada"), and Suzie Ketchum, a mother and athlete Michael Olowokondi's former mate ("*Basketball Wives* 4 Cast Suzie Ketchum"). Although Ketchum is not African American, she has been an integral part of the show for numerous seasons, and she interacts with the African American females on the program. Episodes prior to the fifth season also featured Black women in prominent roles, such as Jennifer Williams, who married athlete Eric Williams and who owns Flirty Girl Fitness in addition to working as a realtor ("*Basketball Wives* 4 Cast Jennifer Williams"); Kesha Nichols, athlete Richard Jefferson's former fiancée who has a dancing troupe ("*Basketball Wives* Kesha Nichols Season 4"); Meeka Claxton, who is wed to former athlete Speedy Claxton and who works in realty in addition to the role as mother ("*Basketball Wives* Meeka Claxton Season 3"); Kenya Bell, athlete Charlie Bell's estranged wife who has musical aspirations ("*Basketball Wives* Kenya Bell Season 4"); Royce Reed, an ex-"cheerleader" who owns the dance troupe Fantashique ("*Basketball Wives* Royce Reed Seasons 1–4"); and Gloria Govan (spouse to athlete Matt Barnes) has "Mexican" in addition to "African American" heritage ("EthniCelebs Celebrity Ethnicity Gloria Govan").

Because of the popularity of the program, there has been lively discourse about the representations of Black females on the show on Internet websites. Although the viewpoints expressed on the Internet sites often acknowledge the prevalence of stereotypes on *Basketball Wives*, there is also a recognition that viewers who watch the program are complicit in supporting these types of representations of Black women because they provide the show with a large audience. For example, according to "Does *Basketball Wives* Really Perpetuate Black Female Stereotypes?," the show promotes stereotypes. The article states, "Amidst the chaos of drink throwing, finger waving, and head slapping, it's easy to look at *Basketball Wives* and reach a verdict that says the show portrays African American women negatively" (Moore). Nevertheless, the article suggests that the show has a large audience because of the portrayals of Black females and the sensational and controversial storylines. Another article, "Are Blacks to Blame for Negative Portrayals of African Americans on Reality TV?," by Terrell Jermaine Starr suggests that responsibility for the depiction of African American individuals on programs such as *Basketball Wives* stems from the support of African American viewers. *Miami New Times* blogs also address stereotypes in an article titled "Does *Basketball Wives* Perpetuate the Stereotype of Women as Gold Diggers?" by Stacey Russell. The article explores whether females on the show are motivated by materialism, and Russell contends that changing the tone or direction of the program would make it boring and uninteresting, which reinforces the idea that the audience for such shows may enjoy the way females are portrayed on the reality program.

Despite the support for the program and its representations of Blacks, some articles emphasize the harmful effects of stereotypes on shows such as *Basketball Wives* and efforts to improve the image of Black women on television. The article, "Women Activists Working to Change Black Stereotypes on Reality TV," claims that the amount of support for stereotypical depictions of Black females has decreased. The article asks, "Could it be that black women are finally getting sick and tired of the 'Crazy Black Reality Chick' meme?" (Abrams). The article claims there is less violent activity on reality television shows because of the prevalence of lawsuits, including the one in which former *Basketball Wives* star Meeka Claxton sued Tami Roman as well as VH1 because of a physical attack from Roman. Another article, "Real World" by Jeannine Amber, which appears in *Essence*, also examines the stereotypical representations of females on shows such as *Basketball Wives* and *Love and Hip Hop: Atlanta*. According to this article, "From the all-out brawls *on Basketball Wives* to the grimy love triangles on *Love and Hip Hop: Atlanta*, reality TV has become a significant force in disseminating images of Black women to the viewing public" (Amber). The representations, however, are problematic because of the stereotypes promoted on these types of programs. As Amber emphasizes, "But to the chagrin of many, these shows seem to feature one type of woman most prominently: She's irrational, unreasonable, oversexed and violent, and more often than not she's so lacking in self-regard she's willing to be humiliated publicly by the man she claims to love." These articles collectively reveal the current debates about the influence of *Basketball Wives* and reality television in general.

Basketball Wives has been on television for several seasons. It can be differentiated from other reality programs because there are so many minority women on the show. It stands in contrast to programs such as *The Real Housewives of Beverly Hills*, *The Real Housewives of Orange County*, *The Real Housewives of New York*, and *The Real Housewives of New Jersey*, which focus on white females and their relationships with each other, mates, and children. Another distinctive aspect of *Basketball Wives* is the connection with the world of professional basketball. At the same time, it is clear from the context of the program that the main claim to fame for some females on the program rests solely in their relationships to the male athletes. In fact, their status as trophy wives is highlighted in the recurring sequence, as mentioned earlier, and when they appear on the show, the name of the male athlete they were or are romantically involved with often appears on the screen. Thus, their identities seem inextricably tied to that of males, and specifically, males who have succeeded in the world of professional basketball.

The fact that the show has, to date, weathered five seasons and generated another program called *Basketball Wives: LA* testifies to its popularity or the interest that it has sustained among the viewers. Viewers can satisfy their cravings for the show from retail outlets, online streaming, and the show's official site that provides viewers and potential viewers with even more information on the show's stars. The *Basketball Wives* website can be instructive in term of its construction of the identities of many on the show in relationship to the depictions of them on *Basketball Wives*. Each Black woman on the show represents or reinforces prevailing stereotypical depictions on the program. These depictions include physical appearance, language, movements, and personality. The show seems to pivot upon the confluence of these stereotypes and the ways in which the Black females interact with friends, mates, and others on the program.

Perhaps the most important person on *Basketball Wives* is Shaunie O'Neal because of her role as a producer and participant on the show. She is arguably connected with the show's most famous athlete, Shaquille O'Neal. In addition, she seems to be at the center of the show in terms of the power dynamics. Despite the fact that Shaunie O'Neal frequently displays traits associated with being a nice, gentle, and friendly person, she also exhibits behavior that displays a confrontational, hostile, and abusive personality. The different aspects of her personality demonstrate the range of emotions O'Neal projects on *Basketball Wives*. The persona she presents on the show varies depending on the context of the situation and whether she is acting in a parental role with her children or interacting with the other adult females on the reality show. For example, sometimes she is shown with her children by Shaquille O'Neal, and it appears that motherhood remains important to her. The show prominently presents her watching her children play basketball and even advising one of her children on how to play basketball better. She is portrayed as a good mother who loves and cares for her children, and the loving, kind, nurturing, and supportive side of her personality becomes an important part of her identity. At the same time, O'Neal is depicted as someone who also revels in time away from her children, and often she is not depicted with the children at all. In fact, unless someone views the show regularly, he or she might not even be aware that she has children, because the screen time for the children is rather limited, and much of the focus is on her relationships with the other Black females or her current dating habits. The depiction of her as a mother takes a back seat to other aspects of her life, including businesswoman, friend, and socialite.

Yet, in addition to her presentation as mother or maternal figure, O'Neal is also presented as an African American female who is easily provoked and who often engages in verbal abuse toward other people because of her perception that she has been mistreated. When she engages in abusive behavior, she reflects the stereotype of a hostile African American female defined by scholars such as Tia Tyree (398) and Jones and Shorter-Gooden (11). In effect, the depiction of O'Neal as the mean Black female on the show is exemplified in an episode when she and others on the program go to a restaurant where Ketchum and Govan are meeting up for a meal. O'Neal and the other women enter the restaurant even though the other women were not expecting them. The episode depicts this action as an act of revenge or aggression. O'Neal then proceeds to criticize, mock, and ridicule Govan about Govan's status with her mate, especially because Govan was earlier depicted on the program as presenting her life as better than that of other women on the show. The way in which O'Neal and others arrive at the restaurant in order to berate someone who did not anticipate their appearance reinforces the idea of O'Neal as the mean or mean-spirited Black female. The incident also is one of the numerous heated encounters on this program, which implies that it is impossible or very difficult for women to have true and lasting and enduring friendships with each other.

The Shaunie O'Neal persona as depicted on a VH1 website runs counter to how she is portrayed on the program when she argues with Govan during the infamous restaurant scene. On a website, she is depicted as independent, successful, entrepreneurial, and gifted at reconciling conflicts ("*Basketball Wives* Shaunie O'Neal"). This description proves to be very revealing because of the irony. The website positions O'Neal as independent and self-made when in fact her former marriage with a basketball star is continually highlighted and emphasized on the show. Despite her previous broadcasting experience prior to wedding Shaquille O'Neal, when she appears on the show her status as his ex-wife regularly appears underneath her name. On the show, Shaunie O'Neal is depicted as someone who really does not possess a separate identity from Shaquille O'Neal, and viewers must keep in mind that her entrepreneurial ventures are intertwined with the fact of who her ex-husband is. Ultimately, her fame or success is predicated upon her association with such a famous man and not on her own skills or merit. She gets lauded for being the mediator of the women, but as was demonstrated in the encounter with Govan, she can be the facilitator of tension on the show. Although it appears that she transitions creatively after her marriage to Shaquille O'Neal, the show emphasizes her connection to him, and the premise of the show rests on her association with her famous former spouse and the world of basketball.

Evelyn Lozada is a woman whose appearance on the show is noteworthy because of her relationship with others on *Basketball Wives*. She has complicated and complex relationships with females such as Lewis, who was featured prior to the fifth season, or Bell, for whom she exhibits a strong disdain and dislike, because of her belief that they have been disrespectful toward her. A *Basketball Wives* VH1 website description makes Evelyn's claims that she was physically assaulted by a spouse appear to be like a game rather than a serious incident ("*Basketball Wives* Evelyn Lozada"). The *Basketball Wives* website account of her also makes her seem a bit materialistic, as if she spent her life seeking money and goods, especially when the account describes her humble background with a single parent ("*Basketball Wives* Evelyn Lozada").

Lozada's relationship problems with Chad Ochocinco and subsequent divorce from Chad Ochocinco because of her claims that she was physically assaulted by him are emphasized in the fifth season, and the attack in particular brings about disturbing observations from the other African American females on the show, such as Marbury, who makes fun of the assault during an episode of the show when she is in a car with Ketchum. The depiction of Marbury making fun of Lozada being physically harmed implies that Black females do not perceive what happened to Lozada to be wrong or inappropriate. Although there is an episode in which Lozada speaks to Marbury to express how she felt about Marbury's attitude toward Lozada's claims that Ochocinco harmed her physically, the show still does not offer or provide an in-depth analysis of the ramifications of domestic violence against women. The storyline represented an opportunity for the program to send a stronger message to viewers that intentional domestic abuse is inappropriate; instead, the program treats a very serious issue as something comical in an earlier episode, and in a later episode, Lozada and

Marbury talk to each other but neither adequately or fully address the serious implications of harming females. As a result, *Basketball Wives* misses an opportunity to seriously and compellingly address an important social issue in an in-depth manner.

Out of all of the women depicted on *Basketball Wives*, Roman is the one who most resembles the stereotype of the mean-spirited and destitute women as identified by Tyree (398) and the recipient of governmental funding as described by Collins (77). She contrasts to other Black females on the show in the sense that she is depicted as being less affluent than Lewis, O'Neal, Bell, and others. Unlike O'Neal, Roman seems to have fallen on hard financial times. In episodes of the show, Roman's experience with food stamps is continually emphasized. The show plays up the income-level disparity between Roman and other Black women, including Williams and later Marbury, who appear to have more money than Roman does and a higher social and economic class. For example, when Roman is depicted as a former recipient of food stamps, Williams claims to be unfamiliar with the type of financial struggles Roman would have endured. She makes a point of mentioning her lack of knowledge about food stamps. Later, in another episode, the income disparity and social and economic differences between the two women comes to the forefront when they argue at an event. The argument stems from Roman's feeling of umbrage over Williams's attitude about food stamps and Roman's struggles. In the midst of the argument, Williams repeatedly says, "I'm not ghetto," which implies that she sees herself as being of a higher social status and class than Roman, and it further highlights the income-level disparity between the two women. The encounter becomes so heated that Roman is restrained, and she is depicted as someone who could be verbally and physically harmful to others. Roman fits Tyree's description of the angry Black woman (398) or mad African American female stereotype because of her words, actions, and deeds on the show.

In a later episode, Roman and Williams are presented as partially reconciling when Roman undergoes surgery to remove fat from her body, and Williams visits her and brings her food stamps. The gesture is seen as Williams's attempt to understand another's social and economic background, yet Roman is amused because these foods stamps do not resemble contemporary ones. The scene provides comic relief, yet it does not provide a serious look at income inequality. Arguably, the scene in which Roman is presented with food stamps by Williams could be viewed as trivializing many people who rely heavily on food stamps, especially those who do not have the option of being on a television show to earn money. The show depicts Roman and Williams as having different class backgrounds, yet the show fails to show in a meaningful way the consequences of such income disparity in the United States of America for Black females. The fact that Roman is presented as the mean Black female with a history of food stamp dependence illustrates how she fulfills a destitute stereotype or the image of "the angry Black woman" as described by Tyree (398) and the recipient of governmental funding depicted by Collins (77).

This kind of interaction between Roman and the other women is mirrored later with Marbury. As was the case with Williams, Roman is also featured as a working-class person of uncouth background when paired with Marbury, especially in the episode at Marbury's house in which she requests a beer, which connotes working class, and Tasha does not have "a cold one" because of her upper-class persona. The beer is available; however, the temperature is not cold. Again, the income-level disparity between the two females leads to a tension. The scene is presented for entertainment value as yet another example of friction between women on the show rather than as a real analysis of the income gap and how to end it among Black females in America.

Marbury exists as a foil for Roman. Marbury lives in a fancy home, and her surroundings suggest a materialistic tendency as well as opulence. She likes to cast an air of gentility, yet this is belied by her attitude on the show. Her description on the VH1 website claims, "She's undoubtedly a dividing presence within the circle, as her high society persona and low tolerance for tomfoolery quickly lead to friction with certain ladies within the group" ("*Basketball Wives* Tasha Marbury Seasons 5"). In Marbury, the viewer sees an upwardly mobile African American female who has tendencies that fall into the mean-spirited woman category. On the show, she appears to consider herself superior to someone such as Roman, and she tries to show a sense of refinement in her physical appearance by dressing in stylish clothing. However, it is important to consider how she diminished Lozada's physical harm by making light of it with Ketchum. The depiction of her high tolerance for abusive behavior against another female suggests, too, a lack of empathy and concern. The depiction of her ridiculing and mocking Lozada in front of and to Ketchum when Lozada was not around reinforces the idea of Black females not being as affected by or responsive to harm against others in an empathetic way.

In addition to O'Neal, Roman, Ketchum, Marbury, and Lozada from the fifth season, an analysis of some of the other women who were featured prominently on earlier seasons is offered. The presence of Reed, Williams, Nichols, Bell, and Claxton reinforces or elicits responses from others that support stereotyping ideas. For example, Reed, who has experience dancing and cheerleading professionally, symbolizes the stereotype of the libidinous and mad African American woman; the show's emphasis on her revealing clothing, body movements, and personality conflicts with that of other females. Her risqué attitude and dancing moves create memorable television, especially when Williams tries to get her to tone down her flamboyant and provocative demeanor via a makeover on the program. Reed also participates in mean behavior on the show with Govan because of personal conflicts between the two of them. Reed dances provocatively, has a series of boyfriends without a lasting relationship, wears revealing clothing, and seems to crave attention from men. In an episode of the show, she wears lingerie for her boyfriend and then is presented engaging in acts of intimacy with him. Reed's depiction on the show combines the two ideas of the erotic and mean Black female. Unfortunately, the depiction of Reed on the show focuses heavily on the racial and sexual stereotypes and downplays other aspects of her life, including her interest in acting, her family, her role as a mother, and her other interests or pursuits.

Like Reed, Bell fulfills a stereotype on the show that emphasizes her body and sexuality. Bell seeks to be a famous recording artist, and she is seen wearing provocative clothing, dancing, and performing. Bell and Reed both reinforce the ideas about Black females as erotic, sexy, and immodest. Other aspects of their lives and experiences are not fully developed on the show because so much of their screen time shows an emphasis on their physical appearance and their erotic nature. Reed and Bell are often presented in a one-dimensional rather than a multidimensional way, and viewers are not as privy to the complexities of their personalities in comparison to other women on the show such as Williams, O'Neal, Lozada, and even Roman. The depictions of Reed and Bell remain an issue because their representations endorse stereotypical ideas about Black females as erotic while downplaying other aspects of their personalities.

Another previous cast member on the show is Williams, who represents the materialistic and mean-spirited Black female stereotype described by Tyree (398). She is prone to becoming upset and has heated encounters with a woman she believes was interested in her mate and with Roman, to whom she acts superior on the show because of the class disparity between the two of them. Williams fits this stereotype by being prone to confrontations with other people, raising her voice, speaking loudly, being verbally critical and judgmental toward other people, and engaging in body language that can be viewed as aggressive because of the positioning of her body and her facial expressions. Williams in effect is displaced in later episodes by Marbury, whose function mirrors that of Williams prior to the fifth season of *Basketball Wives*. The similarities between the two women in comparison with Roman provide highly dramatic scenes showcasing the concepts of the mad African American female. Although Roman may show a working-class perspective and Marbury and Williams may show an upper-class perspective, all three women show a tendency to display abusive behavior and insensitivity to the feelings of other people.

The addition of Kesha Nichols to the show further expands upon the depictions of females. Although Nichols considers herself to be Black, Roman questions her racial identity on *Basketball Wives* because of Nichols's physical appearance. The questioning of Nichols's racial identity reinforces stereotypes about the physical appearance of Black females, suggesting that only women of darker complexions, or complexions darker than that of Kesha, can be Black. In addition, when Nichols travels to her home in North Carolina with other women from the show, the representation of her background also reinforces ideas about social and economic inequity. Ketchum later suggests that Nichols's family has a low income based on the type of housing that they live in, and it suggests a dismissiveness of those who may seem to have low incomes. The inclusion of Nichols on the show had the potential to shatter myths and stereotypes about Black females in regard to skin tones and social class; instead, the show continues to reinforce ideas of racism, sexism, and income-level disparity.

The inclusion of Nichols can be seen as significant, because it testifies to the interracial heritage of many African American females in the United States. On the one hand, *Basketball Wives* is to be praised for acknowledging that Black females can have a variety of skin tones and backgrounds. It presents an argument to viewers that that they cannot or should not have stereotypical ideas about what a Black female can look like in society. On the other hand, the lack of acceptance or understanding of Nichols as a Black woman shows that the program can seem to reinforce stereotyping ideas about Black people, especially in the depiction of how Roman relates to Nichols on the show. Meeka Claxton, who also appeared prior to the fifth season of the show, is another person whose depiction both presents and defies stereotypes of Black females. According to a VH1 website, in contrast with other females on *Basketball Wives*, Claxton remains married ("*Basketball Wives* Meeka Claxton Season 3"). Other females on the show, including O'Neal, Roman, Lozada, Ketchum, Bell, and Nichols, are divorced and/or former mates of professional athletes. In this manner, Claxton may seem to challenge stereotypes about the unmarriageability of Black females, but she also reinforces the idea of the mad African American woman stereotype because of her altercations with her cast mates, in particular, her conflict with Roman within Italy. The women eventually reconciled, yet their reconciliation demonstrates that even the females appearing on *Basketball Wives* at some level recognize that their actions on the show did not present them positively (Black). These representations are classic examples of how *Basketball Wives* is at times refreshing in its approach to portrayals of Black females by showing diversity while at the same time representing a regression, too, in how it serves to reinforce and support stereotypical ideas about Black females in America.

Although *Basketball Wives* is a program that attracted many viewers during the first four seasons because of memorable cast members, the article, "'Basketball Wives' Fired, Jennifer, Royce and Kesha Axed for More 'Balanced' Show," alleges that "Jennifer Williams, Royce Reed and Kesha Nichols have all reportedly been fired and will be replaced in what sources described as a bid to eradicate 'dead weight' from the show, according to TMZ" (Nsenduluka). In addition, the article addresses how actions of individuals affected those who watched the program. It points out, "The reality show recently ignited national debates about bullying, with some viewers arguing that it promotes such behavior following a heated confrontation that took place between Roman and Nichols during episode 13" (Nsenduluka). The article also claims efforts were being made at revising *Basketball Wives*. The article states, "Shed Media, which produces the show along with the Vh1 network, addressed criticisms that the show promotes bullying. They insisted that producers are currently implementing the necessary changes to ensure that the show sends a more positive message to its viewers" (Nsenduluka). However, it should be noted that the content of the program for many of the episodes has relied very much upon physical or nonphysical disputes between females, which can reinforce negative stereotypes.

The females on *Basketball Wives*, their actions, the plot lines, and the events all serve to reinforce stereotyping that occasionally condemns but supports racism, sexism, and income-level disparity. The program serves as a cautionary tale about what can happen when a show that had the opportunity to change people's ideas, concepts, and notions about Black women presents very troubling depictions of them. *Basketball Wives* could have avoided engaging in this kind of depiction by emphasizing non-stereotypical representations. It could have been a highly instructive and useful vehicle for promoting equal rights for individuals. Instead, viewers are left with a program that does a disservice and not a service to Black females in America.

As Tia Tyree has pointed out, "Reality television plays a major role in shaping pop culture. Therefore, it is problematic that reality television includes stereotypical African American participants. It continues the longstanding media practice of reinforcing negative and misleading images of African Americans" (409). *Basketball Wives* in many ways functions as a program that had potential to show more diversity among Black women and to present scenes, situations, and events that provide a more complex and nuanced reflection of Black female experiences in America and abroad. The program needs to emphasize the aspects of the women's lives that defy racial, sexual, and economic stereotypes and less time on conflicts, confrontations, and disagreements that reinforce stereotypical ideas. This representation could be achieved by emphasizing caring, compassionate, and supportive relationships between females. The show could have been truly groundbreaking if it had focused more on emphasizing racial equality, advocating for equal rights for women, and offering a critique and analysis of the income level disparity of women in the United States. Instead, the show highlights racial divisiveness, approves physically harming women, and mocks and ridicules poverty.

Although the show can be applauded for attempting to show the lives of Black females associated with the world of professional basketball and their families, ultimately *Basketball Wives* has proven to be a program that represents a step back rather than a step forward in racism, sexism, and income-level disparity. Any advances that the show has made in highlighting or emphasizing the lives of Black females or minority women on television has been undercut by the reliance on stereotypes. The popularity of the show can have damaging consequences upon viewers because these troubling stereotypical representations can influence how other people perceive African American women or women of color in the United States and abroad. The stereotypes can then lead to assumptions that African American women do not deserve racial, gender, and economic equality. Although there seem to be efforts on the show to challenge racism, sexism, and income-level disparity through the depictions of the females on the program and their activities, events, and observations, *Basketball Wives* all too often relies on stereotypical representations of Black females. The only way that the representations of Black females on television will change is if individuals begin making programs that defy, challenge, and subvert the stereotypical representations of Black females.

Basketball Wives certainly has potential or had potential for that change, but the first five seasons of the program seem to illustrate that the revolutionary aspect of the show is absent, all too often subsumed into the characterizations of Black females who do not provide complex representations of the individuals on the show. In the future, one hopes that there will be a stronger awareness of the need for programs featuring Black females, whether "reality television" or other types of television, that rise to the challenge of proving innovative, inspiring, enlightening, and engaging reflections of Black females on television. Through examining, analyzing, and discussing the representations of Black females on television, this goal can possibly and hopefully be achieved.

In the article "Reality TV Trashes Black Women," Allison Samuels laments the stereotypical representations of this show and others: "Take VH1's *Basketball Wives* and *Love & Hip Hop*, which feature the scorned ex-wives and baby mamas of rich NBA stars and rappers. No episode is complete without a bitchy confrontation or a threat to do bodily harm" (Samuels). This assessment by Samuels shows that *Basketball Wives* connects with a pattern of stereotypical depictions for African American females. As an avid watcher of programs such as *Basketball Wives*, this scholar welcomes television programs that can offer a new and different type of narrative of Black females' lives that does not perpetuate racist, sexist, and classist representations. This new narrative will become increasingly important because of the widespread nature of these types of shows nationally.

Works Cited

Abrams, Sil Lai. "Women activists working to change Black stereotypes on reality TV." From *Clutch Magazine. Grio* 4 Mar. 2013. http://www.thegrio.com.

Amber, Jeannine. "Real World." *Essence* Jan. 2013. Academic Search Complete.

"*Basketball Wives* Season 2 Cast Jennifer." VH1. http://www.VH1.com.

"*Basketball Wives* Season 3 Cast Meeka Claxton." VH1. http://www.VH1.com.

"*Basketball Wives* Season 3 Cast Royce Reed." VH1. http://www.VH1.com.

"*Basketball Wives* Season 3 Cast Suzie Ketcham." VH1. http://www.VH1.com.

"*Basketball Wives* Season 3 Cast Tami Roman." VH1. http://www.VH1.com.

"*Basketball Wives* Season 4 Cast Evelyn Lozada." VH1. http://www.VH1.com.

"*Basketball Wives* Season 4 Cast Kenya Bell." VH1. http://www.VH1.com.

"*Basketball Wives* Season 4 Cast Kesha Nichols." VH1. http://www.VH1.com.

"*Basketball Wives* Season 5 Cast Bios." VH1. http://www.VH1.com.

Black, Elizabeth. "'Hell Has Frozen Over': Meeka Claxton and Tami Roman Make Amends and Hug It Out." VH1 10 Sept. 2013. http://www.VH1.com.

Collins, Patricia Hill. *Black Feminist Thought: Knowledge, Consciousness, and the Politics of Empowerment.* New York: Routledge, 1991.

"EthniCelebs Celebrity Ethnicity Gloria Govan." *EthniCelebs-Celebrity Ethnicity/What Nationality Background Ancestry Race.* http://www.EthniCelebs.com.

Jones, Charisse, and Kumea Shorter-Gooden. *Shifting: The Double Lives of Black Women in America.* New York: HarperCollins, 2003.

Manuel-Logan, Ruth. "Tami Roman Finally Settles 9-Year Child Support Lawsuit." *NEWS-ONE for Black America* 4 Sept. 2012. http://www.newsone.com.

Moore, Michael Langston. "Does *Basketball Wives* Really Perpetuate Black Female Stereotypes?" *Morton Report* 9 Aug. 2011. http://www.themortonreport.com.

Nsenduluka, Benge. "'Basketball Wives' Fired, Jennifer, Royce, and Kesha Axed for More 'Balanced' Show." *Christian Post* 14 June 2012. http://www.christianpost.com.

Russell, Stacey. "Does *Basketball Wives* Perpetuate the Stereotype of Women as Gold Diggers?" *Miami New Times* blogs. 8 July 2011. http://www.blogs.miaminewtimes.com.

Samuels, Allison. "Reality TV Trashes Black Women." *Newsweek* 9 May 2011. Academic Search Complete.

Starr, Terrell Jermaine. "Are Blacks to Blame for Negative Portrayals of African Americans on Reality TV?" *NEWSONE for Black America* Jan. 2013. http://www.newsone.com.11.

Tyree, Tia. "African American Stereotypes in Reality Television." *Howard Journal of Communications* 22 (2011): 394–413. Academic Search Complete.

9

Exploiting and Capitalizing on Unique Black Femininity

• •

An Entrepreneurial Perspective

TERRY A. NELSON

Given the overwhelming popularity of reality TV, it is a natural and effective platform through which a savvy businesswoman may build her personal brand recognition that can be parlayed into successful business ventures. Established celebrities taking advantage of entrepreneurial opportunities is nothing new. However, successfully converting what Sue Collins labels the "fifteen minutes of fame" or "dispensable celebrity" into a sustainable TV personality is a phenomenon that has not stimulated the interest of too many scholars. Foreseeably, a question is "Are these savvy business women capitalizing and exploiting their fifteen minutes of fame to develop new or to enhance current entrepreneurial ventures?"

Particularly disconcerting is the popularity of the African American women–casted reality shows, which is fueled by the glamorization and

ghettoization of Black womanhood (Boylorn). The shows have been criticized for their negative portrayal of Black women (Wilson) with concern
that the mainstream culture will continue to generalize negative stereotypical behaviors across all Black women. Safiya Reid suggests the high content
of verbal and physical aggression in these shows sends a signal that this is
normal behavior. Moreover, considering that individuals tend to use TV as
a proxy for what they know and perceive as the reality of the world (Shanahan and Morgan; Reid), it is not far-fetched that the behavior and actions
in reality shows may augment established stereotypes.

Interestingly, research (Brown; Tomlinson-Burney) has explored the
impact of these negative prototypes on viewers and what motivates them
to watch reality TV, but little if any research has delved into why affluent
African American women would be motivated to curse, fight, roll their
eyes and necks, and point and pop their fingers on national TV. Given
that viewers tend to make social judgments about reality TV personalities
based on their on screen behavior (Reid), it is surprising and contradictory
that the women on *The Real Housewives of Atlanta (RHOA)*, *Basketball
Wives*, *Hollywood Exes*, and *Married to Medicine* are, on average, educated,
worldly, professional, established, successful businesswomen. This schema
is arguably not what one would expect given the disgraceful and outrageous antics the women exhibit on the shows.

Through the use of a theoretical lens, it can be argued that a link exists
between African American women's outrageous behavior on TV reality
shows and entrepreneurial opportunities. Social identity and optimal
distinctiveness theory are utilized to examine their individual motivations to socially identify with a group of women who collectively assume
the persona of a stereotypical Black woman and to understand how some
create unique individual personas involving outrageous behavior that
differentiates them from the rest, and consequently, builds their worth
and currency with the viewers and show producers. To conceptualize and
comprehend the linkage between outrageous behavior and entrepreneurship, I utilize resource-based view (RBV) theory to propose that these
women's individual and unique behaviors are resources that can garner
them additional potential resources such as capital and brand recognition that are needed to overcome the dual disadvantage of gender and
race that hinders the average African American woman in entrepreneurial ventures (Wood, Davidson, and Fielden). In essence, it will take the

unique combination of their questionable talent, on-screen personality, and off-screen business acumen to effectively transfer this culmination into successful entrepreneurial ventures.

This chapter accordingly organizes theory on social identity, unique distinctiveness, and resource-based view. The first exploration is of the behavior of African American women on reality TV as a group using social identity theory. This analysis serves as the foundation for the exploration at an individual level the unique behavior of cast members. Next, the connection between intangible individual resources and tangible external resources such as social and monetary capital necessary for entrepreneurial ventures is discussed. In essence, optimal distinctiveness and resource-based view theories are linked, hence utilizing theories from both the micro- and macro-facets of management. The conclusion addresses theoretical suggestions for future research.

Conceptual Framework: Social Identity Theory

Although voyeurism, entertainment, mood changer, pastime, status, and vengeance have been researched (Ebersole and Woods; Reid) as motivators as to why people watch "fly on the wall" reality TV shows, little if any scholarly research has delved into why ordinary people are eager to let audiences invade their private world. More specifically, why African American women would purposely demean themselves before millions of TV viewers is mentally titillating for researchers but dispiriting when one considers the detrimental effects it has on the societal status and progress of African American women. To explore this paradox, I draw conceptually from social identity theory (SIT). H. Tajfel (1974) defines social identity as an individual's self-concept, which is sourced from his or her membership in a social group coupled with the emotional significance attached to that membership. Simply put, the premise of the theory is that people opt to be a member of a group that reflects their beliefs and attributes, both physical and nonphysical, with similarity in how they relate to and differ from people outside their clique. According to Marilynn Brewer (1991), social identities are chosen by individuals and should not be considered as a membership in a group or social category, which may be voluntary or imposed. This leads one to the question of why African American women would behave in preposterous behavior on TV for the sake of group distinction knowing their behavior substantiates the stereotypical behavior of African American women as a whole.

Executive producers of reality TV shows attempt to predetermine the social identity of these women and their social cliques; however, there is still the matter of the natural evolution of malicious and vindictive chemistry that the producers hope occurs between the cast members. Andy Cohen, executive producer of Bravo's *Real Housewives* (*RH*) franchise, purposely looks for women who are wealthy, have a strong point of view, and are preferably bourgeois housewives or professional women. Augmenting this criteria with serious problems such as divorce, problematic personal and family relationships, bankruptcy, adultery, living beyond one's means, and unrestrained "ghetto fabulousity," one has a recipe for a high-drama show that has made *The Real Housewives of Atlanta* a cash cow for Bravo.

The aforementioned criteria form the foundation of the social identity of the manufactured women's social circle making this phenomenon appropriate for the SIT framework. The purpose of SIT is to comprehend and explicate why individuals desire to adopt and behave in terms of the social identity of a specific group. SIT stems from the social categorization process through which people psychologically place individuals into groups. Categorizing people into groups is a natural process that humans activate to help them understand and predict behavior. When individuals are designated to certain groups, it is assumed they share certain attributes that distinguish them from others (Tajfel 1978).

It has been postulated that the interdependent relationships that are the core of social identity groups are characterized by a mutual concern for the interests and outcomes for the group (Baumeister and Leary; Markus and Kitayama); therefore, members are motivated to benefit each other. The benefit in this case for these types of reality TV shows is members sustaining the popularity of the show for their own individual gains, such as attention, stardom, and money. Collectively maintaining and enhancing the group's welfare benefits all. Moreover, popularity equates to a hefty ad revenue stream for Bravo. It is estimated that between the years 2010 and 2012, Bravo's income from ads ranged from $35.6 million to $162 million for the *RH* franchise. This profit says a lot for the *RH*'s brand, yet Bravo has recently realized that it takes more than a brand for a show to be a success. Taking the *RH* template to different cities does not always translate to success. After one season, the *Real Housewives of DC* was canceled because of the cast's failed chemistry. The women had virtually committed an act of mutiny when all cast members made a pact not to return if cast member Michaele Salahi was allowed to return for another season. In addition, one cast member tweeted after cancellation: "We are too dignified! LOL. its not a bad thing! XO L" (Reality Tea 2011), seeming to imply there was not enough drama to keep the show afloat. *The Real Housewives of Miami* is also exhibiting symptoms of viewers' boredom. According to Nielsen, the average number of viewers has steadily declined since its debut three seasons ago. In season 1, the show averaged 1.16 million viewers; in season 2, 1.06 million; and in season 3, 1.02 million. Hence, the culmination of boring content and low drama and antics can lead to the cancellation of a show, or in some cases, to the release of cast members who do not or no longer embody the nature of the show.

The manufactured social identity of these women groups is key to a show's success. It is challenging for producers to keep the identity intact when so many dynamics occur on and off screen with cast members. Cast members who exhibit aggressive behavior such as bullying and minor violence in conjunction with the ability to instigate heated confrontations and subject others to emotional and psychological abuse are what sells the show and cast members to the audience. Accordingly, producers seek women who can flourish in this type of environment. Apparently, once an individual falls outside the "mean girls' inner circle," she is scrutinized and subject to release. Shaunie O'Neal, executive producer of *Basketball Wives*, released more than half of her cast after season 4. *Sister2Sister* interviewed Shaunie about the releases, and she stated, "Some of the exits were necessary, just because it wasn't clicking anymore. It's hard to continue filming with people that you just have nothing else to talk about or nothing in common with, or that relationship has withered away" (Scott). Likewise, producers of *Basketball Wives: LA* restructured their cast and released six cast members after only two seasons. In this case, four of the released cast members limited camera access to their private lives, therefore limiting content of the show. A main tenet of social identity is that people should identify with their chosen group. Although the four members chose to be participants in the show, their actions indicated they were not willing to assimilate to the social identity as predetermined by the producers.

Using social identity theory to explain the dysfunctional unity of African American women on docu-dramas facilitates the comprehension of their scandalous behavior as an elite group. This theory does not fully explain why particular members of these groups further differentiate themselves from other group members. Whether it is a natural evolution of the group's dynamics or strategic tactics by members, particular members magnify their behavioral antics over and beyond other group members to position themselves as the audience favorite. In essence, the show creates a psychological competitive arena in which cast members vie to be the most prolific and consequently reap the fame and financial benefits that accompanies the status.

In the next section, I theoretically explore the process involved with the African American women cast members' individual shocking and outrageous behaviors employed to distinguish themselves from their counterparts, subsequently increasing their entrepreneurial currency. The premise of RBV theory suggests that these women's individual-specific resources can gain them access to additional resources such as social and monetary capital that are key for successfully launching entrepreneurial ventures.

Resource-Based View Theory

Resource-based view theory maintains that a firm's performance is explained by the differences in firm resources rather than the structure of the industry (Runyan, Huddleston, and Swinney; Wenerfelt); however, in this chapter, it is the individual level of analysis that is the focus. RBV theory generally takes a macro- rather than a micro-approach, but according to Sharon Alvarez and Lowell Busenitz, RBV theorists recognized entrepreneurship as part of the resource-based framework (Connor; Rumelt) more than twenty-five years ago. Additionally, Alvarez and Busenitz contend that both entrepreneurship and RBV employ "resource" as a unit of analysis and resources may manifest in different ways, suggesting RBV can be explored at the level of the individual. Therefore, a reality TV cast member's success may be better explained by her unique individual-specific resources than by the cast member's group's social identity.

Resource heterogeneity is one of the main tenets of RBV, and the assumption is that dissimilarity of resources is one of several components necessary for competitive and sustainable advantages (Alvarez and Busenitz). Resource heterogeneity is also considered a fundamental condition of entrepreneurship (Alvarez and Busenitz; Kirzner). From an entrepreneurial perspective, opportunities may exist when certain individuals are aware of the value of particular resources and elect to exploit and capitalize on the opportunities before others do or better than others would do. Alvarez and Busenitz postulate that the ability to recognize opportunities and opportunity-seeking behavior are resources, which they refer to as "entrepreneurial recognition." Coupling these resources with the aptitude to assemble resources is considered another resource. This theorization is an integral part of the theoretical conceptualization and serves as antecedents to individual-specific behavior.

Entrepreneurship is a combination of discovering, evaluating, and exploiting opportunities, which Alvarez and Busenitz consider an exceptional resource, to create goods and services valued by individuals (Choi and Shepherd; Shane and Venkataraman). In essence, an individual must have an aptitude to make a discovery and to judiciously evaluate the opportunity before assembling the resources necessary to exploit the opportunity. Moreover, the entrepreneur must assemble and systematically establish resources to ensure that he or she extricates the value of the opportunity (Wiklund and Shepherd). Successful TV reality stars who have a recognition and capitalization entrepreneurial disposition use these unique resources to cultivate external resources such as social and monetary capital to launch new endeavors or to enhance current entrepreneurial endeavors.

For cast members to fully reap their potential entrepreneurial opportunities they must possess unique and distinct qualities that their competitors (fellow cast members) do not have, and they must have an aptitude to exploit, cultivate, and sustain these qualities. Intangible individual-specific resources such as having a "ghetto fabulous" attitude and "playing the game" are resources that a cast member must recognize as key for success on Black reality TV shows. Linking optimal distinctiveness and resource-based theories supports the argument that the shocking and outrageous behaviors that Black women employ on reality TV to distinguish themselves from their counterparts, and subsequently increases their stardom and entrepreneurial currency.

Optimal Distinctiveness Theory

The central tenet of RBV is that a competitive advantage can be gained and sustained over one's competitors when the resources are considered valuable, rare, inimitable and nonsubstitutable (Barney). Some individual-specific resources are traits or personality in nature, suggesting that not everyone is gifted with these resources. For example, "playing the game," which is operationalized in more detail later in this section, is more skill based in nature than easily and freely learned. In other words, a cast member must have the desire and wherewithal to learn the game; hence a resource and the ability to transform the resource into other resources for a competitive advantage over her fellow cast members.

As noted earlier, the more colorful and outrageous the behavior on the shows, the more the shows' popularity seems to increase. Subsequently, the more shameful, tasteless, and ghetto fabulous an individual can behave in her clique, the more her star currency increases. Therefore, what social process comes into play that addresses this distinct behavior within a social identity group? Optimal distinctiveness theory (ODT) helps to examine the motivation behind these women's stereotypical antics as they strive to balance a need to socially identify with their "elite" group with the need to develop and maintain an individual distinctiveness.

Optimal distinctiveness theory suggests that people are motivated to attach and to identify with social groups, but people seek to manifest their individual uniqueness within the group. ODT, as paradoxically postulated, suggests "social identity derives from a fundamental tension between human needs for validation and similarity to others (on the one hand) and a countervailing need for uniqueness and individuation (on the other hand)" (Brewer 477). People seek to balance the two diametrically opposing dispositions. Optimal distinctiveness, in this case, occurs when a member identifies with categories that give her a sense of inclusiveness and occurs when an individual establishes equilibrium between her need to be different and her need for assimilation into the group. Consequently, from these two contrasting motives is a social identification that satisfies both needs simultaneously (Brewer). This dual nature of human sociality seems to align with the behavior depicted on screen by African American women on reality TV. What is intriguing about this phenomenon is that the balance between similarity and uniqueness will vary among the members of a group and may facilitate viewers' understanding as to why some women behave more outrageously and outlandishly than other members in their group. This argument suggests that an individual's degree of optimal distinctiveness will also vary.

An important component of ODT is uniqueness. People have a tendency to compare themselves to others in their social groups, and the degree of interpersonal similarity that one perceives relative to other group members is central to uniqueness theory (Brewer). A main tenet of uniqueness theory is that individuals will change their behavior or attitudes when they feel these attributes make them too similar to other people in their group (Brewer; Weir). In essence, people derive satisfaction and enjoyment from expressing attitudes, beliefs, and behaviors reflective of their personal values and their self-concepts (Brewer; Katz) that make them unique. From this perspective, this helps individuals to *establish* their self-identities, and it also can contribute to rewards such as gaining social recognition and/or monetary rewards. Moreover, H. L. Fromkin's study revealed that individuals will resort to unusual activities or outrageous behavior if they feel they are too similar to other people. Indeed, the extent or magnitude of one's self-perceived appraisal of similarity will drive the magnitude of the emotional and behavioral outcomes to differentiate one's commonality with a group. According to Brewer's postulation of uniqueness theorization, when a person perceives highly similar conditions, he or she may look for opportunities to redefine himself or herself from others. This desire may be even more compelling when being unique equates to fame and money. Two individual-specific resources—ghetto fabulous and playing the game—have emerged and correlate to African American women reality stars' success.

Individual-Specific Resources

The most prominent attribute that appears essential for high-profile Black reality TV cast members is ghetto fabulous. Robin Boylorn argues that "the public can't seem to get enough of the glamorized and ghettoization of Black womanhood" (424). Yet, the more flamboyant and outrageous the behavior, the more it whets the public's craving and builds the show's market share, and consequently, builds the women's personal marketability and star currency. Before proceeding, defining the term "ghetto fabulous" may be helpful.

Where and how the term "ghetto fabulous" was coined is somewhat of a mystery. The assumption is the term stems from the definition of *ghetto*, which is defined by *Merriam Webster's Dictionary* as "a part of a city in which members of a particular group or race live usually in poor conditions." Interestingly, *Webster* indicates the term has an Italian origin and was used to indicate where Jews were forced to live around the 1600s. In the twenty-first century, *ghetto* references African Americans who hail from poor neighborhoods and who possess behaviors associated with those neighborhoods. Robin Givhan suggests ghetto fabulous is the merging of ethnic eccentricities with runway chic. In other words, a person is considered ghetto fabulous when "inner-city attitude mixes with Milanese glamour, i.e., Chanel meets Kangol" and the clothing is accompanied with "I'm getting paid" and "Don't mess with me" attitudes. One of *Cassell's Dictionary of Slang* (Green) definitions for *ghetto* is "tough, aggressive, confrontational" (592). Hence, concatenating *ghetto* with the word *fabulous* refers to a certain look and aggressive attitude that some African Americans aspire to, which depending on who one asks can be considered demeaning or enviable. This ghetto fabulous attitude also encompasses a mind-set of living beyond one's means that enables the individual to project a façade of "glamour accompanied by exoticism" (Givhan).

Ghetto fabulous abounds on *RHOA*. The women of *RHOA* frequently broadcast their purchases of couture on the show, which creates a "keeping up with the Joneses" mentality. Take, for example, the episode when Porsha Williams-Stewart purchased a pair of $3,500 designer pumps when she was receiving only $5,000 a month in alimony from her ex-husband Kordell Stewart, a retired NFL player. Other instances are Sheree's purchases of designer dresses and handbags for thousands of dollars while her children slept on inflatable mattresses. Lisa Wu, an original cast member of *RHOA*, purchased a $2.9 million home in Atlanta with her husband at the time, NFL player Edgerton "Ed" Hartwell, in 2007, only months before joining the show in 2008, only to lose the house to foreclosure in 2009 for defaulting on the bank loan.

Ghetto fabulous without aggression is worthless currency on *RHOA*. Possessing an aggressive, confrontational demeanor separates the minor from the major players on *RHOA*. L. Berkowitz (3) refers to aggressive behavior as "any form of behavior that is intended to injure someone physically or psychologically." As newcomers enter the revolving door of the *RHOA*, they are quickly baptized into the group with a psychological confrontation from NeNe. In season 2, NeNe was in the face of newcomer Kandi for no apparent reason, but this was an opportunity to exploit her ghetto fabulous resource and consequently to build her personal brand. Veteran cast members of the show are not insulated from NeNe's aggression and are frequently involved in cat fights with NeNe and are recipients of her backstabbing antics. During a season 1 episode featuring Sheree's independence party, NeNe became loud and offensive bringing much attention to herself, yet steadily building her stardom currency.

Evidently, a ghetto fabulous attitude can go too far. Tami Roman, the ex-wife of retired NBA player Kenny Anderson, has been a cast member of *Basketball Wives* (*BW*) since season 2. Her on-screen physical and verbal altercations are renowned on the show. During one scene Roman aggressively confronts *BW* costar Kesha Nichols, ex-fiancée of Utah Jazz player Richard Jefferson, resulting in Kesha weeping uncontrollably. Fans of the show went quickly to the Internet and created and signed petitions to have Roman removed from the show. Roman did apologize for the encounter, but fans of the show are not a very forgiving bunch. Obviously, the degree of ghetto fabulous that one releases on another cast member is a skill that is learned. Evidently, the audience has compassion and empathy for victims of aggressive confrontations.

People may behave aggressively because they believe the consequences of aggression justifies their actions (Eagly and Steffen). In this case, which may have been obvious to NeNe early on in the first season, the consequences were opportunities to gain additional resources that she could later transform into wealth and stardom. In season 1, NeNe became the series's selling point as "the least snooty, and the funniest and loudest of the five" (Martin). Hence, a cast member's recognition of her magnified ghetto fabulous as a resource is, according to Alvarez and Busenitz, a cognitive ability to frame situations in an opportunistic manner that can be used to organize additional resources that can lead to entrepreneurial opportunities (758).

RBV theory suggests it is a company's ability to bundle unique resources that differentiates it from its competitors, giving the company a competitive advantage. Therefore, when ghetto fabulous is bundled with "playing the game," from a resource-based perspective, this unique bundle of resources can provide cast members with a potential competitive advantage.

Although reality TV shows are espoused as factual, they are contrived to achieve the wow and shock factor that keeps audiences coming back for more. Indeed, reality TV shows are just as contrived as nonreality TV shows (Coyne, Robinson, and Nelson), especially the tactics producers use to evoke certain behavior. According to Deery, producers feed cast members lines to provoke particular behaviors, instigate emotions on and off camera, and in some cases, help to turn cast members against each other. As part of the "game," the producers scheme to evoke certain behavior from cast members, but the game functions better when it is bilateral. In other words, cast members who are apt students of the game quickly jump on board, eagerly bringing additional and intriguing content to the show. Contributing interesting and intriguing contrived situations to the show's storyline increases the cast members' popularity and longevity on the show. Take for example, NeNe's willingness to allow the cameras to showcase her son's brush with the law. The more fanfare and commotion one can bring to oneself and the show, the more adept one is at playing the game. Another example of an ingenious move came from Phaedra Parks when the announcement of her joining *RHOA* was accompanied by revealing her fiancé, Apollo Nida, as an ex-convict. Therefore, even before Parks made her first appearance on the show, she and the producers had creatively stimulated the interest of the fans, hence, wisely playing the game. Indeed, adept players of the game contribute to the show's plot by helping to create personal events to self-promote on their shows.

As a result of some astute group members playing the game and vying for uniqueness, key roles emerge. The most significant and substantial role to surface is the one of the Queen Bee. Queen Bee syndrome is a theory developed by G. C. Staines, C. Tavris, and T. E. Jayaratne that contends that women who obtain success in male-dominated industries are more likely to endorse and facilitate the activation of gender stereotypes. In addition, they see other women in their group as competitors and respond negatively toward them. The contemporary definition of "queen bee" is used by females in reference to the role as the main leader of a group of women. The designation of Queen Bee may be self-bestowed or is a role a woman may strategically and competitively obtain. Queen Bee defined in the realm of reality TV is usually in reference to the woman with the most inflated ego, outrageous, "ghettofied" behavior and the most skillful player of the game. In addition, she is adept at instigating and maintaining emotional chaos between other members and herself. Combine instigator with a gigantic ego, dominant personality, arrogance, and loud and colorful behavior, and a Queen Bee emerges. On *RHOA*, NeNe Leakes had ascended to Queen Bee before the end of the first season. NeNe's superb skill at instigating contention between other cast mates and between herself and others has propelled her to the sovereign level. NeNe strategically kept her relationships with Kim Zolciak and Sheree Whitfield unpredictably hot and cold, milking it for what it was worth to the *RHOA*'s audience. For example, NeNe arranged a casual get-together of the women only a few days after Sheree yanked off Kim's wig, barely giving the women's anger time to subside. In a heated yelling match between NeNe and Sheree, NeNe exclaimed she is "very rich, bitch" attempting to put Sheree firmly in her place as a worker bee. In season 2, Queen NeNe quickly created a confrontation with Kandi before Kandi even had an opportunity to acclimate to the group; hence demonstrating her position as Queen Bee and using the opportunity to continue to build her personal brand. Being the opportunistic person that she is, NeNe does not restrict her antics just to the women of the *RHOA*. In season 3, tensions develop between NeNe and Cynthia Bailey's husband, Peter Thomas, after a heated verbal discussion on the phone.

The path to the position of Queen Bee is not an easy one. Jackie Christie, a cast member on *Basketball Wives: LA* and wife of retired NBA player Doug Christie, had been suspected of masterminding the tension among the cast of women. She was confronted by Draya Michele, a model with a history of dating players, who questioned Jackie's attempt to gain the position of Queen Bee. Draya stated to Jackie during a reunion interview, "You thought that you were going to puppeteer us and have us all fighting, and you were just going to stand and be glorious, the queen bee. That ain't this show, this L.A. The underdog rose to the top on this show" ("'Basketball Wives LA'"). In the end, the other cast members ostracized Jackie. On *Married to Medicine*, Mariah Huq has reached the stature of Queen Bee, and she arrogantly states who is worthy of her friendships: "I'm kinda like Drake," shared Huq. "I don't really do new friends. I do new associates until I got to know them. You have to earn your rights to be Miss Huq's friend. I take friendship very, very seriously" (Scott). Considering Huq is the executive producer and creator of the show, she, like Shaunie O'Neal, executive producer and creator of *Basketball Wives*, is automatically established as the Queen Bee, but that does not necessarily mean the role is not without its challenges. Having the dual roles of executive producer and Queen Bee entails making difficult decisions for the success of the show. In reference to *Married to Medicine* season 2, Mariah stated, "Change is a comin'. Some things just are old and expired and need to go" (Reality Tea).

Obtaining, nurturing, and sustaining the role of Queen Bee is not without cost. NeNe Leakes has stated, "Listen, at the end of the day, I won't let an argument stop me from making money. So I'll get everyone together if that's what it takes" (Martin). Her statement suggests that she will go over and beyond in her behavior to maintain her optimal distinctiveness level. What is revealing here is that an individual's expression of attitudes correlates to her personal values (Katz), which suggests NeNe's expressed personal values are in conflict with her self-proclaimed persona. In an interview with *Essence* magazine, NeNe refuted accusations that she is a mean-spirited, publicity-hungry reality star and suggested the editing of the show makes her appear as an evil person. Yet, she states it is all about the money and she will do what it takes to make money.

As for the rest of the cast, worker bees fight among themselves and with the Queen Bee competing for the next hierarchical position below their monarch. Differentiation through uniqueness becomes more challenging at this level because worker bees tend to be overshadowed by the antics of the Queen Bee. Considering Queen Bees tend to use their power of position to control the nature of their relationships with their underlings, it is difficult for other cast members to rely on their relationship with the queen as a unique attribute. Uniqueness appears to be moderated by situational factors (Brewer); therefore, it is reasonable to expect different variations of unique motivation across a group of people.

The core appeal of reality TV is the dynamics of the interpersonal relationships. The more tumultuous and unpredictable a member's behavior, the more she uniquely contribute to the show's popularity. As with any group formation, people naturally emerge in different roles with some roles having a longer celebrity shelf life than others. For example, a member who takes a role as a back seat harmonizer, one who attempts to reconcile others or mediate confrontation, is released quickly. The *RHOA*'s DeShawn Snow wanted everyone to get along and was cut because allegedly the producers felt she was "too human for a circus show" ("Real Housewives"). In season 1, Snow attempts to reconcile the differences between the women by inviting them to her house for a sunset BBQ. Even during the season 1 Reunion Show, she sat passively listening to others, not offering too much in drama. Incidentally, she did differentiate herself but not in alignment with the show's core appeal, which is bullying, violence, emotional abuse, and degrading behavior. Another *RHOA* cast member who failed to accurately differentiate herself was Lisa Wu-Hartwell. Supposedly, she left the show on her own accord, citing she did not want to deal with drama, hence taking a more passive role. Recently, according to a Bravo insider, Porsha Williams was released from *RHOA* because "she's a mix of boring and annoying, [and] neither is good for TV" (Princ).

Passive and docile demeanors and boring and annoying personal lives are not rewarded in shows such as these that strive for and survive off the explosive and volatile personalities that are typified by the African American women on these shows. According to Reality Steve, perception is "you have to be confrontational to be memorable; if you're a follower, you're not memorable" (Presno). Becoming masterful at bundling "the game" and ghetto fabulous actions sustains a cast member's shelf life on a reality TV show and it opens up avenues for other resources needed to launch entrepreneurial opportunities.

The success of an entrepreneurial venture is not only contingent on intangible individual-specific resources but also on resources that give entrepreneurs access to professional networks and funding. Women entrepreneurs are faced with many barriers that can prevent them from launching a business. Social and monetary capital are two of the most common barriers (Wood et al.). Social capital is the benefit an individual gains from her personal and professional networks, and it is a critical resource that influences the success and profitability of an entrepreneurial venture (McGrath, Wadhwa, and Mitchell). Essentially, social capital is a person's interpersonal relationships with individuals and organizations and the interconnections between them. This network of interpersonal and interorganizational connections provide entrepreneurs with access to a variety of resources that are critical for positive entrepreneurial outcomes (Wiklund and Shepherd). Resources consist of information, advice, and social support. In addition, these networks also create opportunities for exchanging goods and services that may not be governed through contracts and, consequently, opens up avenues to more opportunities (Uzzi). Forming, establishing, and maintaining a well-formed and connected social capital network is challenging for most women. Not surprisingly, women's social network activity is considerably less than men thus hindering women's opportunity to develop influential relationships that can be critical to their entrepreneurial success (Wood et al.).

Social capital and financial capital seems to go hand in hand. Research has determined that for women, social capital is the major disconnect between women entrepreneurs and venture capitalists (Brush et al.). S. Marlow and D. Patton contend that a lack of social and financial capital has a negative relationship on women's ability to generate credit and procure funding from venture capitalists. African American women have a double-prong disadvantage because of their ethnicity and gender. A study conducted by K. Inman and L. M. Grant determined that ethnic minority women had a greater challenge of obtaining social and financial capital than their Caucasian female counterparts.

Successful women reality stars have a built-in advantage for forming and establishing social capital and consequently obtaining financial capital. Cast members who build their stardom currency through the artful bundling of their individual-specific resources benefit from huge media exposure, which equates to a wide following of fans. Many individuals and companies realize the potential commercialization of TV reality stars who have a large loyal fan base and therefore have not hesitated to capitalize on the window of opportunity of the fifteen minutes of fame. Although the formation and establishment of social capital may be easier for female reality TV stars, the instability of their social capital networks are just as fragile or more fragile as those of any female entrepreneur. Former cast members of the *RHOA* averaged only three seasons because many were axed for being boring, annoying, and having declining real-life drama, resulting in low content. All in all, cast members of the *RHOA* have one of the highest longevity averages among the *RH* franchise. As a reality TV celebrity's shelf life expires and starts to wither away, so does her social and financial capital opportunities. Consider Sheree and Lisa Wu, who quickly deteriorated into poverty near the end of their stint on the show. The *RHOA*'s NeNe Leaks and Kandi Burruss and *Basketball Wives: LA*'s Malaysia Pargo, Draya Michele, and Tami Roman are a few of the African American women on reality shows who have expertly exploited their individual-specific resources, which provided them access to social and financial capital to execute their entrepreneurial ventures, giving them a substantial net worth.

An Entrepreneurial Perspective

A RBV theoretical framework explains how some Black female reality TV stars create, shape, and sustain their unique resources accrued during their fifteen minutes of fame as a competitive advantage over less prolific stars. Successful reality TV stars use their unique resources to cultivate additional resources that they will need to launch new endeavors or to enhance current entrepreneurial endeavors. It is helpful to understand the magnitude of the monetary rewards reality TV stars receive for developing and sustaining their unique qualities as a competitive advantage. Although some reality stars are paid minimally, an average of about $5,000 a month, the women of *RHOA* are the beneficiaries of much larger stipends. For example, the prolific NeNe Leakes receives $750,000 to $1,000,000 a season plus bonus (Wolfe). Other cast members who are less prolific receive $300,000 to $450,000 (Wolfe). In comparison to the other *RH* franchise shows, this is a much more lucrative show, reflective of *RHOA*'s appeal to a broader audience. Prolific cast members of other *RH* franchised shows receive $350,000–$650,000 plus bonus, and less captivating cast members receive $55,000 to $400,000 (HuffPost TV), much less than *RHOA*'s members. Salary received from the show is just a nugget of the gold mine that African American women TV reality stars can receive for their short-term fame. Cast members have used their brief fame to promote current and new entrepreneurial ventures. The stars who are fortunate enough to exploit their overnight fame can expand their current brand or build new brands, reaping massive returns on the public invasion into their personal lives.

Well-known white reality TV stars such as Kim Kardashian of *Keeping Up with the Kardashians*, Jillian Michaels of *The Biggest Loser*, and Lauren Conrad of *Laguna Beach* and *The Hills* are pulling in millions of dollars for ventures in skin care, shoes, perfume, video games, workout DVDs, diet pills, clothing, self-help books and autobiographies—the list is almost endless. These women have captured their share of these markets, and some have been successful with quickly responding to their immense popularity and exploiting their brief celebrity shelf life to make millions before the inevitable expiration date. African American women of reality shows have also garnered their fair share of these lucrative markets. Shaunie O'Neal, former wife of NBA star Shaquille O'Neal and a former film marketer, is the creator and executive producer of VH1's *Basketball Wives* and *Football Wives* and owns a shoe line with the Chinese Laundry company, putting her worth at about $35 million ("Reality TV"). Kandi Burruss leads the women of the *RHOA* in wealth with a net worth of about $35 million, but she began the show as a financial success due to her successful music career. Season 6 cast members have the following net worth: Kandi Burruss, $35M; Porsha Williams-Stewart, $16M; NeNe Leakes, $4.5M; Phaedra Parks, $2M; Kenya Moore, $1.5M;

and Cynthia Bailey, $50,000 (Wolfe). Indicative of their net worth, Leaks, Burruss, and Parks seem to have the most entrepreneurial spirit of the *RHOA* cohort. They have parlayed their individual-specific resources on the show to build their social and financial capital networks, and subsequently their wealth.

Specifically, Burruss has effectively used her fame on the *RHOA* to launch several successful business ventures. In essence, she has used just about each season to highlight a business from her burgeoning empire. Besides being a member of the Grammy Award–winning 1990s R&B group Xscape and a songwriter, Burruss has built an appreciable amount of her net worth from her entrepreneurial gigs employing the model described in this chapter—using the *RHOA* series as a platform to start new careers or ventures. During Burruss's stint on *RHOA*, she has launched a successful line of sex toys with the fitting name Bedroom Kandi, the clothing boutique TAGS, the webisode series entitled *Kandi Koated Nights*, and a Bravo TV series, *The Kandi Factory*.

Leakes's solid appearance on the show has also provided her with plenty of entrepreneurial options. She was selected to design a shoe bearing her name for the www.ShoeDazzle.com's *Celebrity Shoe Design Program*; has penned a book entitled *Never Make the Same Mistake Twice* with a coauthor; appeared on the TV show *Glee*; played the lead role in the *RHOA* spin-off, *I Dream of NeNe: The Wedding*, documenting her second marriage to her husband, Gregg; starred in the failed NBC show *The New Normal*; and was a featured star on season 18 of *Dancing with the Stars*. In 2012, Leakes announced a clothing line with global brand licensing agency Beanstalk. The line was scheduled to hit stores in July 2014. Beanstalk's president and CEO Michael Stone summed up the social and financial capital potential of this theoretical business model, "While the fame of reality television characters is often short-lived and fleeting, NeNe Leakes has displayed versatility that has enabled her to transition from being a 'Real Housewives' personality to a featured television star on 'Glee.' NeNe's multi-faceted personality and aspirational style will translate well into products that will emotionally connect with her fans" (McDermott). Supposedly, the company was backing NeNe's venture completely because they were enthralled with her colorful personality, and of course, her large and loyal fan base, which Beanstalk was projecting would help to successfully market the line of clothing. Evidently, the concept of this perfect match between Leakes and Beanstalk was short-lived. On July 28, 2014, Leakes launched her clothing line instead with HSN and most of her styles sold out in a day. Although Leakes has not referenced Beanstalk, she stated, "We took meetings with a lot of different people. And HSN actually felt right." Leakes said, "When they walked into the room we totally clicked" (BET Interactive).

Basketball Wives: LA cast member Malaysia Pargo, wife of NBA Charlotte Bobcats' Jannero Pargo, has an adult line of jewelry and recognizes the link between the reality TV show and her entrepreneurial endeavors. She was asked how being on *Basketball Wives: LA* helped her business. Her response: "It helps me a whole lot. It's pretty much a free commercial. I thank VH1 and the *Basketball Wives* series for this opportunity" ("Reality TV"). Malaysia Pargo's net worth is about $3 million (Williams 2014), but the bulk of her wealth is probably related to her husband's career. Another *Basketball Wives: LA* cast member, Draya Michele, has parlayed her popularity on the show into entrepreneurial ventures such as modeling, clothing, and club appearances. Michele launched Mint Swimwear and FineAssGirls (FAG) clothing and lingerie line and has endorsement contracts with Rocawear and Secret Kisses, a cosmetic line. Draya's net worth is only about $400,000 (Williams 2014). Tami Roman, the more prolific cast member on *Basketball Wives: LA*, has an estimated net worth of $3 million (Williams 2013). Prior to *Basketball Wives*, Roman had a sporadic TV career with recurring and guest roles on television series *Sex, Love, and Secrets; JAG; The Drew Carey Show;* and *Sabrina, the Teenaged Witch*. Since appearing on *Basketball Wives: LA*, Roman has developed multiple entrepreneurial businesses consisting of TR Hair Collection, a line of hair for weaving, TR "Love" cosmetics, a line of lip glosses and nail polishes, and the TR jewelry collection with BFoxy.com. In addition to products, Roman snared a six-figure endorsement contract from NV Sprinkles after dropping twenty-five pounds and publicly announcing NV Sprinkles as the reason for her successful weight loss. NV Sprinkles is a powder that one sprinkles on food to supposedly feel full.

Cultivating and nurturing a group's dysfunctional dynamics creates rich drama that has fattened the personal coffers of African American women on reality shows. The more shocking and shameful the behavior, the more a cast member's marketability and stardom currency increases. Indeed, for some, procuring a role on a popular reality show is profitable, and evidently worth embarrassing oneself in front of millions.

Conclusion

In analyzing the relationship between African American women reality TV stars and entrepreneurship, it is evident that the desire to belong to a social group coupled with the desire to be unique have positioned the more prolific cast members with opportunities to start businesses or exploit current ventures. Utilizing resource-based view and optimal distinctiveness theory, a combination of macro- and micro-theories, to explore this concept enriches the theoretical stance of the proposition presented in this chapter. It is postulated that exploitation of negative stereotypical behaviors of African American women is a viable resource that can lead to lucrative entrepreneurial ventures. The essence of this statement suggests an acceptance of African American women demeaning themselves in order to pursue their goal of owning their own business at the risk of amplifying the mainstream culture's perception of Black women.

As noted in this analysis, African American women face unique barriers, such as the combination of their race and gender, that can hamper their efforts at entrepreneurial ventures. However, as also noted here, some African American reality TV stars are strategically utilizing their unique stereotypical behavior as a resource to overcome the typical and untypical obstacles that they face as they strive to obtain the necessary external resources to succeed as an entrepreneur. African American women entrepreneurs may experience discrimination, like white women entrepreneurs, but the magnitude of the discrimination will vary. As such, my postulation here can apply to white women, but gender discrimination will differ for them and will more than likely be less of an issue in their entrepreneurial endeavors because they do not have the added weight of race discrimination.

Future Research

The nature of ethnic minority entrepreneurs has evolved over the years (Wood et al.) with more opportunities beyond a typical mom-and-pop approach. The passage of years has provided more accessibility to mainstream markets. While there is more accessibility, entrance still requires a strategic approach in order for African American women to gain a relevant share of a market. African American women reality TV stars who are successful entrepreneurs have noted a different approach, and individual-specific resources are required for them. I have noted "ghetto fabulous" and "playing the game" as individual-specific resources, and there are possibly other resources that warrant attention. Future research should focus on uncovering other individual-specific resources that may contribute to an African American reality star's entrepreneurial success.

In addition, considering that most of the women of *RHOA* are professional, educated, and current entrepreneurs, it would be interesting to conduct research to determine whether these variables play a role in entrepreneurial success. According to P. Davidsson and B. Honig, educational levels affect entrepreneurial ventures, and a positive relationship exists between educational level and new enterprise start-up rates. The question is, Does this positive relationship exist across all races and ethnicities of women? Also, work experience and, more specifically, prior entrepreneurial experience can be a factor for success. P. J. Haynes suggests that for women, prior experience can increase the probability of attracting relevant and necessary resources. Here again, does this notion transcend racial and ethnicity boundaries? An interesting future study would examine these factors across white and Black reality TV stars. African American women reality TV stars' success merits additional research. Knowledge gained from this research may be applicable beyond the realm of TV.

Works Cited

Alvarez, Sharon A., and Lowell W. Busenitz. "The Entrepreneurship of Resource-Based Theory." *Journal of Management* 27 (2001): 755–775.

Barney, J. B. "Firm Resources and Sustained Competitive Advantage." *Journal of Management* 17 (1991): 99–120.

"'Basketball Wives LA': Jackie Christie Goes Off on Cast Mates." *Huffington Post* 11/29 2011. http://www.huffington•post.com/2011/11/29/basketball-wives-la-jackie-christie_n_1119031.html.

Baumeister, Roy F., and M. R. Leary. "The Need to Belong: Desire for Interpersonal Attachments as a Fundamental Human Motivation." *Psychological Bulletin* 117.3 (1995): 497–529.

Berkowitz, L. *Aggression: Its Causes, Consequences, and Control.* New York: McGraw-Hill, 1993.

Boylorn, Robin A. "As Seen on TV: An Autoethnographic Reflection on Race and Reality Television." *Critical Studies in Media Communication* 25.4 (2008): 413–433.

Brewer, Marilynn B. "Optimal Distinctiveness Theory: Its History and Development." *Handbook of Theories of Social Psychology.* Vol. 2. Ed. Paul A. M. Van Lange, Arie W. Kruglanski, and E. Tory Higgins. Thousand Oaks, CA: Sage, 2012. 81–98.

————. "The Social Self: On Being the Same and Different at the Same Time." *Personality and Social Psychology Bulletin* 17 (1991): 475–482.

Brown, L. S. "Outwit, Outlast, Out-Flirt? The Women of Reality TV." *Featuring Females: Feminist Analyses of Media*. Ed. E. Cole and J. H. Daniel. Washington, DC: American Psychological Association, 2005. 71–84.

Brush, C. G., et al. "The Role of Social Capital and Gender in Linking Financial Suppliers and Entrepreneurial Firms: A Framework for Future Research." *Venture Capital* 4 (2002): 305–323.

Choi, Young Rok, and Dean A. Shepherd. "Entrepreneurs' Decisions to Exploit Opportunities." *Journal of Management* 30.3 (2004): 377–95.

Collins, Sue. "Making the Most Out of 15 Minutes." *Television and New Media* 9.2 (2008): 87–110.

Connor, K. R. "An Historical Comparison of Resource-Based Theory and Five Schools of Thought within Industrial Organization Economics: Do We Have a New Theory of the Firm?" *Journal of Management* 17 (1991): 121–154.

Coyne, Sarah M., Simon L. Robinson, and David A. Nelson. "Does Reality Backbite? Physical, Verbal, and Relational Aggression in Reality Television Programs." *Journal of Broadcasting and Electronic Media* 54.2 (2010): 282–298.

Davidsson, P., and B. Honig. "The Role of Social and Human Capital among Nascent Entrepreneurs." *Journal of Business Venturing* 18.3 (2003): 301–331.

Deery, J. *Consuming Reality: The Commercialization of Factual Entertainment*. New York: Palgrave Macmillan, 2012.

Eagly, Alice H., and Valerie J. Steffen. "Gender and Aggressive Behavior: A Meta-Analytic Review of the Social Psychological Literature." *Psychological Bulletin* 100.3 (1986): 309–330.

Ebersole, S., and R. Woods. "Motivations for Viewing Reality Television: A Uses and Gratifications Analysis." *Southwestern Mass Communication Journal* 23.1 (2007): 23–42.

"For 'Housewives,' Wallflowers Need Not Apply." *New York Times*. 8 Oct. 2010. http://www.nytimes.com/2010/10/10/arts/television/10real.html?pagewanted=all&_r=0.

Fromkin, H. L. "The Effects of Experimentally Aroused Feelings of Indistinctiveness upon Valuation of Scarce and Novel Experiences." *Journal of Personality and Social Psychology* 16 (1970): 521–529.

Givhan, Robin. "Rapper Attitude in Designer Diamonds and Furs: Ghetto Fabulous Goes Global." *New York Times* 9 Oct. 1999. http://www.nytimes.com/1999/10/09/news/09iht-rghetto.t.html.

Green, Jonathon. *Cassell's Dictionary of Slang*. London: Weidenfeld and Nicholson, 2006.

Haynes, P. J. "Differences among Entrepreneurs: 'Are You Experienced?' May Be the Wrong Question." *International Journal of Entrepreneurial Behaviour and Research* 9.3 (2003): 111–123.

HuffPost TV. "How Much Do 'Real Housewives' Get Paid? Nene Leakes Is Top Earner across Franchise." *Huffington Post* 7 May 2013. http://www.huffingtonpost.com/2013/05/06/how-much-do-real-housewives-get-paid_n_3222457.html.

Inman, K., and L. M. Grant. "African American Women and Small Business Start-Up: Backgrounds, Goals, and Strategies Used by African American Women in the Initialization and Operation of Small Businesses." *International Handbook of Women and Small Business Entrepreneurship*. Ed. S. L. Fielden and M. J. Davidson. Cheltenham, UK, and Northampton, MA: Edward Elgar, 2005. 105–119.

Katz, D. "The Functional Approach to the Study of Attitudes." *Public Opinion Quarterly* 24 (1960): 163–204.

Kirzner, I. "Entrepreneurial Discovery and the Competitive Market Process: An Austrian Approach." *Journal of Economic Literature* 35 (1997): 60–85.

Markus, H., and S. Kitayama. "Culture and the Self: Implications for Cognition, Emotion, and Motivation." *Psychological Bulletin* 98 (1991): 224–253.

Marlow, S., and D. Patton. "All Credit to Men? Entrepreneurship, Finance, and Gender." *Entrepreneurship Theory and Practice* 29 (2005): 717–736.

Martin, Denise. "Queen Bee of 'Real Housewives of Atlanta.'" *Los Angeles Times* 22 Oct. 2009. http://articles.latimes.com/2009/oct/22/entertainment/et-nene09.

McDermott, Tyler K. "Nene Leakes to Create Fashion-Forward and Affordable Fashion Line." 2012.

McGrath, Cohoon, J. V. Wadhwa, and L. Mitchell. *The Anatomy of an Entrepreneur: Are Successful Women Entrepreneurs Different from Men?* Kansas City: Kauffman Foundation, 2010.

"Nene Leakes's HSN Clothing Line a Sell-Out Success: The Savvy Reality Star Makes a 17-Piece Collection for Every Woman." *BET Interactive.* 12 March 2014. 2015.

Presno, Caroline. "Reality Star 101: What the Experts Say It Takes to Make It Big." *The Blog* 9 Nov. 2013. http://www.huffingtonpost.com/caroline-presno/reality-star-101-what-the_b _3560661.htm.

Princ, Lisa. "Porsha Stewart May Be Getting Axed from the Real Housewives of Atlanta." *Reality TV* 18 Dec. 2013. http://realitytvmagazine.sheknows.com/2013/12/18/porsha -stewart-may-be-getting-axed-from-the-real-housewives-of-atlanta/.

"Real Housewives: Where Are They Now." Eonline 17 Jan. 2014. http://www.eonline.com/ photos/8288/real-housewives-where-are-they-now.

Reality Tea. "Bravo Confirms Real Housewives of DC Is Canceled, Housewives React." 8 April 2011. http://www.realitytea.com/category/hot-post/page/3/.

———. "Married to Medicine Returns in February; Mariah Huq and Quad Webb-Lunceford No Longer Friends?" 7 Jan. 2014. http://www.realitytea.com/2014/01/07/married-to -medicine-returns-in-february-mariah-huq-and-quad-webb-lunceford-no-longer-friends/

"Reality TV Decoded: 10 Reality Stars Who Earn." *Black Enterprise Wealth for Life.* 27 April 2012. http://www.eonline.com/photos/8288/real-housewives-where-are-they-now.

Reid, Safiya. "The Reality of Televised Jezebels and Sapphires: Blogs and the Negative Stereotypes of African American Women on Reality Television." Master's thesis. College of Arts and Science, Georgia State University, 2013.

Rumelt, R. P. "Towards a Strategic Theory of the Firm." *Competitive Strategic Management.* Ed. R. B. Lamb. Englewood Cliffs, NJ: Prentice Hall, 1984. 556–570.

Runyan, Rodney C., Patricia Huddleston, and Jane Swinney. "Entrepreneurial Orientation and Social Capital as Small Firm Strategies: A Study of Gender Differences from a Resource-Based View." *Entrepreneurship Management* 2 (2006): 455–477.

Scott, Tracy. "Does Shaunie O'Neal Want Jennifer Williams Back on 'BBW'?" *S2SMagazine. com* 1 Aug. 2013. http://s2smagazine.com/2013/08/01/does-shaunie-oneal-want-jennifer -williams-back-on-bbw/.

Shanahan, James, and Michael Morgan. *Television and Its Viewers: Cultivation Theory and Research.* Cambridge: Cambridge UP, 1999.

Shane, S., and S. Venkataraman. "The Promise of Entrepreneurship as a Field of Research." *Academy of Management Review* 25 (2000): 217–226.

Staines, G. C., C. Tavris, and T. E. Jayaratne. "The Queen Bee Syndrome." *The Female Experience.* Ed. C. Tavris. Del Mar, CA: CRM, 1973.

Tajfel, H. "The Achievement of Inter-Group Differentiation." *Differentiation between Social Groups.* Ed. H. Tajfel. London: Academic Press, 1978. 77–100.

——. "Social Identity and Intergroup Behavior." *Social Science Information* 13 (1974): 65–93.

Tomlinson-Burney, Claudine. "African American Women in the Media." Master's thesis. Communication Management Department, Webster University, St. Louis, MO, 2012.

Uzzi, B. "The Sources and Consequences of Embeddedness for the Economic Performance of Organization: The Network Effect." *American Sociological Review* 61 (1996): 674–698.

Weir, H. B. "Deprivation of the Need for Uniqueness and Some Variables Moderating Its Effects." Unpublished doctoral diss. University of Georgia, 1971.

Wenerfelt, B. "A Resource-Based View of the Firm." *Strategic Management Journal* 5 (1984): 171–180.

Wiklund, Johan, and Dean A. Shepherd. "Portfolio Entrepreneurship: Habitual and Novice Founders, New Entry, and Mode of Organizing." *Entrepreneurship Theory and Practice* (2008): 701–725.

Williams, Dale. "How Much Is Draya Michele Worth in 2014?" *Basketball Wives LA.* 9 Feb. 2014. http://labasketballwives.com/draya-michele-net-worth/.

Wilson, M. K. *The Real Housewives of Atlanta: Propagating Black Male Stereotypes While Enforcing White Male Supremacy.* National Council for Black Studies. 2012.

——"Tami Roman Net Worth in 2013." *Celebrity Bios, Wiki, Net Worth in 2014.* 16 Nov.2013. http://www.NetWorth2013.com.

Wolfe, Lahle. "How Much Do Real Housewives of Atlanta Cast Members Get Paid per Episode?" *Women in Business.* About.com 2013. http://womeninbusiness.about.com/od/rhoa/a/How-Much-Do-Real-Housewives-Of-Atlanta-Cast-Members-Get-Paid-Per-Episode.htm.

Wood, Glenice J., Marilyn J. Davidson, and Sandra L. Fielden. *Minorities in Entrepreneurship: An International Review.* Northampton, MA: Edward Elgar, 2012.

10

Reunion Chapter

• •

A Conversation among
Contributors

JERVETTE R. WARD

Nine of the ten contributors to this book were able to present drafts of
their chapters at the 2014 College Language Association (CLA) Conference in New Orleans, Louisiana. We were able to share our research during
two panel sessions, and it seemed fitting to present at CLA because the
original idea for the book sprouted in my mind at the 2013 CLA conference in Lexington, Kentucky. At the New Orleans conference, we were
able to receive feedback from audience members, and we were able to discuss our chapters with each other. In groups of two or three, we gathered
to talk about our research, and several times, we remarked how amazing
it was to be able to see, meet, and converse with the other book contributors. Several of us have contributed to other edited collections, but none
of us had ever had the opportunity to meet as a group to discuss a collection as a whole. It was an interesting dynamic because many of the group
members did not know each other, but everyone seemed to mesh, and we

easily moved into academic and friendly banter. Once we all returned to our respective homes, we wanted to figure out a way to share the uniqueness of the conference experience with readers. All ten of us were able to gather for a late-night recorded conference call. I asked everyone to relax and to imagine that we were all sitting in one of our living rooms sipping wine while talking about reality TV. Welcome to our conversation:

JERVETTE R. WARD: Many of the popular reality shows have reunion episodes at the end of each season where the stars gather to analyze and to reflect on the past season, so it seems fitting at the end of this book on reality TV that we do the same thing as scholars. Technology has provided us with a unique opportunity to meet across several time zones and states, so thank you all for agreeing to participate in our reunion chapter. I thought it would be unique for us to end this project by gathering digitally to further discuss some of what we have written and to briefly address some topics that maybe we did not write about, but that we think might be important to discuss. Each of you has brought such a special angle to this book, so thank you for contributing your chapters, which leads to my first question. Why did you, each of you individually, participate in a book on Black women in reality television?

SHEENA HARRIS: We talk about reality TV so much. When you brought up the idea of connecting reality TV to what we do as scholars, it was stimulating. You bring this discussion to an academic forum, and I think for me that was appealing, fun, and exciting. It was a breath of fresh air to be able to academically write about something that I talk about regularly.

ALISON D. LIGON: Sheena, I loved the fact that you said that you talk about it regularly. I've never publicly articulated my interest or my viewing habits, and I found it very affirming to have not only a safe collegial space but also very meaningful intellectual conversations with others. The conversations were also humorous ones that gave credence to the notion that I wasn't wasting my time and that I couldn't turn the editor and the critic off in my head while viewing these shows about Black women in a reality space. It was okay to merge the two concepts. So, my participation is solely rooted in that kind of spirit.

TERRY A. NELSON: Jervette challenged me when she approached me about it. I thought, "You've got to be kidding!" I'm not really interested in these show. I watch reality shows like *Hell's Kitchen* and *Project Runway*. She challenged me, and it took me out of my comfort zone. I had an opportunity to examine theories that were not in my wheelhouse, so to speak. I got the opportunity to marry micro- and macro-theories with reality TV. I incorporated a couple of theories that I had never considered before in my research, and even though I wasn't able to send in a proposal to the conference that you all attended, I did submit a version of this to a conference that I hope to attend in the future.

CYNTHIA DAVIS: One of the things that I noticed was a real lack of any critical commentary. There was some discussion of the shows in *Essence* and in *People* magazine—in the popular magazines, but there was just sort of dead silence from the academic community and it seemed like that was a real lack.

WARD: I loved your comment from one of our discussions, Cynthia. You said that if we don't write this book, we, as academics, are shutting ourselves off from real-world opportunities to interact with the public where they are. This is an opportunity to meet people where they are.

DAVIS: Like our students.

WARD: Exactly!

LATOYA JEFFERSON-JAMES: I just need to piggyback off what both of you all are saying. I came to the project with a spirit of frustration because I normally dismiss these shows as fluff entertainment. I would get very frustrated with my students when they would ask me questions like, "Who was Isaac Hayes?" But, then I would ask them about *The Real Housewives of Atlanta*, and they would talk for an hour and fifteen minutes. So, they wouldn't know someone as recent as Isaac Hayes or they wouldn't laugh at a reference that I made to a '90s film like *Class Act*, but they knew every single detail of what was going on in *Love & Hip Hop* or *The Real Housewives of New Jersey*. We can no longer afford in the academic community to dismiss this. We can't afford to dismiss it because our students are suffering from historical amnesia from which Americans occasionally suffer.

HARRIS: There is a thin line between fantasy and reality.

JEFFERSON-JAMES: So, that's why I came. I came out of a spirit of frustration. We can't afford to dismiss reality TV, and we have to meet the students where they are.

PRESELFANNIE E. WHITFIELD MCDANIELS: To connect with LaToya's comment on students having historical amnesia, I don't know if it's historical amnesia. I think that they didn't know the history to begin with.

HARRIS: Right!

MCDANIELS: Part of that is not valuing history or the past. They live for now, and they are consuming the negative things in reality TV. I'll give a quick example because I know we have lots to say. I have a friend who is an event planner, and she said that her work is now super-hard. She has people who are coming to her with gold budgets, but they want a platinum event.

(group laughter)

MCDANIELS: The things that they are describing that they want are things that they watch on reality TV. They're watching these wealthy people, and they're consuming these images every day. They want their wedding to look like NeNe's wedding—they want their wedding to look like this and that, but they have five thousand dollars. So, she's like, "I'm gonna have to come up with a brochure." She said, "I'm gonna give you the gold plan, the silver plan, and the copper plan." Reality TV is affecting everything that everybody does.

(group laughter)

DAVIS: It's not really reality TV; it's really becoming unreality TV in a different way.

SHARON LYNETTE JONES: Well, I have to confess that one of the things that drew me to this project is the fact that I am obsessed with reality TV shows.

HARRIS: Me too!

JONES: I found myself watching a lot of them, and this project gave me an opportunity to use a lot of the critical theories that I had in the past applied to movies or to magazine images. I was able to analyze representations of race, class, and gender in the same way as magazines or motion pictures.

DETRIS HONORA ADELABU: Since my background is in psychology and human development, for me, it was really about focusing on families and children. And, often when we talk about the shows, we talk about them in terms of at least thinking about the impact on African Americans in general, and I really wanted to focus on what does this mean for the African American family, what does this mean for African American children? Also, I wanted to connect to the historical and political aspects of what television has meant to or what television has done to the image of children and families.

MONICA FLIPPIN WYNN: One of the reasons I wanted to get involved is that television is our window of the world. We need to be able to figure out why people are so drawn to this new genre, but also to contribute research so people can understand that there is a big difference between *Love & Hip Hop: Atlanta* and their actual lives. So, I thought we would be able to have a chance to do that by getting everybody together, doing some research and trying to figure this thing out.

WARD: I would say yes to every single one of those things—that's what I was shooting for with this project. When I first started approaching publishers about this idea, there was one publisher who said, "Oh, we really like this idea, but would you do a single-author monograph for this?" I immediately thought "That defeats the purpose of this project!" Maybe I will consider it in the future, but one of the things that I loved about this plan was that we are all coming at this topic from different disciplines, different angles, and we bring these unique thoughts and ideas. I think it's manifested in this conversation right now where we have ten different individuals able to approach this one topic from different disciplines and not always agree. Some of us were like, "I don't watch it—I don't want to watch it—it's trash." To those of us who said, "I watch it every day!" We came from these totally different sides and that's been absolutely stimulating.

LIGON: Right!

DAVIS: You know what kind of strikes me is this is such a dynamic project because the shows are changing as we're writing the paper. I mean I already feel my paper is dated because some of the comments I made about the Real Housewives—you know things have been changing on that show, and so it's a very fluid dynamic environment that we're dealing with.

LIGON: The beauty is that we're capturing a moment in time when we've all but reached a critical mass with the types of shows, and it seems like what else can be generated at this point what kind of subgenres and offshoots and different locales and all of these things. We must take on topics that seem taboo or that others would easily dismiss as not a good terrain for intellectual inquiry.

WARD: During the conference, we received a question about respectability politics that got people a little riled up. Were any of you concerned at all about respectability politics or being labeled as looking down on the shows?

MCDANIELS: I know it came right out of my paper. I remember sending you the draft, and you said, "Go ahead and stop skirting around it; just go ahead and say respectability politics and talk about it." So, when I got to the second draft, I did. But, the reaction in the conference session, it blew me away. It became explosive very quickly, and I don't know if you guys remember the one young lady who had a real problem with the fact that many of us started off by saying we were once ashamed to talk about it. I responded, "No, no, no, you have it wrong—here's Sharon, and she's not ashamed."

JONES: That's right!

(group laughter)

MCDANIELS: But, that issue has come up because I shared this project with a colleague who was actually at CLA in another session during our session. Of course, he wanted to have the session at work when we got back. Interestingly, his former student is the dance teacher on the new show *Bring It* that's filmed here in Jackson. He really wanted to have a conversation because he had some early conversations with her before it was televised, and now that it's on television, he was somewhat outraged on one hand and then on the other hand he said, "Well, at least she is empowering herself by marketing her own thing." He was off and on the fence, going back and forth about it. But, an interesting thing happened just two days ago. It's teacher appreciation week, and one of my former students sent me a text saying, "Happy teacher appreciation week—so glad for what you've done." I replied, "Haven't seen you in a long time, and I haven't seen the girls in a long time. How are they?" She responded, "Oh, well you've probably seen them if you watch *Bring It.* They're on every week." I thought, oh my god, I have to go back and watch some reruns to see what I can see. So, for the first time, it intersected with my real life, and I'm not in Atlanta. If you live in Atlanta, you must have a different feeling about all that's going on. Now that this is actually being filmed in my city, it was a different kind of feeling.

JEFFERSON-JAMES: Returning to respectability politics, when you study all of the diaspora and when you study postcolonial criticism you get a different view of respectability politics. You start to ask yourself, by whose standards is something respectable? One of the characters that I love to teach is from *The Bluest Eye*—the character Geraldine. Those of us who are English professors know this character. She's a dysfunctional character, and she's one of those people who is so caught up in the politics of respectability that she cannot even enjoy sex with her husband. The only sexual pleasure she derives is from a cat sitting in her lap. This is Toni Morrison's way of letting you know that you don't have to be in the ghetto to experience a sense of dysfunctionality—devoting your life to respectability politics is in a sense dysfunctional. How much of your life are you going to devote to being "respectable"? We get into these big huge fights in the English department about what is respectable literature. What can we add to the canon and what cannot be added to the canon? Why can't a Sister Souljah be added to the canon in the say way as say Byron or Shelley or Keats be added to the canon? So, I'm always leery of respectability politics, and I'm always looking for it. I'm always kind of disgusted with it when I hear people dismiss things in the academic arena as not necessarily worthy of academic interrogation. If something is so ubiquitous in our culture as reality TV shows, I do think it's worthy of academic interrogation.

MCDANIELS: There's a flip side to that when you talk about respectability politics, especially in our discipline in English and what goes into the canon. The other side of that is, What makes our Caucasian male counterparts proud to say, "Oh, well, you know, I don't really read African American literature."

Why? And, to say it with a straight face to you, "I just want to let you know that I don't read that."

WARD: Toni Morrison addresses that sentiment in her book *Playing in the Dark.*

HARRIS: Teaching African American history as an African American is sometimes looked at as "Oh, well, that's not really a tough discipline because you're really just teaching about your family and your ancestors who you knew." It's implied that it's not an in-depth discipline, and you're just talking about people who you know in Atlanta. Many people outside of the discipline wonder how "reality television" is scholarly, or how you can tie it into academics. It really is something that you almost have to fight for, especially when you're talking about white males, and even white females in that respect.

DAVIS: If we want something to be part of the canon, we have to fight for it. And, when you think of the whole thing with popular culture, how many people are writing papers about popular culture and skateboard culture and this or that? Who apologizes? I don't see anyone apologizing if they're writing papers on graffiti or skateboard culture.

LIGON: All the more scintillating topics seem to be as far as the boundaries and margins can be pushed within popular culture. Well, then, why not this space, which really I think encroaches upon those questions of boundaries, so it becomes broader than just the question of respectability politics. But, what I think I'm hearing is just the shape shifting of canon and the fact that there are permeable, malleable barriers, and I think that's what our work represents. We often hear people pay lip service to notions of interdisciplinary and cross-disciplinary studies. What it was intended to be is a space that is permeable, but one that is by its design very fluid. It can be very healthy when encouraging our students to interrogate intellectual questions and to interrogate the space with a theoretical grounding.

MCDANIELS: Whether we're talking about respectability politics, or like you said shape shifting of the canon, it is pretty much all relative, then. And that's directly connected to the fact that as African Americans living in the United States, our experiences and our backgrounds are varied. It's just like when you read a text; your interpretations of certain things in the text are colored by who you are. It's colored by what you bring to the table when you sit down as a reader. So, when we think about respectability politics, what's important to one person may not be important to another person. So, then the canon then is always shape shifting, depending on who's teaching what. Correct?

WARD: Yes, absolutely.

DAVIS: LaToya's example made me think of Mrs. Turner in *Their Eyes Were Watching God.* Out on the muck, she was really the anomaly out there with her respectability politics. Yet, the muck was this sort of fluid space with the bohemians and everybody doing their own multicultural thing, but she was trying to hold on in this very anomalous way.

JONES: I'm glad that you brought that up and that we're having this discussion about respectability politics. I was just thinking about the ways in which we could incorporate this kind of discussion of respectability politics, literary texts, and reality TV as texts with our students. I think that might be a really good way to highlight these issues with them especially since so many of them are very familiar with these reality TV shows.

WARD: I've been thinking about respectability politics whenever I work on this book because it is one of my major concerns. I did not want readers to think that we were coming from this high horse of our ivory tower and looking down on the Black women on these shows and telling them that they should be acting this way or not acting that way. Which is interesting because often when people ask me about the book they immediately say, "Oh, are you bashing them?"

(group groans)

WARD: And I respond, "No, that's not even remotely the purpose of what we're trying to do." It's about starting a conversation. It's about looking at it in new ways. It's about making people who monitor the canon understand that the canon is changing. Academics can exist in the real world and not just in our tower reading our Keats and Hemingway. We can talk and relate, and still be academic. In regards to respectability politics, what about those of you who weren't fans of reality television shows before you started writing? Did you think about respectability politics?

ADELABU: So, I will definitely say that I was challenged in writing the chapter. A number of times, Jervette said, "Could you find something good?" We debated the merits of the shows. I had very strong opinions about them even though I'd only seen little snippets of the shows. But, at the same time I think when I started to write, I struggled because on one hand I couldn't really see the merits of the shows or see any positive messages from them. At the same time, I did not want to vilify the families, and my goal in writing the paper was to interrogate what I was watching, but at the same time to do no harm. As a psychologist, it's do no harm. I wanted to be clear and honest about what I saw, but I wanted to write it in such a way that I think folks can read it and walk away with a clear message or understanding of how the shows might impact children and families but I did not want to bash the shows or the families on those shows.

WARD: I think you found that sweet spot of being able to say this is what's going on and this is how it could affect families in these ways while very much avoiding a public bashing of families because that's completely against what we were shooting for.

ADELABU: I didn't even feel comfortable providing very specific examples in the chapter because I felt like by doing that I'm placing families or individuals on trial; I wanted to really speak about the shows in a broad sense.

JEFFERSON-JAMES: I wasn't really concerned with respectability politics. As a matter of fact, I'm going to share with y'all—I had planned on doing a presentation at CLA on the wedding shows and how the wedding shows are a twenty-first-century retelling of the Cinderella story. I belonged to this group on Facebook. It's an all African American group, and they kicked me out of the group because they questioned my academic integrity for even bringing that up. This is an all-black group, and they didn't think that it had any merit.

HARRIS: They unfriended you?

(group laughter)

JEFFERSON-JAMES: Yes, they kicked me out! They banned me from the group. I was trying to explain to the group founder that you never want to say that something this pervasive in our culture doesn't have any academic merit. It's a simple love story. Every culture has a Cinderella story, so how can you say it doesn't have any academic merit? We went back and forth; we had to have a mediator to get me back in the Facebook group.

WARD: Did you throw any Vladimir Propp at her? Give her some *Morphology of the Folktale*—throw some literary theory her way to argue your point?

JEFFERSON-JAMES: When I got back in the group—they kicked me out last summer—I made the announcement that you guys kicked me out of the group for wanting to do a presentation on reality TV shows and now it's a book project.

(group laughter)

JEFFERSON-JAMES: I'm not a heavy consumer of the *Love & Hip Hop* type shows. I do watch the geeky reality shows like *Sex Sent Me to the ER*, and I regularly watched *Say Yes to the Dress*.

HARRIS: Your situation is very interesting because sometimes as academics, it's either all or nothing. You either agree with me, or you are against me. There is rarely this dialogue of okay we don't have to agree, but let's all put it out there. I think this book really does do that. There's growth in not agreeing and there's growth in us really discussing something. What's the fun in doing something and everybody is in agreement?

JEFFERSON-JAMES: Once I returned to the group, we had a good discussion. We even talked about how gay men often play a fairy godmother role while they themselves often can't take part in getting married.

LIGON: I wrote the chapter on the wedding shows, and I had to resist the temptation to write many discursive notes about just that imagery. It's a kind of backward glance at respectability politics and trying to self-censor and keep the text moving forward. I was trying not to look at other images that I saw swirling around and the visual imagery. I'm so shocked that there would be such a response to it occurring—it's all but formulaic if you look at some of these show—many of the men are all but cast—I'm using that term loosely—in these roles but I think it is an expression of the wider culture. Preselfannie made the comment about the friend who is the event planner. I wonder how many have the requisite friend who may serve in that role. It is almost as if the men are being validated on the wider screen when in real life that is not the actuality. There may be an event planner who is a male or someone in the bridal salon who is an assistant. So, it's an adaptation of the Cinderella tale, but as I suggested in my essay, it's a modern revisionist reading of it. And why is that problematic for some?

WARD: As you're talking about the gay sidekick, it of course takes me to our friends in Atlanta. Preselfannie and Sheena, you both have alluded to Atlanta in your earlier comments, but we haven't really talked about Atlanta in particular, even though Atlanta has become this hot zone of reality television. *Hollywood Exes* barely made it to a second season, and now it's going into its third season. They just announced that they're doing a spin-off called *Atlanta Exes* that's supposed to start this year. There are so many shows that feature Atlanta: *Love & Hip Hop Atlanta, T.I. & Tiny: The Family Hustle, Married to Medicine*, and all these other shows—why Atlanta? For example, Preselfannie, I didn't realize, that *Bring It On* was filmed in Jackson until someone told me at the conference. I just assumed it was Atlanta because I thought that's where everybody went!

HARRIS: Well, you know W. E. B. Du Bois did studies where he talked about Atlanta and "Atlanta's elite." A lot of the things that he talked about at the turn of the century are still really relevant in Atlanta today, and not to say that it doesn't exist in other areas, but I think that once you put the cameras on Atlanta it shines even brighter.

MCDANIELS: If you think about all the nicknames or labels that Atlanta has had over the years—some people refer to it as a Black mecca when you think about Du Bois or even Hotlanta when you think about partying or spring break.

WARD: Blacklanta.

MCDANIELS: Yes, yes! You see where I'm going with that. So, it's been historically that when people thought of Atlanta they thought about a predominately Black mecca that had Blacks from all socioeconomic levels from your richest Black people to your poorest Black people. Everything that you were looking for was in Atlanta. I think that's directly tied to consumerism and the way that we objectify everything too.

HARRIS: Atlanta is a southern version of what Harlem was in the 1920s and the 1930s. Everything really gravitated toward that and consumerism really also fuels that as well.

LIGON: I love the historization, Sheena. I was thinking of "Wings of Atalanta" (Du Bois). When you said consumer issues, but specifically the economics, I don't know if many people are aware of the tax credits that are given to many production companies and film companies to film in Atlanta. The state is underscoring and underwriting, trying to entice individuals to come here and to stay for extended periods for movie and television filming. Many of the smaller suburban communities are lending themselves out for the filming of series, so there's something for everyone here. There's a very lucrative financial lure to come to Atlanta.

WARD: That's a really interesting point because there was recently an article lamenting the portrayal of Atlanta in reality TV. There have been these statements made disavowing the portrayal of the city in a lot of these shows. So, how do we mesh those two ideas together where they're saying come, come; oh, but we don't like how you're portraying us.

LIGON: You have state and city questions. The state of Georgia is offering the tax incentives, but the city of Atlanta has to respond to the portrayals.

DAVIS: The image of the city, in *The Real Housewives of Atlanta* is almost like a travelogue because interspersed with the stories they always have some great shots of parks, high-rises, and fabulous architecture. It seems like they go out of their way to really make the city look extremely attractive. And that's very appealing.

LIGON: They put the boundaries on the city limits, too, because even a lot of the stock images that are used to link the segments together are interesting. They'll use recognizable places, but when you speak of it as a travelogue, I'm always intrigued because the suburban areas that many of the housewives of Atlanta frequent, great lengths are taken to conceal the locations of those places. And, only a careful or an informed observer might be able to decode them based upon certain signals or landmarks where they are. So, I'm always reading it in a very interesting way, saying well there's a certain segment of the viewing audience that might not have a clue about these places that are being frequented. The stock images are being used for the public gatherings or iconic buildings like the reunion shows have always been held in the Biltmore Hotel. Atlanta as a city can be consumed through certain images, and it is not really understood that it's very nuanced and very textured in its geographic representation. They talk about it being a city too busy to hate, but in fact, true to form, eleven o'clock Sunday morning, it's probably one of the most segmented and isolating cities within the Southeast.

WARD: I think it's interesting that you brought up this idea of Atlanta being able to be consumed because I would very much argue that Atlanta has become a character in the reality television world. Do you remember that gentleman who came up to us at the conference in New Orleans and talked about how he sees students now applying to the colleges in Atlanta because they watch reality television and they expect to have their college reality television experience? These students are making life decisions possibly from reality television, or what they think is reality television.

LIGON: And, they're basing it on a myth.

WARD: One of the other things that we haven't really talked about, and Terry, you mentioned earlier, were things like competition shows. Most of our book is focused on shows that present the home life or relationships. Our definition of reality shows from the book's introduction marked these shows as off limits, but it might be interesting to discuss some of the shows that gave us our first Black women reality television stars. I'm thinking of people like Omarosa from *The Apprentice* or Fantasia and Jennifer Hudson from *American Idol*. Or even recently, Amber Riley, who won last season's *Dancing with the Stars*.

MCDANIELS: It's really interesting to see the online comments that viewers make about the contestants on competition shows. The comments are awful, and if you were a contestant and you read some of these things, you would be crushed. They're not for the faint of heart.

DAVIS: The comments for *The Real Housewives of Atlanta* can be critical, but they tend to be more engaged and compassionate in that they like to lecture the stars about what they did or what they didn't do or what they should have done. But, I think there's more of an engagement, like you're acting up and I'm going to tell you what the right thing to do here is, rather than really mean comments. I haven't seen really destructive, vicious audience comments because it seems like the viewers they really like most of the characters and want to engage with them.

MCDANIELS: When I was looking at comments on the Braxtons, sometimes fans were mad about their behavior, but the comments were mostly corrective. But, when I looked at comments for the Sheards, it was really interesting because the comments were about the things that were not on the show—things in real life, rumors that were circulating around the city about extra-marital affairs for the pastor, and about the son now having this public relationship with the video vixen, Deelishis. So, the show projected their home life as this churchgoing family, but the comments that were coming out were about the things that you did not see. It appeared to be people in Detroit who knew them.

DAVIS: I wonder if people are very upfront with their behavior, if they don't hide their conflicts, the audience may be more engaged. However, if the audience suspects any kind of hypocrisy, they're going to jump on that.

JEFFERSON-JAMES: Viewers did that with *Preachers of LA.* People went into the show expecting hypocrisy from the commercials. The commercials played on people's expectations of hypocrisy from Black preachers. It's kind of become a caricature in comedies and in movies—this Black preacher who is a predatory member of our community. I think we're all familiar with Leon Lonnie Love from the T.V. show *Martin*; he's a predatory person, and it's funny. The commercials for the new reality show showed these lavish homes and sports cars, and before the show even started there was so much controversy and so many negative comments about the show that two of the pastors went on national television to beg people to watch the show and to give it a chance. The negative comments had already started rolling in, and I can't figure out why producers would choose to advertise the show in that way because it turned off a lot of potential viewers. The Black church is already often perceived negatively. A whole generation, from forty down to eighteen, in a lot of communities is not sitting in the pews. And when you go onto the website, there are so many negative comments there about the preachers' lifestyles, and I know that the editors took some creative liberty in creating the image of the predatory preacher who is just getting the money from his community and supporting his lavish lifestyle. The comments are almost all negative. It even drew ire from T. D. Jakes, and he preached about it in his church.

WARD: There was also that show that only lasted for a short bit of time—it was in Atlanta too.

JEFFERSON-JAMES: *The Sisterhood?*

WARD: Yes.

WARD: The Christian community was very much against that one as well because of the portrayal of Black wives of ministers. It received a similar response to *Preachers of LA.* . . . So, thanks for discussing competition shows, ladies.

(group laughter and apologies)

NELSON: I watch *American Idol*, and I love *The Voice*, but it was difficult for me to pinpoint something specifically about the African American experience on competition shows. It seemed to be that in these competition shows there seemed to be more of a level playing field. And I may be incorrect. I love *Hell's Kitchen*, and a couple of years ago, a young Black woman won it. In *The Voice*, there are a couple of Black people who won, and of course on *American Idol* Ruben Studdard, Fantasia, and Jennifer Hudson did well. So, it seems like they got an equal chance of winning. It seemed like competition shows are more respectable in that it didn't characterize our African American people in a negative way. I don't think that there's a difference between the chances that an African American has versus any other person on there to win. I don't think it comes down to their nationality, or their culture, or their race. It's about how well can you sing or how well can you cook. So, it seemed to me to be more of an even or a more level playing field.

HARRIS: Terry, do you think that the physical image initially played a part with competition shows?

NELSON: Okay, well, let's look at Ruben Studdard.

MCDANIELS: It's different for men than it is for women.

NELSON: It does play a part. Do you remember the lady on *American Idol:* Mandisa? She was phenomenal, but her look wasn't marketable.

WARD: Yeah, she did not have a traditional marketable look, but I think that's the point that could be looked at for these competition shows. African American competitors have the image issue that they're fighting against.

Monica, you might be able to speak to this more than any of us because this is your area of expertise. But if you think about Ruben Studdard, there's only been one winner like him. There isn't a history of having that type of winner on *American Idol*.

NELSON: But, Jervette, how many Caucasian not-the-norm types have won? There's a certain look that people want to see in these contemporary types of singers. I don't even think overweight Caucasians would be acceptable either.

HARRIS: I think that image on both parts, Black and white or any other ethnicity, does play an interesting role in how society accepts them. And especially with a catchy title like *Idol*.

NELSON: Great point.

FLIPPIN WYNN: When we talk about Jennifer Hudson and Fantasia, we must also remember that there was a Caucasian guy who was gay. Clay Aiken didn't really fit what people thought. It's interesting that with *American Idol*, Jennifer Hudson didn't win, but she then went on to win an Oscar. Once that started happening, the images didn't make as much of a difference as they did in the first couple of years and seasons because after that the women are not real thin. They have all different genres. That's what happens with images when they break what our traditional perspectives are. We're more open to looking at things based on the music rather than on what people look like. You're seeing people who look like people now as opposed to initially. The same thing with *America's Next Top Model*— look at the people who are on that particular show and the people who won. It's kind of interesting.

MCDANIELS: Monica, do you see the same thing happening with *The Voice*?

FLIPPIN WYNN: *The Voice* is a different kind of show because they're really not dependent on what's real—it's the audience. If the audience liked you or not, and they could like you or not like you by the way you do your hair or even something as simple as the song you sing and how you sing it.

NELSON: It also comes down to how many people you can get behind you to support you.

FLIPPIN WYNN: Absolutely! I remember voting like seventy-five times for somebody!

(group laughter)

FLIPPIN WYNN: It's not always the best person who wins on these competition shows, and you know the reality of that is they're not winning because they're the best singer, or they're the best songwriter. They have the most glam, or they had the best one liner. The audience falls for that, and they start calling and making their selections. So, you know that in itself is not reality.

NELSON: If you remember, a couple years ago a guy from Conway, Arkansas, won. He was not the best singer, but he was going up against the flamboyant gay guy with the black hair. He beat that guy out.

FLIPPIN WYNN: But you know when *Idol* first came out, the flamboyant never would have worked on it or any of the other shows. But, now the audiences are more receptive, that doesn't seem to be the deal breaker anymore, or the fact that you're not really thin. It looks like they're actually looking at and listening to people and listening to how they sound. The images have changed. How we view the images have changed on some of the competition shows.

NELSON: I'm watching *The Voice* now, and one of the top contenders is this chubby white boy. I'm like, how did you get up there? But, he can sing!

FLIPPIN WYNN: Yeah, and maybe five years ago or eight years ago when it first came on, he wouldn't have made it.

JEFFERSON-JAMES: Chubby Luther can out-sing skinny Luther Vandross.

(group laughter)

MCDANIELS: They both sound the same—God rest his soul.

WARD: Well, since we are talking about men, I have a question. This is a book on Black women, but we've been talking about men and I've toyed with the idea of doing a second book on the portrayal of Black men in reality television. Also, while we were at CLA we got some specific comments and questions about what are y'all going to say about men? Let's pretend we have a book two, what would you want to write about on the portrayal of Black men in reality television?

JEFFERSON-JAMES: I'm a woman who studies masculinity, so I have plenty to say.

HARRIS: There was a man at the conference who was really interested in looking at the perspective of males talking about males in reality TV.

MCDANIELS: My chapter would be on T.O. and T.I.

JEFFERSON-JAMES: I would write about the *Real World* because they always portray the Black man as lazy or they portray him as what Andrew B. Leiter calls the Black beast—predatory and sexual. I stopped watching the *Real World: New Orleans* because the white girl with glasses kept picking a fight, but she always said she felt threatened. You don't feel threatened when you pick the fight, but because the man she was picking the fights with was Black, I guess she felt safe saying before the cameras, "Oh, I felt threatened because I'm a helpless white woman and he's a predatory Black male." It was a recurring theme throughout the *Real World* for them to portray the Black male as a lazy Sambo or someone who just wanted to have sex with everybody.

HARRIS: I would focus on the Atlanta *Housewives*. I don't know how many of you have watched the reunion show, but I thought it was interesting once they brought all of the males out. Not only did they sit the males behind their wives, but they were also only on stage for less than twenty minutes. It really spoke to me of this idea of femininity and masculinity within these reality TV shows.

DAVIS: *The Real Housewives of Atlanta* is one of the shows that appears to present a very positive view of Black men. I mean you know they have their issues, but in general, I think most of the men have come across as very positive in the sense of trying to make it.

WARD: I know that one thing I would be interested in would be looking at how much men watch, say for instance, some of the *Real Housewives* franchises.

I was surprised at the conference at the number of male audience members. I was not expecting that, and then they were some of the first ones to ask questions and to have comments.

JEFFERSON-JAMES: My husband secretly watched the *Bad Girls Club*.

HARRIS: It's not a secret now!

(group laughter)

FLIPPIN WYNN: Males watch reality television because they are also interested in seeing the drama.

ADELABU: You wrote notes on my chapter when I started to talk about the role of fathers, and you encouraged me to stick to talking about the women, but for me the men and women they are all coparenting in the show and to talk about one without talking about the other was challenging. If I wrote another chapter, I would really focus on the role of fathers and not put all of the weight or emphasis on the mothers, the working mothers of the show.

NELSON: I first started looking at reality TV shows when I was watching *Judge Judy*. So, if I were to write about men, it would be about Judge Mathis or Judge Joe Brown.

LIGON: As Detris was saying, I would want to go back and tease out the same things that I mentioned earlier about multiple expressions of masculinity, particularly within the bridal shows. I think that there is something there and there's a reason why certain networks are very comfortable with certain images. It even seems as if there's more latitude given to other expressions of masculinity in other *Housewives* shows, for instance, and that very same kind of privilege or space is not given to men in this very feminine space, the bridal salon. So, I would love to go back—there are a lot of the things I would have loved to expound upon.

JEFFERSON-JAMES: What about the city of Atlanta? Is the possibility to express different masculinities because Atlanta is quickly becoming or quickly getting a reputation for being the Black gay capital of the world?

WARD: Those all sound interesting. The goal is for us to end soon, and I want to try to stick close to that, but just one last thing: What's the one thing that you hope readers take away from this book?

HARRIS: A conversation.

DAVIS: Not to simplify and diminish and stereotype. It's so complex; all of the shows have so many strands.

NELSON: That my argument is from an entrepreneurship perspective rather than a stereotypical perspective.

JEFFERSON-JAMES: I hope that students pick up the book. I hope that they learn to connect the present to the past. Even if they don't value the past, they need to start to learn to make those connections because as Preselfannie said, they are living for the now. They don't see the value in even learning about the past. Like I'm apt to dismiss cultural productions of today, they're apt to dismiss cultural productions of yesterday, and we don't need to do either of those things.

FLIPPIN WYNN: I'm hoping that the book will open up the doors for people to understand that reality shows are not going away even if they hope they would disappear. Our book will become a standard for people, and hopefully, people will build on what we're doing.

LIGON: I hope that this book will help to enrich, deepen, and enliven the conversation. In many spaces, there have been segmented discussions, but I hope in the true spirit in which the editor envisioned this reaching multiple audiences for different reasons that it's a bridge building mechanism and that it creates the opportunity for academics and lay persons or just very interested observers to become more mindful and a lot less disengaged.

MCDANIELS: I hope that it leads to more open-mindedness in the academy.

JONES: I hope that in reading this book people will come away with a better understanding of what they're watching on television and apply some of these ideas that we talked about.

ADELABU: I would certainly agree with LaToya—I hope readers will take away the social, historical, and political implications of these reality shows. And, I would add that reality television isn't reality and that these shows provide such a limited view of African American communities. I think until we are at a place where there are more diverse images, we should be more mindful and careful about what is put out there.

WARD: Sheena, your response of "conversation" is succinctly the goal of this book. We had to end this book with a conversation not just to pay homage to the ubiquitous reunion shows, but also because we are hoping to inspire thoughtful conversations about Black women in reality TV—all over the country, even all over the world because American reality television is of course being exported out to other countries. I hope that conversations will continue to take place and that people will deconstruct reality television and the portrayal of Black women in the genre. This book will allow them to have a better-informed discussion.

Works Cited

Du Bois, W. E. B. *The Souls of Black Folk.* Chicago: A. C. McClurg & Co., 1903.
Hurston, Zora Neale. *Their Eyes Were Watching God.* 1937. Foreword Edwidge Danticat. Afterword Henry Louis Gates Jr. New York: Harper Perennial, 2006.
Leiter, Andrew B. *In the Shadow of the Black Beast: African American Masculinity in the Harlem and Southern Renaissances.* Baton Rouge: Louisiana State UP, 2010.
Morrison, Toni. *The Bluest Eye.* New York: Plume, 1994.
———. *Playing in the Dark: Whiteness and the Literary Imagination.* New York: Vintage Books, 1993.
Propp, Vladimir. *Morphology of the Folktale.* Austin: U of Texas P, 1968.

Appendix

Reality TV Shows That Prominently Feature Black Women

This table is not an exhaustive list of reality TV shows that prominently feature Black women, but it is a useful representative list of the types of shows that feature Black women.

Show Name	Aired	Original Network
All My Babies' Mamas	2013 (never aired)	Oxygen Network
America's Next Top Model	2003–2006/2006–Present	UPN/CW
Atlanta Exes	Aug. 2014–Present	VH1
Bad Girls Club	2006–Present	Oxygen Network
Bad Girls Club: Miami (season 5)	Aug. 2010–Nov. 2010	Oxygen Network
Baldwin Hills	July 2007–Mar. 2009	BET
BAPs	July 2013	Lifetime
Basketball Wives	Apr. 2010–Present	VH1
Basketball Wives LA	Aug. 2011–Present	VH1
Being Bobby Brown	June 2005–Dec. 2005	Bravo
Beverly's Full House	Mar. 2012–May 2012	Oprah Winfrey Network

(continued)

Show Name	Aired	Original Network
Black. White.	Mar. 2006–2006	FX
Blood, Sweat, and Heels	Jan. 2014–Present	Bravo
Born to Dance: Laurieann Gibson	Aug. 2011–Present	BET
Brandy and Ray J: A Family Business	Apr. 2010–Feb. 2011	VH1
Braxton Family Values	Apr. 2011–Present	WE tv
Bring It!	March 2014–Present	Lifetime
Candy Girls	Mar. 2009–May 2009	E!
Chicagolicious	June 2012–Jan. 2013	Style Network
Chrissy & Mr. Jones	Sept. 2012–Present	VH1
College Hill (becomes *College Hill South Beach* in Mar 2009)	Jan. 2004–June 2009	BET
College Hill South Beach	Mar. 2009–June 2009	BET
Daddy's Girls	Jan. 2009–Sept. 2009	MTV
Deion & Pilar: Prime Time Love	Apr. 2008–June 2008	Oxygen Network
Deion's Family Playbook	Mar. 2014–Present	OWN
DMX: Soul of a Man	July 2006–Aug. 2006	BET
Eddie Griffin: Going for Broke	Sept. 2009–Oct. 2009	VH1
Ego Trip's Miss Rap Supreme	Apr. 2008–June 2008	VH1
The Family Crews	Feb. 2010–Mar. 2011	BET
Fantasia for Real	Jan. 2010–Nov. 2010	VH1
50 Cent: The Money and the Power	Nov. 2008–Jan. 2009	MTV/MTV2
Flavor of Love	Jan. 2006–May 2008	VH1
Flavor of Love Girls: Charm School	Apr. 2007–July 2007	VH1
Flex and Shanice	Nov. 2014–Present	OWN
Football Wives	Oct. 2010–Dec. 2010	VH1
For the Love of Ray J	Feb. 2009–Feb. 2010	VH1
Frankie & Neffe	Aug. 2009–Oct. 2009	BET
From G's to Gents	July 2008–Apr. 2009	MTV
Hammertime	June–July 2009	A&E Network
Hollywood Divas	Oct. 2014–Present	TV One
Hollywood Exes	June 2012–Present	VH1
The Houstons: On Our Own	Oct.–Dec. 2012	Lifetime
How I'm Livin'	2001–2004	BET
I Dream of NeNe: The Wedding	Sept. 2013–Present	Bravo
Ice Loves Coco	June 2011–Jan. 2013	E!

Show Name	Aired	Original Network
Ice–T's Rap School	Oct. 2006–Nov. 2006	VH1
I Love New York	Jan. 2007–Jan. 2008	VH1
It's a Mann's World	Jan. 2015–Present	BET
I Want to Work for Diddy	Aug. 2008–Jan. 2010	VH1
The Jacksons: A Family Dynasty	Dec. 2009–Jan. 2010	A&E Network
Kandi's Wedding	June–July 2014	Bravo
Keyshia & Daniel: Family First	Oct. 2012–Dec. 2012	BET
Keyshia Cole: The Way It Is	July 2006–Dec. 2008	BET
Kimora: Life in the Fab Lane	Aug. 2007–Mar. 2011	Style Network/E!
La La's Full Court Life	Aug. 2011–Present	VH1
Life with LaToya	Apr. 2013–Present	OWN
Lil' Kim: Countdown to Lockdown	Mar. 2006–Apr. 2006	BET
LisaRaye: The Real McCoy	Apr. 2010–May 2011	TV One
Love & Hip-Hop	Mar. 2011–Present	VH1
Love & Hip-Hop: Atlanta	June 2012–Present	VH1
Love & Hip-Hop: Hollywood	Sept. 2014–Present	VH1
Love in the City	Apr. 2014–Present	OWN
Love Thy Sister	Jan. 2015–Present	WE tv
Married to Medicine	Mar. 2013–Present	Bravo
Marrying the Game	Nov. 2012–Present	VH1
Mary Mary	Mar. 2012–Present	WE tv
Meet the Smiths	Apr. 2014–Present	TBS
The Michael Vick Project	Jan. 2010–Present	BET
Monica: Still Standing	Oct. 2009–Jan. 2010	BET
One Big Happy Family	Dec. 2009–Aug. 2010	TLC
Preachers' Daughters	March 2013–Present	Lifetime
Preachers of LA	Oct. 2013–Present	Oxygen Network
R & B Divas (name later changed to *R & B Divas: Atlanta* once *LA* aired)	Aug. 2012–Present	TV One
R & B Divas: Los Angeles	July 2013–Present	TV One
Raising Whitley	Apr. 2013–Present	OWN
The Real Housewives of Atlanta	Oct. 2008–Present	Bravo
Run's House	Oct. 2005–July 2009	MTV
R U the Girl	July 2005–Sept. 2005	UPN
The Salt-N-Pepa Show	Oct. 2007–March 2008	VH1

(continued)

Show Name	Aired	Original Network
The Sheards	Apr. 2013–Present	BET
The Sisterhood	Jan. 2013–Feb. 2013	TLC
Sisterhood of Hip Hop	Aug. 2014–Present	Oxygen Network
Six Little McGhees	Dec. 2012–Present	OWN
Snoop Dogg's Fatherhood	Dec. 2007–Jan. 2009	E!
Strange Love	Jan. 2005–Apr. 2005	VH1
SWV Reunited	Jan. 2014 – Present	WE tv
Tamar & Vince	Sept. 2012–Present	WE tv
Thicker Than Water: The Tankards	Nov. 2013–Present	Bravo
Tia & Tamera	Aug. 2011–Sept. 2013	Style Network/E!
T.I. & Tiny: The Family Hustle	Dec. 2011–Present	VH1
T.I.'s Road to Redemption	Feb. 2009–Apr. 2009	MTV
Tiny & Shekinah's Weave Trip	Oct. 2014–Present	VH1
Tiny and Toya	June 2009–June 2010	BET
Welcome to Sweetie Pie's	Oct. 2011–Present	OWN
What Chilli Wants	April 2010–Feb. 2011	VH1

Notes on Contributors

DETRIS HONORA ADELABU is an associate professor of psychology and human development at Wheelock College. She teaches human growth and development, adolescent development, and research methods. She studies factors influencing school achievement among low-income rural and urban African American adolescents. Her work has been published in such journals as *Adolescence, Urban Education*, and the *Journal of School Violence*. She completed her doctorate at the Harvard University Graduate School of Education.

CYNTHIA DAVIS is a professor of English and associate dean of the School of Professional and Career Education (PACE) at Barry University. Her biography of Dorothy West, *Literary Sisters: Dorothy West and Her Circle*, co-authored with Verner Mitchell, was published by Rutgers University Press in 2012. With Mitchell, she is working on a biography of actresses Rose McClendon and Edna Thomas, and a collection of reviews of African-American theatre. Davis, a graduate of Boston College and Georgetown University, received her doctorate from the University of Maryland at College Park.

MONICA FLIPPIN WYNN is an assistant professor of mass communications at Jackson State University. She received her PhD in communication at the University of Oklahoma, and she has professional experience in producing and editing for several radio and television stations. Her current research covers such topics as connectivity, racial socialization, and instructional teaching. She is currently working on projects involving social media and engagement, race and agenda setting, and research and undergraduate students.

SHEENA HARRIS is an assistant professor of history at Tuskegee University. She completed her PhD in African American history at the University of Memphis. Her research and teaching interests are in African American history, US history, women's history, and West African studies. Harris is in the final stages of completing her monograph on the life and times of Margaret Murray Washington—Booker T. Washington's third wife.

LATOYA JEFFERSON-JAMES is an assistant professor of English at Rust College. She completed her doctorate at the University of Mississippi where she studied African American and African diasporic literature in a postcolonial theoretical framework. She is currently completing her manuscript on Black masculinity in comparative Black literature of the African diaspora.

SHARON LYNETTE JONES is a professor in the Department of English Language and Literatures at Wright State University in Dayton, Ohio. She is the author of *Rereading the Harlem Renaissance: Race, Class, and Gender in the Fiction of Jessie Fauset, Zora Neale Hurston, and Dorothy West* and *Critical Companion to Zora Neale Hurston: A Literary Reference to Her Life and Work*. She coedited *The Prentice Hall Anthology of African American Literature* with Rochelle Smith. She also edited *Critical Insights: Zora Neale Hurston*. She earned her PhD from the University of Georgia.

ALISON D. LIGON is an assistant professor of English at Morehouse College. Her most recent publications and current research activities focus on sociopolitical subtext found in historical fiction from the African diaspora, primarily the Anglophone Caribbean. She is especially partial to reading and writing about the *bildungsroman* in contemporary Caribbean fiction. Some of her most recent publications appear in refereed journals such as *Caribbean Vistas: Critiques of Caribbean Arts and Cultures*, the *Journal of Africana Composition and Rhetoric*, and the *Journal of South Texas English Studies*. Ligon, a graduate of Hampton and Duke Universities, completed her doctoral studies in humanities with a concentration in African American studies at Clark Atlanta University.

PRESELFANNIE E. WHITFIELD MCDANIELS is an associate professor of English at Jackson State University in Jackson, Mississippi. She completed her PhD in English at Louisiana State University. Her areas of study include twentieth-century American, African American, and women's literature with an emphasis on the novel. McDaniels has recently published articles on mothering in twentieth-century novels, service learning, capstone pedagogy, and the work of poet C. Leigh McInnis. Her recent publications also include book chapters in *Presenting Oprah Winfrey, Her Films, and African American Literature* (Tara T. Green, ed.) and *Constructing the Literary Self: Race and Gender in Twentieth-Century Literature* (Patsy J. Daniels, ed.).

TERRY A. NELSON is an assistant professor of leadership at the University of Alaska Anchorage. She conducts research in leadership, cross-cultural issues, diversity, and work stress and coping. She has published in *Cross Cultural Management: An International Journal, Journal of Business and Entrepreneurship*, and *IEEE Engineering Management Review*. She recently coauthored the book *Work Stress and Coping in the Era of Globalization* with Rabi S. Bhagat and James Segovis. Nelson earned her BBA and MBA from the University of Arkansas at Little Rock and completed her PhD at the University of Memphis. Her scholarly background is enhanced with more than seventeen years in leadership roles with two Fortune 500 companies, Kroger and Coca-Cola Enterprises, and a large regional bank, First Tennessee Bank.

JERVETTE R. WARD is an assistant professor of English at the University of Alaska Anchorage. She earned the PhD in English—literary and cultural studies from the University of Memphis. Her research and teaching areas focus on African American women's literature and American literature. She recently published the article "In Search of Diversity: Dick and Jane and Their Black Playmates," in *Making Connections: Interdisciplinary Approaches to Cultural Diversity*; the introductory essay, "Zora Neale Hurston: Coming Forth as Gold," for the book *Zora Neale Hurston: An Annotated Bibliography of Works and Criticism*; and the book chapter "Seraph on the Suwanee: Hurston's 'White Novel'" in the book *Critical Insights: Zora Neale Hurston*. She is currently writing a book in response to the novel and film *The Help*.

Index

CPSIA information can be obtained at www.ICGtesting.com
Printed in the USA
LVOW06s2356051015

457034LV00001B/53/P